Beckett and Embodiment

Other Becketts – Series List

Published
Creative Involution: Bergson, Beckett, Deleuze
S. E. Gontarski

Beckett's Thing: Painting and Theatre
David Lloyd

Samuel Beckett and the Terror of Literature
Christopher Langlois

Samuel Beckett's How It Is
Anthony Cordingley

Posthuman Space in Samuel Beckett's Short Prose
Jonathan Boulter

Beckett and Embodiment: Body, Space, Agency
Amanda M. Dennis

www.edinburghuniversitypress.com/series/ORBT

Beckett and Embodiment
Body, Space, Agency

Amanda M. Dennis

EDINBURGH
University Press

Edinburgh University Press is one of the leading university presses in the UK. We publish academic books and journals in our selected subject areas across the humanities and social sciences, combining cutting-edge scholarship with high editorial and production values to produce academic works of lasting importance. For more information visit our website: edinburghuniversitypress.com

© Amanda M. Dennis, 2021, 2023

Edinburgh University Press Ltd
The Tun – Holyrood Road
12(2f) Jackson's Entry
Edinburgh EH8 8PJ

First published in hardback by Edinburgh University Press 2021

Typeset in 11/13 Adobe Sabon by
IDSUK (DataConnection) Ltd

A CIP record for this book is available from the British Library

ISBN 978 1 4744 6299 0 (hardback)
ISBN 978 1 4744 6300 3 (paperback)
ISBN 978 1 4744 6301 0 (webready PDF)
ISBN 978 1 4744 6302 7 (epub)

The right of Amanda M. Dennis to be identified as the author of this work has been asserted in accordance with the Copyright, Designs and Patents Act 1988, and the Copyright and Related Rights Regulations 2003 (SI No. 2498).

Contents

Series Editor's Preface	vi
Acknowledgements	vii
List of Illustrations	x
List of Abbreviations	xi
Introduction: Embodied Agency: Towards an Ecology of the Subject	1
1 From Cartesian Ruins: Rocking Chair Phenomenology	21
2 Short-Circuited Rationalism, or How the Body Means	51
3 From Dialectics to Infinity: Life Cycles in *Molloy*, *Malone Dies* and *Endgame*	85
4 Radical Indecision: Aporia and Embodied Agency in *The Unnamable*	114
5 Style and the Violence of Passivity: *How It Is*	134
6 Compulsive Bodies, Creative Bodies: *Quad* and Agency	161
7 The Body and Creation: *Worstward Ho*	176
Conclusion: Embedded in the World: Beckett, Late Modernism, Earth-Body Art	201
Bibliography	216
Index	235

Series Editor's Preface

In 1997 Apple computers launched an advertising campaign (in print and on television) that entreated us to 'Think Different', and Samuel Beckett was one of Apple's icons. Avoiding Apple's solecism, we might modify the appeal to say that *Other Becketts* is a call to think differently as well, in this case about Beckett's work, to question, that is, even the questions we ask about it. *Other Becketts*, then, is a series of monographs focused on alternative, unexplored, or under-explored approaches to the work of Samuel Beckett, not a call for novelty *per se*, but a call to examine afresh those of Beckett's interests that were more arcane than mainstream, interests that might be deemed quirky or strange, and those of his works less thoroughly explored critically and theoretically, the late prose and drama, say, or even the poetry or criticism. Volumes might cover (but are not restricted to) any of the following: unusual illnesses or neurological disorders (the 'duck foot, goose foot' of *First Love*, akathisia or the invented duck's disease or panpygoptosis of Miss Dew in *Murphy*, proprioception, or its disturbance, in *Not I*, perhaps, or other unusual neurological lapses among Beckett's creatures, from Watt to the Listener of *That Time*); mathematical peculiarities (irrational numbers, factorials, Fibonacci numbers or sequences, or non-Euclidian approaches to geometry); linguistic failures (from Nominalism to Mauthner, say); citations of or allusions to contrarian aesthetic philosophers working in a more or less irrationalist tradition (Nietzsche, Bergson, or Deleuze, among others), or in general, 'the simple games that time plays with space'. Alternative approaches would be of interest as well, with foci on objects, animals, cognitive or memory issues, and the like.

S. E. Gontarski, Florida State University

Acknowledgements

My first debt of gratitude is to Stan Gontarski, who approached me about submitting a manuscript to Edinburgh University Press's *Other Becketts* series and whose comments, in addition to those of anonymous reviewers at the press, helped sharpen and shape the work, pushing me to explore the ramifications of Beckett and phenomenology for ecological thought. Jackie Jones showed enthusiasm and support for the project from the beginning, and Ersev Ersoy kept things running smoothly and enjoyably over many months. Working with Edinburgh has been a pleasure thanks to the energy, intelligence and professionalism of everyone at the press with whom I've worked.

This book, like many first academic books, has its seed in my doctoral dissertation, which I submitted to the University of California at Berkeley and which also grew out of my study at the University of Cambridge. Though very little of that work survives in the present volume, I would like to acknowledge the professors and mentors who not only refined the line of argument I pursue in this book but strengthened my habits of thinking and questioning. I'm grateful to Judith Butler for directing my dissertation and especially for her incisive reading and generative conversations, in Berkeley, Cambridge and Paris, which enabled me to alight upon and pursue the link between the body and agency. Ramona Naddaff and Anthony Cascardi modelled philosophical-literary scholarship, and they offered encouragement and continued support. I'm grateful also to Suzanne Geurlac, who reread Husserl with me, and to Kaja Silverman, in whose seminar I first read Merleau-Ponty.

The generosity of the Gates Cambridge Trust supported this project in its early stages and introduced me to a global community of scholars across the sciences and humanities that remains a source of inspiration and friendship. I gratefully acknowledge support from Trinity College Cambridge, which enabled me to spend a year at the École Normale Supérieure, and Berkeley's International Postdoctoral Fellowship gave me a year of research funding and the opportunity to teach in Madrid. The expertise of Jean Khalfa and Ian James at Cambridge was invaluable as I worked through the history of phenomenology and its relationship to French theory. I owe a special thanks to my undergraduate advisor at Princeton, Michael Jennings, who gave me my first copy of Beckett (*First Love*) and who encouraged me to pursue the intersection of philosophy and literature.

Earlier versions of Chapters 4 and 6 and a portion of Chapter 2 have appeared in print in slightly different form. The *Journal of Modern Literature* and the *Journal of Beckett Studies* have kindly granted permission to reuse the following material: 'Glitches in Logic in Beckett's *Watt*: Toward a Sensory Poetics', *Journal of Modern Literature* 38:2 (2015), pp. 103–16; 'Radical Indecision: Aporia as Metamorphosis in *The Unnamable*', *Journal of Beckett Studies* 24:2 (2015), pp. 180–197; 'Compulsive Bodies, Creative Bodies: Beckett and Agency in the 21st Century', *Journal of Beckett Studies* 27:1 (2018), pp. 5–21.

Seminars, conferences and working groups provided occasions to think through much of the material for this book. I'd like to thank the organisers of the Samuel Beckett Summer School, Nick Johnson and Sam Slote, for inviting me to give a plenary lecture in 2015, which laid the groundwork for Chapter 7. I would also like to thank Cassandra Falke and Hana Meertoja for inviting me to present at the 'Hermeneutics of Violence' workshop in Turku in 2019, part of *Interpreting Violence: Narrative, Ethics and Hermeneutics*. This generated much of the material that became Chapter 5. My work has also benefited from support provided by the international Beckett community for early career researchers to attend conferences, and I'd like to thank Sean Kennedy for spearheading this effort in Halifax.

Beckettians are a community of scholars of which I'm glad to be a part, and I'd like to thank in particular, for their conversation and encouragement, Patrick Bixby, Jonathan Boulter, Michael Coffey, Michael D'Arcy, Jose Francisco Fernandez, Scott Hamilton, Ulrika Maude, Mark Nixon, Laura Salisbury, Hannah Simpson, Paul Stewart, Dirk Van Hulle, Joe Valente and Feargal Whelan. I'm grateful to Jean-Michel Rabaté for his support over many years, for asking the right questions, for book recommendations, for colourful anecdotes and walks through Paris. And to Dan Gunn, a friend and now colleague at the American University of Paris, for the opportunity to help annotate Beckett's letters, for so many enjoyable conversations and for lending me books from his personal library as I endeavoured to finish this during a pandemic.

Leon Chai, Lauren Elkin, David Nowell-Smith, Grégoire Chamayou and Christopher Dennis read and commented on early drafts, and Douglas Atkinson offered, in addition to generative conversations about Beckett, an island refuge for writing part of this book. I'm grateful to him and to Smaranda Boros for roasting octopus and for being wonderful hosts. Thanks also to Sam Leader and Dina Nayeri for the most wonderful writing desk in Provence, to Rachel Donadio and Aysegul Savas for driving me to Beckett's house in Roussillon and to the Luberon Commune for your laughter and friendship. Emmanuel, thank you for your patience, steadiness and sense of adventure. Finally, I'd like to thank my brilliant mother, Vicki Mahaffey, who read draft after draft, reminded me why it mattered and rekindled motivation through her conversation and questions, again and again, my whole life long.

Illustrations

Figure 8.1 Giuseppe Penone, *Continuerà a crescere tranne che in quel punto* (*It Will Continue to Grow Except at That Point*), 1968. © 2021 Artists Rights Society (ARS), New York / ADAGP, Paris.   211

Figure 8.2 Ana Mendieta, *Imagen de Yagul*, from the series Silueta Works in Mexico 1973–1977, 1973 © 2021 The Estate of Ana Mendieta Collection, LLC. Courtesy Galerie Lelong & Co. / Licensed by Artists Rights Society (ARS), New York.   213

Abbreviations

CD   Merleau-Ponty, Maurice (1993), 'Cézanne's Doubt', trans. Michael B. Smith, in Galen A. Johnson (ed.), *The Merleau-Ponty Aesthetics Reader*. Evanston, IL: Northwestern University Press, pp. 59–75.

CP   Beckett, Samuel (1995), *The Complete Short Prose, 1929–1989*, ed. S. E. Gontarski. New York: Grove Press.

CPEF   Beckett, Samuel (1977), *Collected Poems in English and French*. New York: Grove Press.

E   Beckett, Samuel (2009), *Endgame & Act Without Words I*. New York: Grove Press.

G   Beckett, Samuel (1954), *Waiting for Godot*. New York: Grove Press.

Go   Beckett, Samuel (1952), *En Attendant Godot*. Paris: Minuit.

H   Beckett, Samuel (1964), *How It Is*. New York: Grove Press.

IL   Merleau-Ponty, Maurice (1993), 'Indirect Language and the Voices of Silence', trans. Michael B. Smith, in Galen A. Johnson (ed.), *The Merleau-Ponty Aesthetics Reader*. Evanston, IL: Northwestern University Press, pp. 76–120.

LB1   *The Letters of Samuel Beckett, vol. I, 1929–1940* (2009), ed. Martha Dow Fehsenfeld and Lois More Overbeck. Cambridge: Cambridge University Press.

LB2   *The Letters of Samuel Beckett, vol. II, 1941–1956* (2011), ed. George Craig, Martha Dow Fehsenfeld, Dan Gunn and Lois More Overbeck. Cambridge: Cambridge University Press.

LB3 *The Letters of Samuel Beckett, vol. III, 1957–1965* (2014), ed. George Craig, Martha Dow Fehsenfeld, Dan Gunn and Lois More Overbeck. Cambridge: Cambridge University Press.

M Beckett, Samuel (1957), *Murphy*. New York: Grove Press.

NH Beckett, Samuel (1996), *Nohow On: Company, Ill Seen Ill Said, Worstward Ho*. New York, Grove Press.

PP Merleau-Ponty, Maurice (2012), *Phenomenology of Perception*, trans. Donald A. Landes. Abingdon and New York: Routledge.

Ph Merleau-Ponty, Maurice (1945), *Phénoménologie de la perception*. Paris: Gallimard.

PTD Beckett, Samuel (1999), *Proust: Three Dialogues*. London: Calder.

TN Beckett, Samuel (1965), *Three Novels: Molloy, Malone Dies, The Unnamable*. New York: Grove Press.

VI Merleau-Ponty, Maurice (1968), *The Visible and the Invisible*, ed. Claude Lefort, trans. Alphonso Lingis. Evanston, IL: Northwestern University Press.

Vi Merleau-Ponty, Maurice (1964), *Le visible et l'invisible*, ed. Claude Lefort. Paris: Gallimard.

W Beckett, Samuel (1953), *Watt*. New York: Grove Press.

Introduction
Embodied Agency: Towards an Ecology of the Subject

> Just think of it, living flesh, for in spite of everything I was still living flesh.
>
> Beckett, 'The End'

Bodies in Beckett are no strangers to pain, dismemberment, compulsive spasms and decrepitude. Stuck in jars or trash bins or mounds of earth, or wandering unprotected from nature's fury, their own stink and the scorn of others, bodies in Beckett might strike us, quite reasonably, as abject, with no wish greater than to shuffle off this mortal coil. To some, the body in Beckett has appeared as an impediment to the mind's pursuit of rational perfection.[1] Although this view has been rightly criticised for overlooking Beckett's avid mockery of transcendence in all its forms, the discomfort associated with bodily being in Beckett makes the question animating this study seem, at first, counterintuitive. I ask: what possibilities are enabled in Beckett by assuming (rather than denying or transcending) the material limitations and embeddedness of the physical body?

My interest in embodiment and agency in Beckett grew out of an encounter with his bizarre 'ballet' for television, *Quad* (1981), at a Beckett centennial exhibition in Paris. Watching the four figures in colourful robes interweaving frantic patterns on a white square felt like watching a time-lapse video of a traffic intersection crossed with Nietzsche's eternal return of the same: bathetic and sublime. Beneath the supple fabric of the robes, one can just make out the contours of a knee or a shoulder, reminders that these are indeed bodies executing a perversely mechanistic design. *Quad* is often understood as dramatising the impossibility of human agency, as its players follow circuits set out in advance and cannot but repeat their trajectories *ad infinitum*.[2] But kaleidoscopic forms twist into view as the players form patterns invisible to them, swept up in a self-moving structure that includes and exceeds them. Constrained by their courses, the bodies nevertheless admit a volatile energy into their circuits. It made me wonder more generally about the fraught foregrounding of the body in Beckett, as well as our human possibilities for acting back on the structures (environment, culture and language) in which we are implicated.

Across the span of Beckett's work the human body is represented as antagonistically and intimately entangled with its material environment: buried to the waist then to the neck in a mound of earth packed hard under a scorching sun, crawling through mud or lying face down in a ditch, pummelled by rain. There are composite body-objects: heads potted in jars, bodies speaking tonelessly from urns (rims fit snugly to their necks), tied to rocking chairs and going stiff and wooden like the furniture. When they are not in danger of merging with or dispersing into the environment – crushed in the landscape's 'mighty systole, then scattered to the uttermost confines of space' (CP 99) – Beckettian bodies are confined in closed spaces, their movement restricted or compulsively repetitive, like *Quad*'s players riveted to their iterating series and May's metronomic walk in *Footfalls* (1976). In the late theatre and prose, the body is disarticulated, its parts isolated: Mouth in *Not I* (1972) and the 'worsening' shades in *Worstward Ho* (1983). Even the ghost-like bodies of the late plays draw attention to the body's (de-materialising) materiality. Insofar as the body inheres within its material environment, it seems to suffer for it, hindered by its own object – abject – nature.

Bodies in Beckett seem passive, impressed and affected by the vicissitudes of their environments: temperature, weather and the tempers of those who molest and displace them. They seem, at times, to (e)merge not only within their physical environments but also within language, the discursive material element in which they find themselves: 'words pronouncing me alive' (TN 335); 'I'm in words, made of words, others' words' (TN 386); 'I say it as I hear it' (H 7). Famously, Beckettian bodies 'go on' speaking or moving in the absence of recognisable signs of subjective intention or rational control, determined by structures (including language) of which they are a part. But if we shift our perspective to consider the body as experienced (rather than reified), a different story emerges: we find bodies involved in collaborative negotiations with their material surroundings, both physical and linguistic. In moving 'back', as it were, from a poststructuralist to a phenomenological perspective, I join scholars interested in Beckett and embodiment (Garner 1993; Maude 2009; McMullan 2010).

In a general sense, embodiment refers to the body as lived rather than as viewed from outside. In the history of philosophy, embodiment sets certain bodies apart from dead matter, for while we may speak of bodies like stones or asteroids that are not the bodies of any particular subjects, to 'speak of embodiment by contrast is always to speak of a subject that finds itself variously inhabited, or captaining, or being coextensive with, or even being imprisoned in, a body' (Smith 2018: 1). In phenomenology, Husserl distinguishes between the body as lived (*Leib*) and the body as matter (*Korper*), while his successor, Maurice Merleau-Ponty, puts embodiment at the centre of his phenomenology: 'One's own body is in the world just as the heart is in the organism; it continuously breathes life into the visible spectacle, animates it and nourishes it from within, and forms a system with it' (PP 209). In contemporary theory, embodiment has come to refer not only to the experience we have of our bodies – what it is like to be or live our bodies – but to the 'process whereby collective behaviors and beliefs, acquired through acculturation, are rendered individual and "lived" at the level of the body' (Noland 2009: 9). Embodiment, then, is how we assimilate the impressions of cultural practices and norms by living them.[3]

Insofar as it resists abstraction, embodiment has also been read in terms of its potential for subversion. 'The body', for Katherine Hayles, is an abstract concept, but embodiment is always specific and embedded, 'generated from the noise of difference' (Hayles 1999: 196–7). Embodiment becomes a site of resistance: 'Whereas the body can disappear into information with scarcely a murmur of protest, embodiment cannot, for it is tied to the circumstances of the occasion [. . .] Along with these particularities come concomitant strategies for resistances and subversions, excesses and deviations' (197–8).[4] Reading Beckett through the perspective of embodiment discourages us from viewing the body as wholly passive. Beckettian representation of embodiment suggests an active passivity (or passive activity) whereby what is inherited is assimilated and rearticulated. Wedged in earth or peering out of trash bins, jars, urns or ditches, Beckett's personae seem to ask what possibilities exist for (inter)acting within a world in which we are inextricably embedded. I argue that the body's embeddedness within its material world suggests a limited agency that stresses our embodied relationship to earth. Drawing on phenomenology, posthumanism and eco-criticism, I read in Beckett's representations of the body a 'passive' agency that challenges the voluntarism that has dominated post-Enlightenment thought, while avoiding the poststructuralist tendency to attribute agency to systems rather than individuals.[5]

A major achievement of poststructuralist readings of Beckett has been to demonstrate the extent to which his work unravels the idea of a voluntarist subject. Beckett's personae, unable to control the voices that speak them alive and course through them, remind us – often comically – of the limits of individual human control. A wave of scholarship in the 1990s aligned Beckett's work with that of Derrida, Deleuze and Foucault, dismantling the idea of the sovereign subject on which earlier, existentialist readings depended. Poststructuralist readings also account elegantly for the play of repetition, deferral and self-cannibalising narratives that characterise Beckett's prose (Connor 1988; Hill 1990; Tresize 1990; Katz 1999; Uhlmann 1999).[6] Such readings are compelling also because they situate Beckett's work within a theoretical milieu that engages explicitly with Beckett (Connor 2007: xii). Foucault's 'What is an Author' famously takes direction from Beckett's *Texts for Nothing* – 'What matter who's speaking, someone said what matter who's speaking' (Foucault 1977: 115; CP 109). Here the speaking subject is subordinated to its utterance, folded into a field of iterative citations. A writer does not express a thought, but, rather, writing itself 'implies an action that is always testing the limits of its regularity, transgressing and reversing an order that it accepts and manipulates' (Foucault 1977: 115–16). The writer is deprived of agency, which is conferred on writing itself, which creates 'an opening where the writing subject endlessly disappears' (116).

It could be that Beckett's work boldly presents the impossibility of human action in the face of linguistic, cultural, historical and material structures in which we are embedded. Elizabeth Barry (2006; 2008) and Steven Connor (1988), in different ways, amplify a crisis of agency in Beckett's work. Steven Connor looks at repetition across Beckett's oeuvre in relation to difference. As the place where 'certain radical instabilities' appear, repetition can induce generative variation (Connor 1988: 1). In poststructuralist fashion, Connor's reading situates agency within the workings of a transpersonal structure (like language).[7] Barry considers agency in relation to authority and to language, arguing that Beckett's work repurposes old forms – clichés – to revitalise language. More relevant to my topic, she indicates the body as a site where agency is problematised, calling attention to grammar constructions like the 'agentless sentence' that appear in connection with bodily processes: 'processes of living and dying are described in language that elides the question of agency, something that only emphasises the protagonists' failure to control their own physical existence' (Barry 2008: 121). She demonstrates that the problem of agency is everywhere in Beckett and unresolved (Barry 2006: 185). And yet the dynamic rapport that Beckettian bodies have with their environs – sucking stones or identifying with objects like hats, stools, boats and pencils – presents the human body in a ludic exchange with the material world, checking the idea that the body is incapable of (inter)action.

One of the most salient critiques of poststructuralist theory in general turns on the problem of agency. Traditionally, this critique has been framed in terms of ethical and political responsibility: How do we conceive of ethics in the absence of subjective interiority? To whom or what might ethical and political responsibility attach itself? In *Who Comes After the Subject?*, editors Eduardo Cadava, Peter Connor and Jean-Luc Nancy claim that one of the major theoretical problems we face after the twentieth century's challenge to the idea of an autonomous, willing subject is to arrive at an account of agency robust enough to survive, if not the death of the subject, then at least its imbrication in complex social structures and environments (Cadava et al. 1991: 4). In *Giving an Account of Oneself*, Judith Butler asks 'how a theory of subject formation that acknowledges the limits of self-knowledge can serve as a conception of ethics' (2005a: 19–20). She urges that lack of total self-knowledge cannot license us to abandon responsibility.[8] More recently, questions about human agency and its corollary (responsibility) are being reconsidered in light of anthropogenic climate change, which makes collective human (re)action both necessary and urgent (Coole and Frost 2010: 16).

Recently, theorists have turned to embodiment to find a middle way between the agentic impasse of poststructuralism (which evacuates the human, attaching agency to the play of transpersonal structures) and a voluntarism that confers upon the human subject an unrealistic power. Carrie Noland frames her interest in the moving body (and her work on agency and embodiment more generally) as an attempt 'to find a way beyond the impasse of constructivist theory', which she takes to be 'the inability, after Foucault, to produce a convincing account of agency' (2009: 9). Similarly, Diana Coole argues that descriptions of subjectivity as an effect of power or performative iteration make it 'difficult to envisage what kind of political agency could even in principle materialise and what its motivations or ambitions might be' (2005: 126). Both Coole and Noland find a way out of this impasse by recourse to embodiment, and both avail themselves of the theoretical tools made available by French phenomenology, in particular the work of Maurice Merleau-Ponty. In her rethinking of agency, Coole begins with the reflexivity Merleau-Ponty attributes to the body; in trying to touch itself while being touched, the body achieves a 'kind of reflection' that distinguishes it from objects (2005: 132). Noland links the possibility of agency to the awareness a body brings to its performance of cultural gestures, arguing that this awareness is 'agentic' in the sense that it plays a role in what a subject does and feels (2009: 16). 'Kinesthesia', or feeling the body move, can encourage experimentation, variation and even rejection of cultural routines. Noland defines agency as the power to alter collective behaviours and beliefs, acquired through acculturation and embodied 'for purposes that may be reactive (resistant) or collaborative (innovative) in kind' (9). For both Coole and Noland, embodiment provides the foundation for a non-voluntarist version of agency, a self-reflexivity that, arguably, extends beyond the human body to animate other forms of matter.

Like Coole and Noland, I view Merleau-Pontian phenomenology as offering viable possibilities for rethinking agency after poststructuralism – a project made particularly urgent as we renegotiate our (human) relationship with nonhuman species, technologies and the environment (Braidotti 2013). As phenomenologically oriented critics of Beckett have demonstrated, Merleau-Ponty's theory of embodied subjectivity reveals in Beckett's work a persistent foregrounding of the material, fleshy body and its role in cognition and in the construction of identity (Maude 2009: 135). My aim is to show that Merleau-Ponty's thought may also reveal a different, expanded mode of agency in Beckett, a move that phenomenologically oriented scholars of Beckett have either resisted for fear of returning to early 'affirmative' existential-humanist readings (Maude 2009: 71) or made in the context of performance, which limits the power of imaginative re-embodiment to Beckett's work for the stage (McMullan 2010).[9] Beckett criticism before the turn of the twenty-first century moved sharply between viewing Beckett's work in terms of voluntarist agency and seeing individual agency evacuated or beholden to the iterative movement of structures like language. What Merleau-Pontian phenomenology offers is a middle way: an understanding of agency that avoids the poles of voluntarism and poststructuralism by attending to the physical body's kinship with its material environment.

Etymologically, phenomenology means the study of what is given in appearances (*phenomena*) or directly accessible to the senses. Rather than two worlds – one of sensory appearances, the other of objective realities – phenomenologists see only one world of appearances with their different modes of appearing. The study of how phenomena reveal themselves gives us their truth (Zahavi 2018: 14). This privileging of perceptual experience over scientific abstraction appealed to Merleau-Ponty, whose most important contribution to twentieth-century thought was to replace the 'transcendental ego' with a 'body-subject' which 'acts' only in collaboration with the material environment of which it is a part. Following his engagement with structuralism in the 1950s, Merleau-Ponty applies this idea to language. As in Beckett, language itself becomes a navigable terrain, an 'environment' that spawns selves and worlds. But what distinguishes this kind of thinking from structuralism and poststructuralism, which similarly suggest that subjectivities are formed within language, is the importance attached to the physical body, which organises spatial and linguistic terrain by moving within it. The body, for Merleau-Ponty, far from being an obstruction to transcendental knowledge, becomes the precondition for an embodied agency that avoids the extremes of voluntarism (the subject is sovereign) and poststructuralism (the subject is that through which structural forces act).

Though they shared the cultural, political and intellectual milieu of Paris from 1928 to 1961 and the environment of the École Normale Supérieure from 1928 to 1930, it is unlikely that Beckett and Merleau-Ponty knew each other personally. In a letter to Lois Oppenheim, Merleau-Ponty's wife reports that Merleau-Ponty's library contained books by Beckett, though these books did not make an appearance in Merleau-Ponty's reading notes. The two also had a number of friends in common, through whom Beckett may have become acquainted with ideas important to French phenomenology: Jean Beaufret, Georges Duthuit and Alberto Giacometti.[10] Rather than tracing direct influence, my focus here is the theoretical value of pairing aspects of Merleau-Ponty's thought with Beckett. The theoretical overlay is rich: Merleau-Ponty's theory of subjectivity as embodied perspective, inextricable from its surrounding environment, presents Beckettian bodies, exaggeratedly embedded in their world, as exploring different possibilities for (re)acting, not by transcending their material limitations but by reshaping them by their interactions: a more robust, if limited, material agency.

Though Merleau-Ponty's emphasis on embodiment puts him at the centre of a turn to phenomenology in Beckett studies, Husserl, Sartre, Heidegger and other figures feature in the volume *Beckett and Phenomenology* (Feldman and Maude 2009).[11] It is only natural, after two decades of poststructuralist critique that tended to reduce the body to a texture of signs, that critics should move to interrogate the body as lived experience. As Steven Connor writes, '[t]hose contemporary critics who have turned to phenomenology have often done so in order to make out a more intimate and inward sense of embodied experience than poststructuralist criticism seemed to make possible, looking for a "phenomenological body" to supplement post-structuralism's body of signs' (Connor 2014a: 28). Indeed, Ulrika Maude's *Beckett, Technology and the Body* (2009) praises poststructuralist critics for recognising the 'textual foregrounding' of the body in Beckett's work, but she takes aim at a 'poststructuralist bias, which has emphasized the discursively produced body at the expense of the material fleshly one' (Maude 2009: 2). A phenomenological approach enables Maude to attend to the lived experience of the 'maimed and visceral' body in Beckett, which she does by focusing on sensory experience, devoting chapters to vision, hearing and touch as well as to motility and to the role of technological prosthesis in mediating the senses – of no small importance to Beckett.

Maude's work valuably illuminates the importance of the lived body in Beckett – a body that is visceral, mortal, capable of sensation, pain and secretions – and it breaks ground insofar as it dispenses with the existentialist-humanist view of the body as an impediment while avoiding the poststructuralist tendency to reduce the body to a collection of signs. Maude's work inaugurates a turn to the (fleshy and sensing) body in Beckett, and she aptly applies Merleau-Ponty's idea of incarnate subjectivity to Beckett's work. Her materialist study of the senses demonstrates the extent to which Beckett 'grounds' subjectivity in the body but it stops short of exploring what kind of agency this might afford the body-subject, breaking with phenomenology at this crucial juncture. She writes: 'Over and over again in his work Beckett emphasises the incarnate nature of subjectivity, while simultaneously demonstrating how vision, hearing, touch and technologically enhanced forms of perception expand the limits of the body, facilitating the subject's transgression beyond itself' (Maude 2009: 137). The subject's 'transgression beyond itself' and the expansion of the 'limits of the body' suggest a body-subject capable of interacting in collaboration with its world – an agentic capacity. Yet Maude insists that Beckett differs from Merleau-Ponty by refusing to find in the body 'a new locus of meaning' (22). For Maude, Beckett's work 'radically departs' from that of Merleau-Ponty 'in its stern refusal of all forms of transcendence' (22). This claim becomes more fraught when it is repeated later in the book: 'Although Beckett's work denies all forms of transcendence, and hence, unlike Merleau-Ponty's writing, refuses to posit the body as a new locus of meaning, his focus on sensory perception suggests that, in a disenchanted world, sensuality emerges as a new, albeit subtle source of value' (137). What sort of 'value', then, emerges from sensuality? Maude is careful to point out – perhaps to avoid being read as reverting to existentialist-humanist, 'affirmative' readings left behind in the 1990s – that 'the affirmative nature of Merleau-Ponty's thinking is lost on Beckett' (22). And while Maude is right to mark the differences between Merleau-Ponty's phenomenology and Beckett's writing – amply apparent in their tones and sensibilities on the page (in Beckett there is a horror of merging with the world that is nowhere present in Merleau-Ponty) – I argue that Merleau-Ponty's early development of the body-subject as well as his late ontology of the flesh reveal a radical interrogation of agency in Beckett. Merleau-Ponty's 'flesh of the world', a material element that joins the body with its material environment and with other bodies, entails an ontology of immanence, emphasising the body-subject's inherence within its world. Maude's reading valuably demonstrates the extent to which what we think we *will* is founded on what is non-agential (nonconscious bodily processes), but it leaves room to investigate the body's agentic possibilities, particularly in connection with Merleau-Ponty's late work.

My project builds on the body-focused work of Ulrika Maude as well as that of Anna McMullan, whose book *Performing Embodiment in Samuel Beckett's Drama* (2010) also engages with Merleau-Pontian phenomenology. McMullan does locate a version of agency in embodiment, particularly in the context of performance. For McMullan, there is a subversive element to Beckett's drama, which 'produces new modes of intercorporeal embodiment out of the materials of subjection and vulnerability' (McMullan 2010: 9). McMullan prefers the term 'embodiment' to 'body' because it not only accommodates 'the unstable and uncanny incarnations in Beckett's work, such as a mouth, a voice or even just an intake and outtake of breath' but also because it evokes the subjective experience of being a body while still 'engag[ing] a history of the ways in which bodies have been represented, imagined, analysed and regulated' (4). McMullan's conception of embodiment bridges a view of the body as marked by cultural and conceptual frameworks (including language) with the body as lived. This duality of the body (as represented and as experienced) enables McMullan to ask: 'To what extent is the individual body subjected to authority, and to what extent does the subject assert agency through imaginative re-embodiments – the embodied subject imagining his or her embodiment?' (4). Discussing the play *Catastrophe* (1982), McMullan writes that the body 'emerges as a site of struggle between the agency of the self, the other and the inherited grammar of language and movement' (109–10). As we perform embodiment, we explore our power to recompose ourselves and those legacies we necessarily inherit. For McMullan, it is the 'experiential framework of performance' that allows Beckett to present and work through such questions (110). Building on McMullan's work, I consider how embodiment across Beckett's oeuvre (not only in performance) engages its environment to support a limited, material agency.

McMullan aptly describes Merleau-Ponty's sense that 'the embodied subject is both determined by the world and remakes the world' (McMullan 2010: 11), but Merleau-Ponty's agency-oriented philosophy should not be written off as a return to 'transcendence'. The body-subject's inherence in the material world – as a thing among things and as part of the element Merleau-Ponty calls the 'flesh' – distinguishes his thinking from Husserl's transcendental idealism.[12] For Merleau-Ponty, meaning and structure emerge within matter as immanent reconfigurations, such that consciousness, subjectivity or mind are just reifications of the contingent capacities to structure and stylise the world that develop from bodily interactions (Coole 2010: 102). To say that Merleau-Ponty's agency-oriented philosophy is relevant to a reading of Beckett is not to say that Beckett's work must have meaning or to reinstall subjective agency under different terms. Rather, it is to emphasise that only as a collaboration with the material environment is agency possible. Recent 'postcognitivist' studies of Beckett argue that Beckett's fictional minds are grounded in interactions with their fictional environments (no matter how diminished these environments may become in the late prose) (Beloborodova 2020: 63; Van Hulle 2012). Postcognitivist theories of mind are akin to Merleau-Ponty's thought insofar as they emphasise embodied cognition. Enactivism, for example, is explicitly indebted to Merleau-Ponty. It rejects representational accounts of cognition and argues instead that cognitive processes take place through interaction with one's surroundings (such that cognitive systems both shape and are shaped by their worlds) (Beloborodova 2020: 63).[13] A Merleau-Pontian reading highlights in Beckett a material agency identified also by cognitive literary theorists. Beckett's amalgams of bodies, objects and earth, of human forms entangled with their environments, intimate that only in collaboration with the world can anything (including literature) be made at all.

While this project builds on previous phenomenological approaches to Beckett, part of where it differs is in its attempt to connect the abstract notion of 'an organism's spatial environs' (Merleau-Ponty) or 'lifeworld' (Husserl) to our contemporary environment in peril.[14] At the same time, I aim to illustrate how Merleau-Ponty's thinking anticipates theories of material agency that underpin contemporary efforts to rethink relations between the human and the nonhuman – efforts grouped under the heading 'posthumanism'. Phenomenology's focus on the interrelation between an organism and its environment is so pertinent to ecology that the contemporary phenomenologist and Merleau-Ponty scholar Ted Toadvine writes that 'phenomenology, led by its own momentum, becomes a philosophical ecology' (Brown and Toadvine 2003: xiii). The cross-section of phenomenology and ecological thought has led to the flourishing subfield 'eco-phenomenology', which David Wood defines broadly as 'the pursuit of the relationalities of worldly engagement, both human and those of other creatures' (2003: 151).[15] Where eco-phenomenology differs from other forms of eco-criticism is in its attempt to find a middle way between naturalist causality (which phenomenology was created to resist) and simple intentionality (our connection to things and the implicit idea that what we see comes into being through our interaction with it). In this context, Merleau-Ponty's situation of the body-subject within its world, and his theoretical elaboration of the 'chiasm' to describe the body's complex attachment to its material environment (neither opposed to it nor fused with it), may help us reconceptualise our human relationship with (and responsibility to) the environment (Toadvine 2009, 2017). Insofar as he understands the human as embodied, as part of the materiality of the earth, Merleau-Ponty questions modernity's separation of the human from nature. His thinking undermines 'resourcist, technological, economic, and managerial approaches to environmental problems', revealing in them a 'modernist instrumental rationality' (Toadvine 2017: 174). Among phenomenology's contributions to environmental ethics, Toadvine includes also 'its aim to articulate a post-metaphysical conception of the self-world relation and an alternative ethos appropriate to our experience of nature' (175). Merleau-Ponty's body-subject, consubstantial with its environment, founds a more diffuse and provisional version of subjectivity – one that contrasts sharply with the Enlightenment humanist subject. Might Beckett's work also model human-environment interrelations that resist the modernist and metaphysical paradigms of separation and exploitation?

The body-subject, in contrast to the humanist subject, or the subject of modernity who severs himself from nature, already implies a less hierarchical rapport between humans and the environment. In his celebrated book *We Have Never Been Modern*, Bruno Latour criticises modernity's sharp divide between the human and the natural world, which led to human domination and exploitation of the environment. Latour's thinking, along with that of Donna Haraway and others, has been influential for contemporary theorists grouped loosely under the headings 'posthumanism' and 'new materialisms' (Coole and Frost 2010).[16] In contemporary theory as in phenomenology the 'material environment' expands to encompass technology, which interpenetrates the biological, fleshy body – a hybridisation relevant also for Beckett.[17] The thinkers associated with posthumanism vary in their orientations and methods, but they share an interest in material subjectivity, in renegotiating the boundary between the human and the nonhuman and (for many) in reconceptualising agency ontologically and politically.[18] For Rosi Braidotti, 'the common denominator for the posthuman condition is an assumption about the vital, self-organizing and yet non-naturalistic structure of living matter itself' (2013: 2). To attribute to nonhuman matter vital capacities for organisation is to erode modernity's divide between an 'active' subject and a 'passive' object and to encourage a rethinking of agency. Jane Bennett (2010) attributes 'agentic capacities' to things – edibles, commodities, storms, metals – in such a way that differs from Katherine Hayles's more cognitivist account of distributed cognition, yet both extend agency beyond the human. Karen Barad's 'agential realism' borrows from quantum physics to reconceptualise agency as interaction (entities emerge from their interactions rather than pre-existing them) (2007, especially chapter four). The idea that individual agencies emerge through interaction or entanglement recalls the way Merleau-Ponty's perceiver and perceived are mutually constituted through the intertwining of the flesh.

Many thinkers associated with posthumanism and new materialism engage explicitly with Merleau-Ponty, recognising the extent to which their work resonates with a phenomenology of embodiment. Astrida Niemans, for instance, proposes a 'posthuman phenomenology' that extends the experience of embodiment beyond subjectivised humans to other bodies, for instance 'bodies' of water (2017: 23–4). Diana Coole argues that, in his late unfinished writings, Merleau-Ponty 'was envisaging a radically new materialism' insofar as he sought to explain 'a generative, self-transformative, and creative materiality without relying on any metaphysical invocation of mysterious, immaterial forces or agencies' (2010: 93). Posthumanism, like eco-phenomenology, illuminates the relevance of Merleau-Ponty's work for rethinking agency and environmental ethics; the effort to theorise material agency is a phenomenological project highly relevant to contemporary theory. Although the present study is grounded in Merleau-Pontian phenomenology rather than in eco-criticism or posthumanism, both of which are vast and varied fields, the relevance of phenomenological embodiment to these approaches enables me to gesture towards how Beckett's hybrid bodies, vital landscapes and parodies of anthropocentrism may anticipate and inform efforts to reimagine the rapport between the human and our nonhuman environment.

Although there have been studies of Beckett and ecology (Davies 2006; Garrard 2011; Lavery 2018) and engaging forays into Beckett and the posthuman (Boulter 2019; Rabaté 2016; Tubridy 2018), there has been little concerted attention to how representations of the body in Beckett might be understood in light of these approaches. My focus on embodiment brings together elements of phenomenology, posthumanism and ecocriticism to investigate material agency in Beckett's work. Greg Garrard's ecological reading of *Endgame* takes up the unrepresentability of climate change, drawing on Timothy Morton's idea that 'ecological thought makes our world vaster and more insubstantial at the same time' (Morton 2010 as qtd in Garrard 2011: 394). As demonstrated by my ecological readings of 'The End' (Chapter 1) and *Endgame* (Chapter 3), my focus is less on the problem of representing climate change than on the human's inherence within its environment and the implications this has for agency. Engagements with the posthuman in Beckett studies, though provocative, tend to be siloed; in his study of posthuman space, Jonathan Boulter (2019) uses a Heideggerian approach to suggest a radical 'dismantling' of the idea of the human, while Jean-Michel Rabaté interrogates the 'limit' of the human using a conception of the posthuman he derives from James Joyce's description of Molly Bloom in a letter from 1922. Rabaté connects Molly's association with the 'posthuman figure of the revolving earth' to Beckett's admiration of anti-anthropomorphism in Jack Yeats's paintings (2016: 37–9). Rabaté jokes that the 'posthuman' today 'calls up analyses of subjectless technology, cyborgs, and mutants or post-Deleuzian organic machines and "bodies without organs"' and emphasises (rightly) Beckett's reluctance 'to push the speaking and desiring subject beyond the human altogether' (41). More sympathetic to contemporary posthumanism – to Braidotti's claim that posthumanism does not reject the human but moves beyond anthropocentric humanism – Derval Tubridy, arguing that Beckett opens up a space for subjectivity beyond the human, lays 'the groundwork for further developments in our thinking of Beckett in terms of the posthuman: the materialist, vitalist and relational subject' (2018: 202). Building on this work in Beckett studies, I consider also how eco-phenomenology and posthumanism mobilise phenomenological ideas to respond to an environment in crisis. These approaches, with their strong ties to phenomenology, reveal not only how Beckett's work exposes the brittleness of an

Enlightenment subject, separate from its world, but also – and this has been less extensively discussed – how representations of bodies as embedded (often horrifically) within their material environment may startle us into a more agile conception of agency – an agency rooted in embodiment.

Therefore, the abject, decrepit body in Beckett does not, as some have argued, signal the impossibility of agency, but demands its reconceptualisation. My interrogation of the power to do and act in Beckett proceeds through an analysis of the body as it is represented throughout his work, focusing on four moments in his career: his early parodies of Descartes, his inter- and postwar writing, the stylistic innovation in the 1960s (*How It Is*) and the late prose. At these junctures, Beckett's representation of the body changes, moving from a critical excoriation of disembodied rationalism in *Murphy* (1938) to a meditation on the body as a limit that enables the work of creation and de-creation in *Worstward Ho* (1983). This study favours Beckett's prose, considering his drama and television work only insofar as it illuminates aspects of his literary experimentation. One reason for this is that much prior work on Beckett and phenomenology has focused on the late drama and television plays (Garner 1993; McMullan 2010; McTighe 2013), though Maude's 2009 study does attend to the prose, as well as radio plays and *Film* (1965). Another reason is my interest in exploring Merleau-Ponty's surprising conception of language as a spatial environment as it plays out in Beckett. Four salient ideas in Merleau-Ponty's thought will serve as anchors in this study: the body-subject, his theory of style as an effect of perception, the chiasm (which illustrates a reversibility between perceiver and perceived) and the flesh of the world.

Chapter 1 traces both thinkers' ambivalent engagement with Descartes: Beckett's parody of Cartesian rationalism in *Murphy* and Merleau-Ponty's revision of the *cogito* as he develops the 'body-subject'. Both thinkers replace a transcendental subject with an embodied one, figured horrifically and comically (in Beckett) as part of its material world. This gesture is reprised in Beckett's anti-anthropomorphic fable 'The End' (1946), which I read as a coda to *Murphy*.

With reference to Merleau-Ponty's essay 'Cézanne's Doubt' (1945), Chapter 2 shows how paradox in Beckett provokes the jarring of 'incompossibles', creating space in which objects become visible from multiple perspectives. In Beckett's interwar novel *Watt* and in Lucky's speech in *Waiting for Godot*, written in French in 1948, language is revitalised by its connection to the sensing body. Intellection is revealed as bodily, passive as well as active, challenging assumptions that undergird humanist agency.

Spatiality is the focus of Chapter 3, which argues that Beckett's postwar writing replaces dialectical progress with the body's wandering in space, shattering faith in the predictable progress of thesis-antithesis-synthesis. Merleau-Ponty's theory of space as elastic, as malleable, supports a reading of *Molloy*, *Malone Dies* and *Endgame* as reshaping textual and physical space, not least by fusing beginnings and endings. Molloy begins at the end of his quest, in his mother's room, replacing teleology (or destination) with the idea that subject and place co-constitute (room as womb). Detained by Lousse, a Circe figure allied with the body, Molloy's materiality intertwines him with others and with his surroundings, while Malone's meta-fictional emphasis dramatises the scene of writing and opens a realm of play. Finally, *Endgame* joins immanence with infinity, the discomfort of which suggests an ethics of bodily endurance.

The theme of bodily endurance extends to Chapter 4, a study of how aporia operates in *The Unnamable* to question the value of a certain kind of spatial politics. To explore how *The Unnamable* exploits contradiction to generate alternative ways of moving and meaning, I draw on Merleau-Ponty's reinvention of the dialectic as the chiasm (or reversibility) and on Derrida's writings on aporia. With what seems like a divestiture of humanist agency comes an ethics of endurance – underscored by Merleau-Ponty's embedding of subjectivity in the flesh – and a renegotiation of the conditions of passage.

In the 1950s, influenced by structuralism, Merleau-Ponty extends his theory of the body-subject to language, which he describes as a spatial environment amenable to shaping by the operation of 'style'. If style corrupts independent agency for the young Beckett (his early letters associate it with involuntary transmission of influence), it is, for Merleau-Ponty, the manifestation of a deeper, passive agency and the engine of (creative) variation. Chapter 5 explores how style, in Merleau-Ponty's radical sense, as bodily signification, operates in Beckett's *How It Is* (1961). The novel's setting in mud accents what the body's orientation of space and the linguistic emergence of meaning have in common: the task of form-giving (mud is linked to the dust from which, according to Genesis, humans were formed by God). But Beckett's unflinching descriptions of torture and sexual violence accent the pain of bodies belonging to a common element in a way that Merleau-Ponty never works through.

Chapter 6 turns to *Quad*, where bodies in space create a non-verbal 'language' that means by repetition and variation. *Quad*'s repetition, like the repetition found in certain rites and rituals, disturbs the comfortable opposition between compulsion and creative invention. *Quad* demonstrates how the body's compulsive repetition, despite its uncomfortable closeness to addiction, may harness a loss of individual control that expands the parameters of agency.

In Beckett's late prose, closed space is a precondition for creation, as it enables a self-reflexivity that Merleau-Ponty associates with sentience. Chapter 7 begins with a discussion of Merleau-Ponty's late ontology of the flesh, then turns to Beckett's *Worstward Ho*, which invents a peculiar language and takes spatial direction as its theme. I argue that the self-referential language of *Worstward Ho* (phrases vary their precedents according to a pattern) shares the self-reflexive structure of the flesh described by Merleau-Ponty. Words and phrases, as part of the 'flesh' of language, unmake and remake meaning as they unmake and remake the text's human forms, joining the project of world-creation in language to the more general project of being.

In Beckett, the physical body's capacity to reconfigure its surroundings renders viable a version of material agency that permits us to vary determining structures (spatial, linguistic, technological and cultural) from positions within them.

Notes

1. See Ulrika Maude's critique of Hugh Kenner, whose famous 'Cartesian Centaur' argument, according to which Molloy's body is juxtaposed against the rational perfection of his bicycle, presents the material body as obstacle in Beckett's work. Such a reading, for Maude, ignores moments in Beckett that invest value in embodied experience and Beckett's 'repeated, albeit often reluctant, realization of the unsustainable nature of transcendental thought' (2009: 2).
2. My description borrows from Bryden (1995) and McMullan (2010), for whom the 'excess' of the material body complicates *Quad*'s movement towards abstraction. For a reading of *Quad*, see Chapter 6.
3. Carrie Noland takes inspiration from Merleau-Ponty to propose 'a theory of agency fully implicated in embodiment', where embodiment is the 'ambiguous phenomenon in which culture both asserts and loses its grip on individual subjects' (2009: 16).

4. Anna McMullan connects embodiment with subversion in the context of Beckett's theatre, which 'presents a radical transvaluation of vulnerability and otherness, using the public space of the stage to interrogate the laws and norms that judge and marginalize non-normative identities and bodies' (2010: 10).
5. Voluntarism, in this context, refers to the philosophical idea that the will is the fundamental principle or dominant factor in the individual or in the universe (*OED*).
6. In *Into the Breach*, Thomas Tresize voices the critical commonplace that poststructuralism replaces phenomenology. He describes a 'general economy of signification that conditions and exceeds the universe of phenomenology' (1990: 160). Stanton B. Garner rightly objects that the version of phenomenology Tresize rejects is 'a polemical construction' based narrowly on Derrida's critique of Husserl. This caricatured version of phenomenology ignores Merleau-Ponty's phenomenology of embodiment and its refashioning of the humanist subject in a way that is different from but complementary to poststructuralism's linguistic/textual problematics (Garner 1993: 446). On poststructuralism's debt to phenomenology, consider also Christopher Norris's claim: 'Derrida is as far from "rejecting" Husserl as he is from simply dismissing the linguistics of Saussure or the structuralist anthropology of Levi-Strauss' (*Deconstruction: Theory and Practice* p. 48 as qtd in Garner 1993: 447).
7. It is interesting to note Connor's shift from a poststructuralist reading that arguably ignores the body by reducing it to signs (Connor 1988) to a materialist reading of the body in Beckett via Sartre (Connor 2014a) to his most recent work, which he characterises as 'against agency'. *Giving Way: Thoughts on Unappreciated Dispositions* (2019) considers human-inhuman ecological awareness, and 'in a world that promotes assertion, agency, and empowerment, [. . .] challenges us to revalue a range of actions and attitudes that have come to be disregarded or dismissed as merely passive' (3). The conscientious passivity Connor describes and the 'imperious humility' he attributes to Beckett are more in line with what I am suggesting here.
8. Ten years later, Butler reformulates the issue, writing that 'norms, conventions, institutional forms of power, are already acting prior to any action I may undertake [. . .] The task is to think of being acted on and acting as simultaneous, and not only as a sequence' (2015: 6). Butler's theorisation of this active passivity may be a response to critics like Diana Coole, who writes that 'difference' has 'substituted for agency in these anti-humanist approaches, sustaining certain agentic qualities (notably generativity) in the absence of agents. Butler [. . .] explains the productivity of power as "inadvertently generative" due to the "functions of differential relations"' (Coole

2005: 140). Carrie Noland also disputes Butler's early description of agency: 'all signification takes place within the orbit of the compulsion to repeat; "agency", then, is to be located within the possibility of a variation on that repetition' (Noland 2009: 145). For Noland: 'as soon as Butler denies "the fiction of the ego" and places agency squarely in the "orbit of the compulsion to repeat" resistance becomes a very slippery project indeed' (188).

9. Derval Tubridy goes some way towards stitching together the divide between Beckett's drama and his prose, building on Anna McMullan's work to suggest that Beckett achieves a form of embodied relationality in his plays, which then 'influence the development of his prose as it evolves the taut viscerality that voices a material subjectivity' (Tubridy 2018: 201). I find this argument compelling, but I suspect that the influence moves in both directions.

10. In her 1995 letter, Merleau-Ponty's wife wrote: 'je ne sais pas si Beckett et mon mari se sont connus à l'ENS, mais ce dont je suis sûre, c'est qu'il n'y a pas eu de vraies relations entre eux au cours des années pendant lesquelles j'ai vécu avec mon mari [. . .] Mon mari connaissait certainement l'œuvre de Beckett, il y a plusieurs livres de lui dans la bibliothèque, mais je n'ai pas trouvé de notes de lectures dans ses papiers' (Oppenheim 2000: 207). For more detailed accounts of the biographical connections between Merleau-Ponty and Beckett, see Oppenheim (2000: 94–120) and Maude (2009: 5).

11. Stanton B. Garner (1993) first pairs Merleau-Ponty with Beckett in his study of the late drama. Lois Oppenheim (2000) draws on Merleau-Ponty in her study of Beckett and visual art. The twenty-first century has seen a more concerted interest in Beckett and phenomenology, particularly around issues of embodiment (Maude 2009; Feldman and Maude 2009; McMullan 2010; McTighe 2013). Interest in Merleau-Ponty in Beckett studies reflects a turn to phenomenology in modernist studies more broadly, as evidenced by books such as *Modernism, Phenomenology and Beyond* (2010) and *Understanding Merleau-Ponty, Understanding Modernism* (2018).

12. Whether or not Merleau-Ponty's philosophy qualifies as transcendental is debatable. Certainly, Husserl conceived of phenomenology as a transcendental mode of investigation; he sought pure, unchanging structures of experience and to provide empirical science with non-empirical philosophical grounding. But although Merleau-Ponty occasionally uses the language of transcendence, his thinking doesn't ultimately make claims of a transcendental kind (Inkpin 2017: 27). Merleau-Ponty's contestation of a self-present, self-transparent subject aligns his work more closely with poststructuralism than with transcendental idealism.

13. Dan Zahavi and Shaun Gallagher point out that Merleau-Ponty offers one of the best examples of how phenomenology can play an important role in the cognitive sciences. With the advent of embodied approaches to cognition (beginning in the 1990s), scientists and philosophers have appealed to Merleau-Pontian ideas to develop their objections to disembodied cognition, countering 'functionalism', the idea that 'cognition could be instantiated in a disembodied computer program, or "brain-in-a-vat"' (Gallagher and Zahavi 2012: 5).
14. Anna McMullan's most recent book, *Beckett's Intermedial Ecosystems: Closed Space Environments Across the Stage, Prose and Media Works*, forthcoming as the present volume moves into production, promises a fascinating account of human agency within the closed space 'ecosystems' developed in Beckett's work.
15. Toadvine argues further that 'an adequate account of our ecological situation requires the methods and insights of phenomenology' (Brown and Toadvine 2003: viii). Husserl, Heidegger, Merleau-Ponty and Levinas are the phenomenologists evoked most often by eco-phenomenology. On Merleau-Ponty and ecology see Toadvine (2009), Cataldi, ed. (2007) and notes from Merleau-Ponty's 1950s course on nature at the Collège de France (2003a and 2003b).
16. Braidotti is careful to mention that the 'posthuman' does not imply a rejection of the human but rather 'an enlarged sense of community, which includes one's territorial or environmental interconnections' (2013: 190). Even so, the prefix *post-* implies a move 'beyond'. Donna Haraway takes distance from this term in her recent work, seeking 'to refuse human exceptionalism without invoking posthumanism' (Haraway 2016: 13). Playfully recycling 'post', Haraway uses the term 'compost' to describe the human as complexly interwoven within a material environment that includes other beings. She writes: 'Natures, cultures, subjects, and objects do not preexist their intertwined worldings' (13). Though the term 'posthuman' is imperfect, I use it here to designate the confluence of recent attempts to part ways with social constructivism (while avoiding reversion to naturalism).
17. The phenomenologist Don Ihde explicitly reimagines the lifeworld to include technology in *Technology and the Lifeworld* (1990); in Beckett studies, Yoshiki Tajiri's *Samuel Beckett and the Prosthetic Body* (2006) questions the borders of the human body vis-à-vis the nonhuman, material world.
18. For instance, Braidotti's theorising of subjectivity as a 'process of auto-poiesis or self-styling, which involves complex and continuous negotiations with dominant norms and values and hence also multiple forms of accountability' means that political agency does not always have to be 'critical in the negative sense of oppositional' (2013: 35).

CHAPTER I

From Cartesian Ruins: Rocking Chair Phenomenology

Cartesian rationalism is a point of departure for both Beckett and Merleau-Ponty, though neither can accept the bedrock of the self as a thinking thing, split off from the body and its world. In opposition to a dominant philosophical climate of intellectualism in early twentieth-century France, Merleau-Ponty refashions Husserl's phenomenology to amplify the importance of the body and senses. Against the idea that the body makes us less human (our senses distracting us from pure ideas), Merleau-Ponty argues that it makes us more so. He argues: 'there would be for me no such thing as space if I did not have a body' (PP 104). In contrast to the disembodied subject proposed by Cartesian and neo-Kantian philosophies in fashion at the time, he proposes a body-subject, whose position in the world structures space into perspectives. In this way, the body in space usurps the task philosophy has traditionally assigned to the transcendental subject: the task of creating meaning.

Beckett's early parodies of Descartes – particularly Murphy's catastrophic success at ridding himself of his body – suggest similarly that subjectivity cannot be severed from the body's position and perspective. If Descartes is radically refashioned by Merleau-Ponty, he is sharply parodied by Beckett, who spins out the consequences of dualism beyond the point of absurdity. Although Beckett resists the inclination to set up positive theses and his parodies are famously ambivalent, I suggest that his engagement with seventeenth-century rationalism leads him, paradoxically, to exaggerate the body's oddities, its capacity for sensation and its embodied agency – a limited, material agency hinted at in the final scene of *Murphy* (1938), when Mr Kelly flies his kite in Kensington Gardens.

Anglophone Beckett criticism since the 1950s has foregrounded the influence of Descartes, calling Beckett a 'Cartesian' writer and attributing to him 'a life-long obsession with Descartes' (Scruton 1983: 123; see also Mintz 1959; Kenner 1959). Critics were equally swift to notice that Beckett's ambivalent parody extends to Descartes' contemporary Arnold Geulincx, whose dualism led him to attribute all causal agency to God. The powerlessness of the human to effect change in the world comes with an ethos of humility for Geulincx, who connects this humility to the absence of desire: *ubi nihil vales, ibi nihil velis* (where you are worth nothing, there you shall want nothing). Although Beckett's philosophy notes suggest a range of influences other than Descartes and Geulincx (Feldman 2006), Beckett's early fiction engages seriously with rationalism as it probes the relation between mind and world. Where Merleau-Ponty emphasises the primacy of the body and perception, Beckett's Murphy endeavours to restrain his body to 'free' his mind. Murphy's attempt to control what of the world he takes in culminates in the body's destruction and distribution across its material world. With *Murphy*, I read Beckett's anti-anthropomorphic fable 'The End' (1946), in which the narrator is crushed in the landscape's mighty systole. A Merleau-Pontian reading suggests that even Beckett's early fiction situates the body-mind within the material world of things, engaging ambivalently with Descartes to precipitate the fall of the transcendental subject. In its place emerges an embodied subject, ecological insofar as it is figured (horrifically and comically in Beckett) as part of its material landscape.

Merleau-Ponty revises the Cartesian *cogito*, separate from the world it seeks to know, and conceives of a 'body-subject', oriented within the world of which it is a part. With the body-subject, Merleau-Ponty brings meaning-making out of the realm of the transcendental, down to earth and into the life of the body. His major work, *Phenomenology of Perception* (1945), demonstrates how the body induces direction (*sens*) in its surrounding space. The idea that meaning emerges in the interaction between body and world challenges the sufficiency of a definition of agency as the activity of a willing subject.[1] It is appropriate, in light of this, that Beckett's much-anticipated Godot evokes *godillot* or *godasse*, French slang for shoe, playfully linking bodily movement (walking) to a meaning-making typically assigned to the ultimate transcendental subject, God.[2] Beckett's leitmotif of onwardness, which appears with increasing frequency in his later work (especially *Worstward Ho*), further suggests the body's involvement in a partly involuntary form of meaning.

Phenomenology's arrival in France entailed a reworking of Husserlian ideas to accent the lived experience of the body. Like his contemporaries Jean-Paul Sartre and Simone de Beauvoir, Merleau-Ponty sought to restore philosophy's contact with sensory experience, so that philosophy might take as its object something as quotidian as the taste of an apricot cocktail at a Montparnasse café.[3] Dissatisfied with the Cartesian intellectualist philosophy taught at the École Normale Supérieure where he was a student, Merleau-Ponty responded, with Sartre and de Beauvoir, to Husserl's call in his 1929 Paris Lectures to return 'to the things themselves'.[4] By 'things' Husserl refers not to material objects but to the ideal forms and contents of experience (Carman 2012: viii). He calls for a suspension of the scientific and conventional frameworks through which we understand experience in order to glimpse its underlying structures. One such structure is intentionality in the specialised sense that it is used in phenomenology: the idea that consciousness must always be *about* something. Intentionality in this technical sense differs from its everyday meaning; it refers not to an intention to do something but to the directed nature of consciousness. Husserl's phenomenological reduction, or *époché*, brackets the 'natural attitude' in which the world appears to us to open a 'new region of being never before delimited in its own peculiarity' (Husserl 1983: 62–4). In his first book of *Ideas* (1913), Husserl instructs that: 'at each step we faithfully describe what we see, from our point of view and after the most serious study, actually see' (235). This emphasis on first-person description and the idea that radical subjectivity can lead to objectivity carries over into Merleau-Ponty's thinking, which shifts to posit the body's perspective as the foundation for subjectivity.[5]

A version of transcendental idealism supported by Merleau-Ponty's teacher, Leon Brunschvicg, held that the world exists as the work of the constituting consciousness of its perceiver, before which it appears with complete transparency, a view consistent with Kantian and Cartesian views of the subject.[6] For Merleau-Ponty, perception is not the work of a constituting consciousness, a position he criticises as 'intellectualism'. The body, moreover, far from hindering the intellection of pure forms, is the means by which experience is possible and the condition for linguistic expression and abstract thought. The primacy that Merleau-Ponty attributes to embodied perception leads him to his most concise and oft-quoted formulation of the body-subject: 'the body is a natural myself and, as it were, the body is the subject of perception' (le corps est un moi naturel et comme le sujet de la perception) (PP 213; Ph 249). Although Merleau-Ponty retains the language of subjectivity and selfhood (le moi, le sujet), his body-subject is more than an ersatz for the transcendental subject, as some critics suggest.[7] Merleau-Ponty's occasional use of intellectualist vocabulary (such as the word 'subject') effectively alters our understanding of these terms. Merleau-Ponty scholar M. C. Dillon observes that there is a 'half-truth, become commonplace, that Merleau-Ponty replaced the transcendental subject with the lived body' (1991: xiv). Dillon maintains that even though the body-subject retains a transcendental function (it becomes the 'ground' of the constitution of the world), its 'thing-like' attributes (the body is part object) distinguish it significantly from the transcendental subject of Husserl and Kant. A body-subject situated in the world, in some ways object-like but nevertheless capable of inducing meaning within its surroundings, contests notions of subjectivity as a constituting consciousness, transforming not only our understanding of subjectivity but also subjective agency.

In a particularly vivid passage of the *Phenomenology*, novelistic in its descriptive detail, Merleau-Ponty rewrites the Cartesian *cogito* by emphasising rather than stripping away sensory detail. He describes the paper under his hands (the manuscript of the *Phenomenology* on which he is working) and the view from his window: 'I am thinking of the Cartesian *cogito*, wanting to finish this work, sensing the coolness of the paper under my hand, and perceiving the trees of the boulevard through the window' (PP 387). This section, titled 'The Cogito', cites and varies the scene of Descartes' first meditation. Merleau-Ponty's gazing out the window at the trees contrasts sharply with the dark room and fire described by Descartes: 'I am here, sitting by the fire, wearing a winter dressing gown, holding this piece of paper in my hands' (Descartes 1988: 78). Merleau-Ponty further situates himself within the philosophical-cultural tradition he seeks to alter, comparing the *cogito* to the objects (in a familiar setting) in relation to which his body orients itself (PP 387). Merleau-Ponty performs what he describes, refashioning the intellectual *cogito* by emphasising the subject's embodied being in the world.

If Descartes' *cogito* exists outside of space and time, Merleau-Ponty's body-subject belongs to the world. Its temporal and spatial situation incites one critic to refer to it as the 'Claudelian *cogito*'.[8] Instead of blocking the senses, stopping his ears and shutting his eyes as Descartes does in his third meditation, the man in the street in Paul Claudel's *Ars Poetica* (1929) looks at his watch and wonders where he is. Claudel's emphasis on the situation of the body in space (and time – he looks at his watch) mirrors Merleau-Ponty's insistence on the body's spatial position as the condition for perception: 'the body [. . .] is required for perceiving a given spectacle' and the 'gearing of the subject into his world [cette prise du sujet sur son monde]' is the 'origin of space' (PP 263; *Ph* 299). Meaning is less the purview of an intellectual or transcendental subject than a result of the body's interaction with its surroundings. The double meaning of *sens*, which blends spatial direction with signification, calls further attention to role of the body in space in the ordering of experience (*sens*).

The body-subject includes within itself pockets of opacity that frustrate total self-transparency, allowing for change and growth. Cartesian dualism separates subject from object, such that we have the 'transparency of a subject who is nothing other than what it thinks it is' (PP 204) and an opaque, thing-like object. The experience we have of our bodies, by contrast, 'is opposed to the reflective movement that disentangles the object from the subject' (PP 205). The experience of being a body exceeds the knowledge a subject has of itself, and this leaves open the possibility of its transformation: '[the body] is always something other than what it is' (PP 205; *Ph* 240). Merleau-Ponty describes the body as 'like a natural subject, or a provisional sketch [esquisse provisoire] of my total being' (PP 205; *Ph* 241). The idea that the body combines subjective being with being-as-object, and that it is a 'provisional sketch' of one's total being (rather than everything laid out in advance), connects the more passive elements of subjectivity to the possibility of a subject's variation; not everything is known in advance. Embodied experience reveals in the subject's dependence on its object-being the potential for its transformation – for change or for variability.

Metaphors for subjectivity in the *Phenomenology* emphasise the fact that it includes a measure of object-like passivity, but this does not collapse the distinction between subject and object. Merleau-Ponty insists on reversibility (not identity) between the body's being-as-subject and its being-as-object. The necessity of maintaining this difference (*écart*) results in the visually compelling figure of the intertwining (*entrelacs*) or chiasm.⁹ Metaphors compare subjectivity to a *shipwreck*, a *flaw* (in a diamond) and a *fold* in being – three illustrations that accentuate the passivity, object-nature and alterity at the heart of a subject to which metaphysics attributes total self-presence. Merleau-Ponty writes: 'the world ceaselessly bombards and besieges subjectivity just as waves surround a shipwreck on the beach' ([le monde] vient sans cesse assaillir et investir la subjectivité comme les vagues entourent une épave sur la plage) (PP 215; *Ph* 251). The image of subjectivity as a wreck softens boundaries between the subject and its world, figured as waves seeping through cracks in its hull – an image similar to the one we find in Beckett's 'The End'). By describing the subject as acted upon by the world, Merleau-Ponty calls into question the idea of the subject as actively investing the world with meaning from a position outside it.¹⁰ Borrowing from Paul Valéry, Merleau-Ponty goes on to describe perception as a 'flaw' in a diamond, such that 'the picture of the world will always include this lacuna that we are and by which the world itself comes to exist for someone' (PP 215). Perception as a flaw (*défaut*) emphasises the impossibility of total vision (associable with a diamond's transparency) and the idea that the subject is *part of* the world she perceives.¹¹

Merleau-Ponty's most striking metaphor for the subject varies an image he attributes to Hegel – the subject as a 'hole in being' – by figuring it as a fold (*creux, pli*): 'I am not, to recall Hegel's phrase, a "hole in being", but rather a hollow, or a fold that was made and that can be unmade' (Je ne suis donc pas, selon le mot de Hegel, un «trou dans l'être», mais un creux, un pli qui s'est fait et qui peut se défaire) (PP 222–3; *Ph* 259–60).¹² The fact that the body-subject is endowed with terrestrial weight, that it is a fold or hollow rather than pure nothingness, hints at its ephemerality and vulnerability; a 'fold' in being lasts only as long, we assume, as a human life. This veiled admission of the subject's mortality – in death it will become entirely object – further distinguishes the body-subject from the intellectual subject.

Merleau-Ponty's conception of the body-subject necessarily changes the way we understand meaning, which can no longer be attributed to a willing agent.¹³ Merleau-Ponty describes discovering 'a new sense of the word "sense"' (un nouveau sens du mot «sens») (PP 148; *Ph* 182), which derives not from a constituting consciousness but from the body's interaction with its world. Throughout the *Phenomenology*, Merleau-Ponty insists that 'our body is not primarily in space, but is rather *of* space' (notre corps [. . .] est *à l'espace*) (PP 149; *Ph* 184 – my emphasis). The body-subject is neither a thing among things nor a self-transparent consciousness, and this means that its movements can organise space to induce meaning as orientation. As bodies, we alter our environment by our movements, 'polarizing' it by means of our needs and desires: 'Already the mere presence of a living being transforms the physical world, makes "food" appear over here and a "hiding place" over there, and gives to "stimuli" a sense that they did not have' (PP 195). Merleau-Ponty further describes how the body structures its environment by means of the body schema (*schéma corporel*).

The body schema was first introduced by the English neurologist Henry Head, who characterised it as an internal representation of our body that allows us to situate ourselves in space (Head 1896).[14] Psychologists Paul Schilder and Jean Lhermitte later modified this definition in ways that were important to Merleau-Ponty's thinking. Merleau-Ponty begins his discussion of the body schema by pointing out that our body is not an object like other objects. We would never think of our arm as *next to* the ashtray in the way that the ashtray is next to the telephone (PP 127). Rather, the body is a system of parts that envelop each other; a change in one affects all the others as well as the form of the whole. The ability of the body schema to record and react to changes in any part of the body is an important feature of Head's definition of the body schema as a 'combined standard against which all subsequent changes of posture are measured before they enter consciousness' (Head as qtd in Schilder 1950: 11) – a definition that Schilder paraphrases when he describes the body schema as a 'store room of past impressions' and ghostly 'schemata' that modify present sense impressions (1950: 11).

But this account of the body schema cannot account for one of its most widely observed and studied effects: the experience of a phantom limb. An amputee's lingering sensation of pain in her lost limb, or her sense that she might still use a part of her body that is missing, remains mysterious if the body schema is defined as a global consciousness of its parts. For Merleau-Ponty, the body schema is ultimately not a Gestalt form but an organisation of space relative to the body's tasks and desires: 'my body appears to me as a posture towards a certain task, actual or possible' (PP 102). Merleau-Ponty's sense that the body schema derives from the body's possibilities for acting in the world rather than from an internal sense of its parts leads him to redefine it as follows: 'If my body can ultimately be a "form" [. . .] this is insofar as my body is polarized by its tasks, insofar as it *exists toward* them [. . .] the "body schema" is, in the end, a manner of expressing that my body is in and toward the world' (PP 103; *Ph* 130). In other words, the body schema configures its environment in view of its opportunities for (inter)action. Any change is predicated upon the body's inherence in and participation in the world.

Merleau-Ponty redefines the body schema as the dynamic experience of one's body in relation to its possible tasks. The dynamic quality of the body schema is important insofar as it implies a mutual modification of body and world. The body schema changes constantly as it acquires new habits, and habits enable the body to extend its possibilities for acting in the world through the use of new 'instruments':[15]

> To habituate oneself to a hat, an automobile, or a cane is to take up residence in them, or, inversely, to make them participate within the voluminosity of one's own body. Habit expresses the power we have of dilating our being in the world, or of altering our existence through incorporating new instruments. (PP 145)

These 'new instruments' are not limited to material objects. Rather, the instruments that the body annexes to itself include language: 'sometimes the signification aimed at cannot be reached by the natural means of the body. We must, then, construct an instrument, and the body projects a cultural world around itself' (PP 148).[16] Language, or the word, then, is one of the body's possible activities: 'I possess its articulatory and sonorous essence as one of the modulations or one of the possible uses of my body' (PP 186). If the word exists as a possible use of the body, then the body can expand its being by inhabiting the space of language, which, for Merleau-Ponty, 'borrows' the structure of physical space. Meaning in language, or signification, is similarly modelled on the body's orientation of its surroundings: 'the phonetic gesture produces a certain structuring of experience, a certain modulation of existence, just as a behavior of my body invests [. . .] the objects that surround me with a certain signification (PP 199).[17]

Merleau-Ponty founds the possibility of meaning (*sens*) and the thinking subject more generally on the embodied subject's possibilities for action within its environment (PP 99).

Intellectual or abstract thought is therefore founded on the possibilities presented to the body by its spatial surroundings. Citing A. A. Grünbaum, author of 'Aphasie und Motorik' (1930), Merleau-Ponty describes the body's power of movement – 'motricity' (*motricité*) – as possessing the 'elementary power of sense-giving (*Sinngebung*)' (PP 143). Merleau-Ponty's idea of motricity as 'original intentionality' means that consciousness 'is originarily not an "I think that", but an "I can"' (PP 139). The *Phenomenology* remodels the *cogito* as spatially and temporally located, like Claudel's man in the street eager to know his coordinates in space and time. The body-subject, moreover, links the emergence of meaning (even in language) to the body's power to order its surroundings. The body-subject subverts the idea that signification is the work of a willing subject, a view that is similarly troubled in Beckett's oeuvre. Merleau-Ponty's notion that meaning – or what replaces it – issues from the body's negotiation of space finds an analogue in Beckett's work from the 1930s.

From 1928 to 1930, as a *lecteur d'anglais* at the École Normale Supérieure, Beckett took copious notes on Descartes' life and work. Through Jean Beaufret, a philosophy student at the time and the model for Lucien in *Dream of Fair to Middling Women* (a wildly gesticulating Frenchman with whom Belacqua discusses Leibniz, Galileo and Descartes), Beckett also encountered the philosophical climate of intellectualism in which Merleau-Ponty received his training (Merleau-Ponty graduated from the École Normale in 1931). In their study of Beckett's library, Dirk Van Hulle and Mark Nixon note that Beaufret's copy of Descartes' *Choix de textes* remained in Beckett's library until his death (Van Hulle and Nixon 2013: 131). Beckett also copied passages about Descartes some years later from Wilhelm Windelband's *A History of Philosophy* (Beckett's favourite synoptic sourcebook for philosophical concepts), in particular the line: 'Everything must be true which is as clear and distinct as self-consciousness' (TCD MS 10967 as qtd in Van Hulle and Nixon 2013: 132). While other archival scholarship cautions against overestimating the influence of Descartes at the expense of other philosophers (such as Schopenhauer, Spinoza, Democritus, Berkeley and Arnold Geulincx) (Feldman 2006), Beckett's early work is engaged in a rigorous (and farcical) grappling with the relation between mind and world – a grappling that requires at least some reckoning with Descartes.

The irony with which Beckett presents the mind-body split in *Murphy* makes it clear that he, like Merleau-Ponty, saw the absurdity of a mind without its world. But in *Murphy*, bodies merged materially with their environments receive the same measure of parody as 'lives immured in mind' (M 180). Perhaps an alignment between Beckett and Merleau-Ponty goes only as far as a shared distaste for disembodied rationalism. But Merleau-Ponty's body-subject recruits the materiality of the body in what replaces the agency of the subject, making it possible to read Murphy's periodic merging with his surroundings as playfully evoking an earthbound humility, whereby demotion of the will suggests other possibilities for interacting with the environment – possibilities according to which the mind has less control than it would wish.

Most scholars of Beckett and philosophy admit that while philosophical elements (such as the *cogito*) may be explored, dramatised and satirised in Beckett's fiction, they are neither accepted nor rejected (Morot-Sir as qtd in Feldman 2006: 53). Even *Murphy*, an excoriating satire, isn't designed to prove or disprove. Rather it exacerbates the live tension between bodies embedded in the material world and minds severed from substance, pushing each to its logical extreme. Beckett's early fiction explores philosophical shortcomings by means of serious parody, his engagement with Cartesian rationalism leading – paradoxically – to a foregrounding of embodied experience that is, I argue, abundantly present in *Murphy*.

According to James Knowlson, Beckett worked diligently on Descartes in the months before he composed 'Whoroscope' (1930), a 98-line poem penned in a single evening for a contest run by the Hours Press. The fact that Beckett didn't hear about the contest until the day of its deadline didn't stop 'Whoroscope' from winning (Knowlson 1996: 116). To write the poem, Beckett leafed through his notes, assembling biographical arcana culled from Adrien Baillet's *La Vie de Descartes* and especially from a slim biography written by a professor at Trinity College Dublin, J. P. Mahaffy (Doherty 1992). 'Whoroscope' is striking for its subversion of Cartesian ideas, which it performs by including biographical particulars and sensory detail. It is a sharply physical poem that situates Descartes within his concrete, lived environment, resisting the winnowing away of the sensory world that Descartes felt was necessary to reach the bedrock of the *cogito*. Taking on the persona of Descartes, the poem's 'I' makes much of the philosopher's bizarre predilection for consuming eggs hatched between eight and ten days – 'How long did she womb it, the feathery one?' – his six-year-old daughter's death from scarlet fever – 'Her little grey flayed epidermis and scarlet tonsils!' – his valet, Gillot, to whom he gave his easier problems in analytic geometry and the Queen of Sweden's insistence that Descartes (used to sleeping late) give her lessons at 5 a.m., which led him to catch a chill and die: 'the murdering matinal pope-confessed amazon,/Christina the ripper' (CPEF 1–6). Though the poem's weave of allusions is dense enough to be fairly opaque without Mahaffy's biography to hand, the poem's charm is in its grounding of even the airiest philosophical doctrine (Plato's forms) in the material world (the edible reality of omelettes): 'In the name of Bacon will you chicken me up that egg./ Shall I swallow cave-phantoms?' (CPEF 3). The young Beckett – twenty-four when he wrote 'Whoroscope' – humorously suggests that the pursuit of pure forms might leave us hungry.

According to Mahaffy, Descartes did not want his birthday known for fear that it might 'exercise idle people in superstitions about his horoscope' (qtd in Ackerley and Gontarski 2004: 133). Beckett's poem betrays any implied injunction to ignore the life and person of the thinker, and its title merges the (abstract) starry fates with the fleshy body, its perfidiousness (and Beckett's own poetic, anti-rationalist gesture) humorously evoked by the figure of the whore. Beckett's strategy of refusing to divorce philosophy from the particular life in which it developed not only violates Descartes' method (of paring away the personal and incidental to reach the universal bedrock of the indubitable), but also anticipates Merleau-Ponty's more earnest rewriting of the *cogito* in the *Phenomenology*, where he includes his embodied point of view, describing the feel of the paper and the leaves on the boulevard, in contrast to Descartes shutting out the senses.[18] Beckett's own rewriting of the *cogito* – '*Fallor, ergo sum!*' (CPEF 4) – mixes Saint Augustine's wording with Descartes' to suggest, like Augustine, that it is our error and not our knowledge that assures our existence (Ackerley and Gontarski 2004: 30–1).

Beckett's no less ludic but philosophically more engaged staging of Descartes, along with subjective idealism, *amor intellectualis*, Occasionalism, Greek atomism, Schopenhauer and psychoanalysis, occurs when he begins writing *Murphy* in 1935, in London. Early Beckett critics showed alacrity for describing Beckett as a

Cartesian writer, reading illustrations of dualism into *Mercier and Camier* (Cohn 1965: 117) and comparing the style of *Discourse on Method* and the *Meditations* to passages in the trilogy (Kenner 1961; Cohn 1962). Critical consensus soon shifted to emphasise the irony with which Beckett engages Cartesian ideas.[19] As Chris Ackerley and S. E. Gontarski write, Beckett's novels 'are Cartesian in their premises but ironic in their method' and *Murphy* in particular 'implies a questioning and thus subversion of dualism' (Ackerley and Gontarski 2004: 135). This subversion is perhaps most evident in chapter six of the novel, which interrupts the narrative to discourse on the nature of 'Murphy's mind'. Murphy is set on 'freeing' his mind, an exercise that requires 'appeasement of the body' (M 2). For this purpose (appeasing the body), Murphy binds himself naked with seven scarves to his rocking chair. Immobilising his body is the only way for Murphy to 'come alive in his mind' (M 2). Like Descartes and later Husserl, Murphy brackets the body and senses, putting them out of commission. Celia, the beautiful prostitute with whom Murphy is in love and who loves Murphy, distracts from the project of subduing the body, as does Murphy's love of ginger biscuits and his desire for friendly recognition from the schizophrenic, inward-looking Mr Endon, a parody of rationalism who regards everything with a 'chessy' eye (M 241–2).

Murphy's freedom of mind culminates, at the end of the novel, in the incineration of his 'body, mind and soul' (M 275), undercutting a rationalist view of freedom as self-determination. Without the body, there is nothing at all. Or, as Merleau-Ponty writes: 'The body is our general means of having a world' (PP 147). Beckett's novel takes aim also at the dualist idea that the body and mind are different substances (*res extensa* and *res cogitans*):

> Thus Murphy felt himself split in two, a body and a mind. They had intercourse, apparently, otherwise he could not have known that they had anything in common. But he felt his mind to be bodytight and did not understand through what channel the intercourse was effected nor how the two experiences came to overlap. (M 109)

Murphy's experience of his mind as 'bodytight' mocks the idea of a mind sealed against the world, 'hermetically closed to the universe without' (M 107). We find a jab at subjective idealism and an articulation of the dualist conundrum: how do body and mind communicate? The mind-body problem leads Descartes to suggest that this communication happens through the pineal gland, or conarium, and early in the novel Neary surmises that Murphy is unable to love because his 'conarium has shrunk to nothing' (M 6). Second-generation Cartesians, like Geulincx, posit God as the force that enables communication between mind and body (Occasionalism), and Spinoza evokes the intellectual love with which God loves himself. Beckett's epigraph to chapter six – *Amor intellectualis quo Murphy se ipsum amat* [the intellectual love with which Murphy loves himself] – substitutes Murphy for God in Spinoza's dictum (M 107). What is perhaps most clear in the novel is the vigour with which dualism is pilloried. The ridiculousness of binding himself to a chair aside, the 'end' of Murphy's efforts to quiet his body culminate in his total destruction. We see in Beckett's excoriation of Cartesian rationalism an insistence – similar to Merleau-Ponty's – on the primacy of the body and its perception.

Recent postcognitivist Beckett scholarship has emphasised the fact that Murphy loses his mind as well as his body when he burns to death in a garret, pointing to 'a fundamental unity of mind, body, and the world they operate in' (Beloborodova 2020: 14). Dirk Van Hulle, remarking that developments in cognitive science have undermined the Cartesian image of the mind as an interior space (Van Hulle 2012: 277), suggests that Beckett's realisation of the untenability of a Cartesian and Geulingian mind/world split – 'Cartesianism (in whatever form) is not the answer' – motivates Beckett to 'keep looking for other models to investigate how our body is moved by the mind and how the mind is moved by our body and by bodies existing outside us'. Van Hulle credits Beckett with 'intuitively' hitting upon principles of extended cognition (2012: 281 as qtd in Beloborodova 2020: 30). Although postcognitivism is concerned less with embodiment *per se* than with how the brain interacts with its environment more generally, its theories resonate with Merleau-Pontian phenomenology insofar as both view the mind as embedded within and interacting with a concrete, material environment.[20]

It may be sufficient to stop here, having demonstrated that Beckett's excoriation of Cartesian rationalism in *Murphy* is the comedic analogue of Merleau-Ponty's abandonment of intellectualism – an abandonment that leads him to reinvent phenomenology around the idea of embodied consciousness. But I wish to suggest that Beckett doesn't stop at parody, and that *Murphy* is involved in investigating how a body interacts with its world to create order or meaning, a world that 'makes sense' from a certain perspective. The novel's first line announces its interest in the problem of agency: 'The sun shone, having no alternative, on the nothing new. Murphy sat out of it, as though he were free' (M 1). In addition to pitting freedom against determinism, the opening accents a reversibility between human subjects and things. The sun shines, as if it were capable of deliberation but has exhausted its alternatives, while Murphy is inert. A few lines later, Murphy's rocking chair is described as made of 'undressed teak' (M 1). *Things* undress and run out of alternatives, while characters are inert like inanimate objects, deluded about their freedom.

Hints at determinism pervade the novel – 'So all things limp together for the only possible' (M 235) – and character motives take diagrammatic, geometrical form. 'Our medians [. . .] meet in Murphy' (M 213), Wylie says of the secondary characters. Indeed, any motive or intention in *Murphy* seems like a comical, stilted affair. Characters go about their loving and searching mechanically – Cooper follows commands automatically, no matter who gives them – and many speak with a stilted arch-literary allusiveness that makes them puppet-like: 'Let our conversation now be without precedent in fact or literature, each one speaking to the best of his ability the truth to the best of his knowledge' (214). The novel's profusion of 'doing' in the absence of intending – Murphy takes a job as a nurse at the Magdalen Mental Mercyseat because it aligns with his horoscope – might suggest a deterministic universe where fates are set in the stars and Suk's prophesy holds the future already laid out. But there is mockery in this determinism, and the stiffness of character movements is at times undercut by what is unpredictable: the 'surd' in the system, elements of the irrational. Upsurges of human spontaneity in the novel overwhelm its philosophical allusions, revealing them as detached from the life of the body.

Murphy, unlike the minor characters, 'is not a puppet' (122). He is endowed with an interiority described in the idiom of the novel as the 'little world'. In *Murphy*, the 'little world' of the human mind can seem irremediably separate from the 'big world' of shared reality, and this pokes fun at subjective idealism (for which Murphy is bathetically striving). Murphy finds solace among the 'little worlds' at the Magdalen Mental Mercyseat, lunatic minds severed from the big world, and he loathes 'the complacent scientific conceptualism that made contact with outer reality the index of mental well-being' (176). Wishing to be 'of the little world', Murphy wonders how to survive the big world, where he has little control, little chance at (rational) perfection:

> How should he tolerate, let alone cultivate, the occasions of fiasco, having once beheld the beautiful idols of his cave? In the beautiful Belgo-Latin of Arnold Geulincx: *Ubi nihil vales, ibi nihil velis.*
>
> But it was not enough to want nothing where he was worth nothing, nor even to take the further step of renouncing all that lay outside the intellectual love in which alone he could love himself, because there alone he was lovable. It had not been enough and showed no signs of being enough. (M 178–9)

The word 'fiasco' with its evocation of failure and ignominy leads Murphy to Geulincx's ethos of humility (*ubi nihil vales, ibi nihil velis*). Yet the idea that human powerlessness to effect change in the world should lead to cessation of desire is of little help to Murphy, nor is Spinoza's 'intellectual love' that mirrors divine self-love. Nothing, not even Murphy's bondage to his rocking chair, is enough to 'clinch' the little world, for he remains 'deplorably susceptible' to Celia, to ginger – in short, to the life of the body and its desires, implicated in the 'big world' of material reality (179). Murphy suspects, moreover, from the expressions of pain, rage and despair among the mental patients, that there 'is a fly somewhere in the ointment of the Microcosmos' (179).

Nevertheless, Mr Endon (Greek for 'within') kindles Murphy's longing for a 'little world' so ordered and immaculate as to be free of messy desire. After ending their chess game, Murphy swoons. His senses 'found themselves at peace, an unexpected pleasure. Not the numb peace of their own suspension, but the positive peace that comes when the somethings give way, or perhaps simply add up, to the Nothing' (246). This Nothing is the 'absence (to abuse a nice distinction) not of *percipere* [to perceive] but of *percipi* [to be perceived]' (246).[21] Murphy's escape from the phenomenal world does not last long, for the material world intrudes; Murphy notices Mr Endon missing and must recover him. Later, Murphy finds his own image 'horribly reduced, obscured and distorted' in the eye of Mr Endon. He understands himself as a thing seen (*percipi*), or, rather, 'a speck in Mr. Endon's unseen' for the latter is 'immune' 'from seeing anything but himself' (249–50). Instead of an unperceived soul, Murphy recognises himself as a thing seen, reduced and distorted. As Merleau-Ponty writes: 'I the seer am also visible' (VI 113). Abandoning night duty, Murphy goes outside, where he raises his face to the starless sky, 'abandoned, patient, the sky not the face, which was abandoned only' (M 251). Here again Murphy changes places with the material world; to the sky is attributed the human quality of patience, whereas Murphy is merely abandoned. Taking off his clothes, Murphy lies down in a 'tuft of soaking tuffets' and tries to imagine Celia. But he 'could not get a picture in his mind of any creature he had met, animal or human' – only 'scraps of bodies, of landscapes, hands eyes, lines and colours evoking nothing' (252). Murphy's encounter with Mr Endon's hyper-rationalism sends him to the opposite extreme – mystic union with the earth, where only chaotic visions commingle. His self-immolation, likewise, fuses him with the night sky through his skylight and with the gas fire by his feet. On the face of it, materialism seems to fare no better than rationalism in Beckett's parody.

But, often in the novel, Murphy finds pleasure as he relaxes into the material world, feeling himself a part of the landscape and the world of things and of animals. These episodes of earthy fusion are no less rigorously parodied than Murphy's seedy solipsism or hermetically sealed mind, but they echo other moments in Beckett's oeuvre in a way that hints at a working through of the body-mind's situatedness within its material world. In Beckett's early story 'Assumption', published in 1929 in *Transition*, a young artist receives a visit from a woman that culminates in a sense of release; he becomes 'irretrievably engulfed in the light of eternity, one with the birdless cloudless colourless skies, in infinite fulfilment' (CP 7). As at the end of *Murphy*, ecstatic commingling of body and world ends in death, and the woman is found 'caressing his wild dead hair' (CP 7). In the postwar story 'The End' (1946), to which I will turn shortly, Beckett's narrator is similarly subsumed in the landscape. Murphy, reduced to ashes at the end of the novel, assumes the grey colour of the earth with which his remains are mingled (on the floor of a London saloon): 'before another dayspring grayened the earth [the body, mind and soul of Murphy] had been swept away with the sand, the beer, the butts, the glass, the matches, the spits, the vomit' (275). Even if death is the culmination of a body's merging with its environment, Murphy finds pleasure in exploring the object side of his being in intermediate ways; he longs to lie down – 'any old clod of the well-known English turf would do' – 'and enter the landscapes where there [was] only himself improved out of all knowledge' (79). In the Cockpit in Hyde Park, he remarks on the 'ecstatic demeanour of the sheep' (100), 'with whom he felt in close sympathy' (104) and 'composed himself on the hollow of his back for the torpor he had been craving to enter for the past five hours' (105). He slips away from 'the pensums and prizes, from Celia' (105) and feels 'the will dust in the dust of its object, the act a handful of sand' (105). Here Murphy relaxes into the elements (dust, sand, earth). Suspending will and desire, he temporarily rejoins the world he perceives.

Murphy's merging with his environment in Hyde Park gives him an experience of his body's objecthood and a connection to his surroundings. He claims to understand the sheep in the park, who eat only at certain hours, and when he feels the moon's yellow 'ooze' 'into his skull' he cites a passage from Beaumont and Fletcher's *The Maid's Tragedy*, where the moon goddess, jealous of the sun, complains that too few look at her – only those with 'unquiet eyes' (Ackerley 2004: 115): *'Gazed on unto my setting from my rise/Almost of none but of unquiet eyes'* (M 106). In communion with the sheep, ventriloquising the moon, Murphy thinks of 'caged owls in Battersea Park, whose joys and sorrows did not begin till dusk' (M 106); he feels himself connected to, or in communion with, the natural, material environment.

Such moments of thing-like passivity find a correlate in the deepest layer of Murphy's mind explored in chapter six: the dark zone, 'a flux of forms; a perpetual coming together and falling asunder of forms [. . .] the world of the body broken up into the pieces of a toy [. . .] forms becoming and crumbling into the fragments of a new becoming' (112). This passage has been read convincingly alongside myriad philosophical traditions (Bergso-Deleuzian, Schopenhauerian, Democritan, psychoanalytic), but it also evokes the nonhuman (pre- or post-human) world of creative matter, forming and reforming, the hard rock of the earth turning, indifferent to the drama of human minds: 'Here [Murphy] was not free, but a mote in the dark of absolute freedom' (112).[22]

Feeling his own imbrication within the world of matter is agreeable to Murphy. Celia too, when she imitates Murphy in the rocking chair, experiences a 'silence not of vacuum but of plenum' (M 148). But what, if anything, does Murphy's embeddedness in his environment afford, given that he slips from consciousness when he swoons? How do such moments of communion between body and world speak to the problem of agency expressed in the novel? Certainly, such moments offer an alternative to the subjective idealism and Cartesian dualism the novel is engaged in questioning, for an embodied subject is flexible enough to pass into objecthood (and back). Murphy's coupling with the material world undermines voluntarism – 'the will dust in the dust of its object' (M 105) – but the fact that communion with the world of things ultimately deprives Murphy of body, mind and soul seems to imply that no agency, however limited, can follow from these periodic cesurae in his being-subject. Yet Murphy intuits a creative power linked to matter in these moments, a non-teleological movement in which he participates as body: 'forms becoming and crumbling into the fragments of a new becoming' (112). S. E. Gontarski convincingly reads this moment in *Murphy* in terms of Bergsonian and Deleuzian ideas about the creativity of an *élan vital* that works through matter (Gontarski 2015: 97). In the end, Murphy seems unable to harness such energy, which ultimately consumes him (as chaos), but scenes of the body's imbrication in its world echo forcefully throughout Beckett's oeuvre. In Beckett's later work, I argue, the body's merging with its environment does culminate in a movement towards creation, an emergence of form. I take up these questions further in Chapter 7 of this volume, on *Worstward Ho*.

Despite Murphy's demise, the final scene of the novel does gesture towards a version of non-voluntarist agency linked to the body's being in the world (as both subject and object of perception). One mild, sunless day in autumn, Celia wheels her grandfather, Mr Willoughby Kelly, to Round Pond in Kensington Gardens to fly his kite. Mr Kelly is as fond of his wheelchair as Murphy had been of his chair, and Mr Kelly evokes the recently incinerated Murphy also in that he 'burned with excitement' at the prospect of kite flying (M 276–7). Mr. Kelly is a skilful kite flyer: 'in five minutes he was lying back, breathing hard and short, his eyes closed of necessity but in ecstasy as it happened, half his line paid out, sailing by feel' (M 279). The kite's motion in Beckett's tongue-in-cheek rendering is not only the result of Mr Kelly's nimble management of winch and wind, but it mimics the movement of history: 'out, back a little, stop; out, back a little, stop. The historical process of the hardened optimists' (M 279). Later, Mr Kelly lets out a rush of line: 'the industrial revolution' (M 279–80). Humorous as this is (human progress compared to the ascent of a kite agreeably mangles our sense of scale), it nonetheless points to the idea of agency not as individual will but as part of a larger movement. The chapter ends with dusk falling and the rangers clearing the park – '*All out. All out*' – and Mr Kelly, having fallen asleep, 'not dying but dozing' (281), losing control of his kite. Celia sees the winch spring from his hands; the 'end of the line skimmed the water, jerked upward in a wild swirl, vanished joyfully in the dusk' (282). Failing to recover the winch, Mr Kelly 'went limp' in Celia's arms. She wheels him back up the hill, thinking of the levers of his wheelchair as 'the tired heart'. Agency passes from Mr Kelly's embodied 'sailing by feel' to the kite 'joyfully' freeing itself from his control as Celia meditates on the fatigue of the heart.

In a letter to his friend Thomas McGreevy in September 1935, soon after beginning work on *Murphy*, Beckett describes watching 'little shabby respectable old men' kite-flying in the park: 'My next old man, or old young man, not of the big world but of the little world, must be a kite flyer. So absolutely disinterested, like a poem, or useful in the depths where demand and supply coincide' (LB1 274). The scene of kite flying in *Murphy*, what James Knowlson calls a 'powerful image of freedom and release' (1996: 196), not only models a 'moving with' forces outside the self, necessary to literary creation, but the kite's escaping Mr Kelly's grasp underscores the fact that recognition of the limits of one's control is part of agentic power. The fact that the lost line vanishes 'joyfully' into the dusk extends agency beyond the human (which the novel has done all along, through its playful reversal of humans and things), but we still might catch currents as they come. This is not passivity, nor relinquishment of agency in a deterministic universe; rather, it is the realisation that our power to create depends on our material rapport with the environment in which we, as bodies, necessarily inhere.

A decade later, living in Paris after the war, Beckett writes – in French – a story with an ending that mirrors the climax of *Murphy*: a body ecstatically fused with its environment, not 'swept away with the sand, the beer, the butts' (M 275) but 'scattered to the utmost confines of space' (CP 99). Like Merleau-Ponty, Beckett rejects (by mockery) the idea of a transcendental subject, separate from the world, and in 'The End' (1946) we find a subject not merely embodied but ecological insofar as it is embedded within – and then scattered across – its material environment. To read 'The End' in this context, paired unorthodoxly with *Murphy*, sheds light on how embodied subjectivity evolves in Beckett, as horror at our bodily imbrication within our surroundings gives onto a particular vision of literary creation.

'The End' is Beckett's earliest extended prose work in French, and it launched his 'seige in the room', the period of heightened creative activity after the war. 'The End', or 'La Fin', was the first of four short stories in French, all narrated in a tonally quirky first-person voice that extends and develops in the trilogy. Beckett did not set out to write the 'nouvelles' in French. He began 'The End' in February 1946 in English, and after twenty-nine pages drew a line across his notebook page and continued the story in French (Knowlson 1996: 325). *Les Temps Modernes*, a young review at the time, which listed Merleau-Ponty among its contributors, agreed to publish 'La Fin', but an editorial misunderstanding meant that only the story's first half was published, and Simone de Beauvoir refused to rectify what Beckett saw as a 'mutilation' of his work (Knowlson: 325–6). Despite this setback, Beckett wrote three more stories before the end of the year: 'L'expulsé' ('The Expelled'), 'Premier Amour' ('First Love') and 'Le Calmant' ('The Calmative').

The nouvelles stage a subversion of Romanticism in that they challenge the possibility of a dialogue between the human and the landscape and mock the habit of projecting human emotions onto the natural world. Mark Nixon describes Beckett's parody of pathetic fallacy in 'Lightning Calculation' (an unpublished text from the 1930s that became part of *Murphy*) and discusses Beckett's general scorn for the 'itch to animise' (Nixon 2006: 62). The nouvelles don't stop at parody, but sketch an alternative, less hierarchical rapport between the human and its nonhuman environment. The Romantic fantasy of a union with the natural world is literalised and made egalitarian, for instead of inseminating or impregnating the landscape with their emotions or needs, the narrators are themselves impressed by animals, landscapes and material objects. The narrator of 'First Love', rather than having intercourse with Lulu-Anna, finds himself in her room – figured in the story as a womb insofar as the word 'fibrome' (a growth on the uterine wall) springs to the narrator's mind.[23] In 'The End', the sky, instead of extending, generating space for the human imagination, presses upon the narrator: 'I felt it weighing softly on my face, I rubbed my face against it, one cheek after the other, turning my head from side to side' (CP 93). The breakdown of the usual divisions between self and world that enable subjective mastery over the environment has led Ulrika Maude to compare the landscape of 'The Calmative' to the 'dehumanized, de-anthropomorphized landscapes of Cézanne, which disrupt, rather than confirm, our point of view' (2009: 38). The nouvelles, and 'The End' in particular, might be aptly described as anti-anthropomorphic fables.

In 'The End', as in *Murphy*, humans become as wooden as objects, and objects and features of the landscape take on an eerie sort of life. To objects, and to the earth itself, are attributed agentic qualities, and the thinning of the boundary between the human body and the material world anticipates the story's cataclysmic end. Instead of projecting himself onto exterior space by arranging things, the narrator is subject to an encroachment of objects. He reflects on the company of furniture, particularly a wooden stool: 'At times I felt its wooden life invade me, till I myself became a piece of old wood. There was even a hole for my cyst' (80). The attribution of agent-like qualities to material objects as well as to the environment – the earth is said to 'make a sound as of sighs' (80) – evokes Jane Bennett's sense that agentic capacities extend beyond the human and operate within the material world. Bennett argues that 'vibrant' matter has the capacity 'not only to impede or block the will and designs of humans but also to act as quasi agents or forces with trajectories, propensities or tendencies of their own' (2010: viii). She evokes childlike experiences in which the world is populated by animate things rather than passive objects (vii) – an experience we find also in 'The End'. Beckett's narrator is also implicated within the material world in such a way as to suggest a non-hierarchical relationship between the human and the environment. Much as he has difficulty orienting himself within his strange-familiar surroundings, he finds a bench he knew in former times 'shaped to fit the curves of the seated body' (M 82). This mutual shaping or collaboration between body and world echoes Cézanne's provocative statement, quoted by Merleau-Ponty: 'The landscape thinks itself in me, and I am its consciousness' (1993: 67). The idea that the landscape thinks itself through the human (rather than vice versa) inverts elements of Romanticism as it troubles human efforts to dominate and master the landscape.

The narrator has difficulty with mastery. Attempts to fashion a home and to domesticate livestock result in failure, plunging the narrator further into abjection. The narrator of 'The End' is successively evicted from various dwellings; he is forced out of a 'charitable institution' (perhaps a mental asylum) only to be swindled out of his subsequent lodgings to make room for a pig. He finds shelter in a cave by the sea, but, unable to stand 'its splashing and heaving, its tides and general convulsiveness' (89), he moves to a ruined cabin in the mountains, where he encounters a cow. When he tries to milk her, the cow drags him across the floor covered in dung, stopping only to kick him. 'I didn't know our cows too could be so inhuman' (90), the narrator quips, a dig at the hypocrisy of French postwar humanism.[24] He later regrets a lost opportunity for animal husbandry: 'More master of myself I might have made a friend of her. She would have come every day, perhaps, accompanied by other cows. I might have learnt to make butter, even cheese' (90). This episode reflects a general failure on the part of the narrator to cultivate his environment, to bend the material world to his needs and desires. In Merleau-Ponty's terminology, this is tantamount to a failure to make meaning in collaboration with one's world, ordering one's surrounds in relation to one's possibilities for action. But an eco-phenomenological reading might credit the narrator for refusing an extractive, managerial approach to his environment, even though eschewing an instrumental framing of the earth costs him a measure of dignity in the context of the story (Toadvine 2017). A moment later, the narrator is more earth-like than ever. His face is malformed by wrinkles, a 'mask of dirty old hairy leather, with two holes and a slit' (CP 91). The narrator's leathery face evokes the hide of the cow he failed to domesticate, solidifying his belonging to the world of animals and nature. At the height of his abjection, the narrator lies down on the road 'at a narrow place' to increase the likelihood that a cart would run him over 'with one wheel at least, or two if there were four' (91). The humorous exactitude of this calculation distinguishes the narrator, even in his abject state, from a natural world indifferent to his survival, for he cares how efficiently he might be demolished.

Following this episode, the story mentions Arnold Geulincx's *Ethics*, a gift from the narrator's former tutor who died in a particularly undignified way (infarctus in the water closet, 'his clothes in awful disorder'). Pairing Geulincx with instances of bodily indignity (the narrator's as well as his tutor's) rivets attention to the relation between the human and humility. Geulincx's *Ethics* calls for a 'disregard of the self' that stems from the idea that the human will is powerless to effect change, so that causality or any change in the material world is attributed to God.[25] The narrator of 'The End', supine on the road, his face a 'mask of leather', demonstrates humility in the etymological sense, as closeness to earth (from *humus*).

When the narrator attempts to master nature by force, he fails, but at moments when the narrator 'acts passively' in concert with the world of nonhuman matter, he has more salutary interactions with his surroundings. Rather than attempting to master his environment, to bend it to his will (as he did unsuccessfully with the cow), the narrator decorates himself with trappings from the natural world: 'I stuck leaves in my hat, all the way round to make a shade. The night was cold. I wandered for hours in the fields. At last I found a heap of dung' (86). We find a certain 'disregard of self' – sleeping in dung – as the narrator recognises himself as part of the world he organises by his needs. The narrator begins begging and fits himself out a board to wear:

> I got a kind of board or tray and tied it to my neck and waist. It jutted out just at the right height, pocket height, and its edge was far enough from my person for the coin to be bestowed without danger. Some days I strewed it with flowers, petals, buds and that herb which men call fleabane, I believe, in a word whatever I could find. I didn't go out of my way to look for them, but all the pretty things of this description that came my way were for the board. They must have thought I loved nature. (92–3)

Here the narrator has relaxed his will – 'I didn't go out of my way to look' (93) – but he is receptive, using what comes his way. The image this scene evokes, of the narrator wearing a board adorned with flowers, petals, buds and fleabane, underscores his imbrication within the natural world. This non-hierarchical mode of interacting with the environment further parallels the ethical stance implied by eco-phenomenology, with its rejection of anthropomorphic and dualist attitudes. Insofar as the narrator's experience of the natural world guides his interaction with it, 'The End' aligns itself more aptly with phenomenology than with naturalism or Guelingian Occasionalism, since the narrator does effect change in his environment by living with/in it. His actions are those of an embodied perspective, and they impact the environment only indirectly, in ways he could not have willed.

The narrator's most successful inhabitation is also, ironically, that which brings about his ecstatic, deathly fusion with the landscape. In a shed (*remise*) on an abandoned estate, the narrator finds a rowboat, which he fills with stones and pieces of wood to make his bed. To keep out rats, avid for 'living flesh' (95), he fits out a lid for the boat-bed, now coffinlike. As with his begging board, the narrator adapts 'whatever tools and material I chanced to find' (96). From his boat in the shed, the narrator sees 'gulls ravening about the mouth of the sewer near by' and hears 'the lapping of water' and 'the open wave' (97): 'I [. . .] felt less boat than wave, or so it seemed to me, and my stillness was the stillness of eddies. That may seem impossible' (97). Despite his enclosure within the coffin-bed-boat, the narrator feels himself a part of his extended environment – 'less boat than wave' – and its movement.[26] Like Murphy, the narrator restricts his movement, retreating within the boat, and this leads paradoxically (or mystically) to visions: 'I was in my boat and gliding on the waters. I didn't have to row, the ebb was carrying me out [. . .] I drifted with the current and the tides' (98–9). Carried by the current, the narrator is beset by scenes from his childhood – walking with his father, naming the mountains, watching gorse burning on the hillsides. As he reaches the open sea, he finds that he is chained to his boat, and pries out a plug from a hole in the floorboard:

> Back now in the stern-sheets, my legs stretched out, my back well propped against the sack stuffed with grass I used as a cushion, I swallowed my calmative. The sea, the sky, the mountains and the islands closed in and crushed me in a mighty systole, then scattered to the uttermost confines of space.

This vision of ecstatic union and self-dispersal – the narrator is crushed in the heartbeat of an anthropomorphised landscape, subsumed into a body that is like his but 'mightier', before being scattered – parallels Murphy's incineration, but with a grander feel. The progression of ascetic restriction and explosive dispersal might similarly experiment with putting the body out of action to enable the mind to wander freely among ecstatic visions.

But the story does not end with the narrator scattered to the 'uttermost confines of space' but with the more sober line: 'The memory came faint and cold of the story I might have told, a story in the likeness of my life, I mean without the courage to end or the strength to go on' (99). The tale we have been reading is revealed here to be one among many possible stories, expressive of the impossibility and necessity of going on. We find that the ecstatic end of 'The End' is a false end, in that it returns us to the more sober duty of going (living) on. The story's last line picks up on a number of metafictional seams dangled before us earlier in the story; the narrator takes a rag from his greatcoat, before remembering that he no longer has a greatcoat: 'of my coat then' (92). A few lines later, he slips and mentions the greatcoat again: 'what's the matter with me' (92). Describing the abandoned estate proves too much for the narrator – 'Only the ground-floor windows – no, I can't' (95) – and he leaves off his description. The fictional story world insists on the fact that it is contingent; it might have been made differently. We find this technique extended in the trilogy at the beginning of *The Unnamable*, when Beckett's characters swirl about, revealed as so many avatars (TN 293). If the 'I' in the last line of 'The End' referred, somehow, to Beckett the author, we might return to a Cartesian universe where the I that thinks is separate from the world that is thought and so provides a backstop against infinite variations. But we have every reason to believe, especially given the metafictional hiccups throughout the story, that it is the narrator of the story who utters this line, self-reflexively aware of his situation as part of textual material that can be made and unmade. If the perspective that gives us this last line is immanent to the story – if it is the narrator's voice, which it must be – then we have not a Cartesian story but a phenomenological one, in that awareness of one's embeddedness within one's surroundings (including language) opens possibilities for moving within and shaping them.

The Merleau-Pontian body-subject reimagines subjectivity not as a view from nowhere or a 'hole' in being, but as a fold, implicated within the material world it perceives. This reconfiguration of the relation between an embodied subject and its world suggests a more complex view of agency, and it exaggerates the difficulty dualism faces in determining how a mind, cut off from the substance of the world, might effect change. In Merleau-Ponty's thinking, we find a body-subject interacting with its environment, inducing order on the basis of its possible actions. The parody of dualism in *Murphy* suggests that without a body there can be no world, as Murphy's attempts to quiet his body and come alive in his mind culminate in his transformation into non-sentient matter strewn across a pub floor. More interesting, and less discussed, is how Murphy's earlier episodes of communion with the environment not only prefigure his catastrophic end but also introduce a more egalitarian rapport between the human subject and the world of things; Murphy's subjectivity emerges as a provisional detachment from his non-sentient environment. Possibilities for a collaborative rapport with the environment emerge in the context of Mr Kelly's kite-flying, which ends in frustration, since material agency is necessarily limited in scope and in time (to the span of a human life). Like *Murphy*, 'The End' interrogates the body's relation to its material surroundings, toggling between ecstatic fusion of the body with its environment and a non-instrumentalising approach whereby the body structures its surroundings based on its possibilities for action. The story's allusion to literary creation in its final line extends the idea of material agency to the spinning of stories, to finding within the materiality of language a particular, contingent tale, which can be made and unmade.

Notes

1. Michel Foucault draws attention to this aspect of Merleau-Ponty's thought, identifying in the *Phenomenology* a 'body-organism' [. . .] 'linked to the world through a network of primal significations, which arise from the perception of things' (1980: 170).
2. *Godillot* (later *godasse*) is named for Alexis Godillot (1816–1893), maker of military boots. On the subject of bodily agency, Tim Ingold describes how the hand, associated with the wilful manipulation of objects, has ousted the foot in the development of human culture. Ingold argues for a more 'grounded' approach to human movement (2004).
3. Simone de Beauvoir recounts an anecdote about Sartre's encounter with phenomenology at the Bec de Gaz in Montparnasse: 'We ordered the specialty of the house, apricot cocktails; [Raymond] Aron said, pointing to his glass: You see, my dear fellow, if you are a phenomenologist, you can talk about this cocktail and make philosophy out of it! Sartre turned pale with emotion at this. Here was just the thing he had been longing to achieve for years – to describe objects just as he saw and touched them, and extract philosophy from the process' (*La force de l'âge* as qtd in Schmidt 1984: 18–19).
4. Husserl's Paris Lectures were published in 1931 as *Les méditations cartésiennes* by Armand Colin, then by Vrin in 1947, translated from German by Emmanuel Lévinas and Gabrielle Peiffer. For discussion

of the conflict between intellectualism and phenomenology in early twentieth-century France, see Vincent Descombes's *Modern French Philosophy*.
5. Merleau-Ponty was also influenced by the work of Henri Bergson, who, like Husserl, sought direct intuition, free from symbolic and mathematical methods. Wary of false problems set up by intellectual reasoning, Bergson conveys the leap from intelligent to intuitive thinking by means of the metaphor of a swimmer; only by jumping into the water and experiencing the unique kind of resistance it affords do we learn to move in it (Bergson 1998: 192–4).
6. For further discussion of Brunschvicg's idealism and Merleau-Ponty's criticism of it, see Gary Gutting's *French Philosophy in the Twentieth Century* (2001: 40–9). Gutting also specifies that Merleau-Ponty understands Husserl's reduction in a *non*-idealist sense (in an idealist sense, it would be 'a return to a pre-personal transcendental subject before which the entire world appears with complete transparency'). Merleau-Ponty sees the reduction as revealing intentionality, our body's being directed towards things and its inherence in the world (187).
7. At the end of the lecture, '*Le primat de la perception*', in which Merleau-Ponty summarises his argument in the *Phenomenology*, Jean Beaufret suggests that Merleau-Ponty did not go far enough in his rejection of intellectualism because he conserves its terminology: 'Mais tout le problème est précisément de savoir si la phénoménologie poussé à fond n'exige pas que l'on sorte de la subjectivité et du vocabulaire de l'idéalisme subjectif comme, partant de Husserl, l'a fait Heidegger' (Merleau-Ponty 1989: 151). Similarly, Renaud Barbaras criticises the *Phenomenology* for reinstalling the subject-object divide, citing a working note in *The Visible and the Invisible* in which Merleau-Ponty criticises his earlier work for not going far enough to unravel the opposition between consciousness and its object: 'Les problèmes posés dans *Phénoménologie de la perception* sont insoluble parce que j'y pars de la distinction «conscience» – «objet»' (*Vi* 252 as qtd in Barbaras: 30). On the other hand, Françoise Dastur claims that Merleau-Ponty's thinking about subjectivity is closer to Derrida than to Sartre despite his intellectualist vocabulary. She argues that the *Phenomenology* remains attentive to authentic phenomenological description even if it retains an intellectualist vocabulary (2001: 30).
8. Emmanuel de Saint Aubert's attribution of a 'Claudelian *cogito*' to Merleau-Ponty is inspired by André Vachon and Georges Poulet, who observe: 'Pour aboutir à son *Ergo sum*, Claudel est parti de la question *Où suis-je?*' (*Le temps et l'espace dans l'œuvre de Paul Claudel* 244 as qtd by de Saint Aubert 2003: 259n).

9. For discussion of Merleau-Ponty's notion of the *écart* (between subject and object) in relation to Derrida's concept of *différance*, see Dillon 1991: xviii–xxii.
10. Merleau-Ponty follows this passage with a polemic against the transcendental ego: 'In intellectualism, that place outside of the world – which the empiricist philosopher merely implied, and where he tacitly placed himself in order to describe the event of perception – now receives a name [. . .] This place is the transcendental Ego [. . .] The entire system of experience – world, one's own body, and empirical self – is subordinated to a universal thinker, charged with sustaining the relations among these three terms. But since this universal thinker is not engaged in this system, the terms remain what they were in empiricism, namely, causal relations laid out on the level of cosmic events' (PP 215).
11. Merleau-Ponty borrows this image from Valéry's '*Le cimetière marin*'. The poem's lyric subject is that which interrupts self-transparency and absolute knowledge; the 'I' of the poem introduces the possibility of change (*Je suis en toi le secret changement*) as well as the limitations that undermine the idea of a self-transparent, constituting consciousness.
12. This phrase is most likely drawn from Alexandre Kojève's Hegel lectures, which Merleau-Ponty attended between 1933 and 1939 in Paris. The notion of the subject as 'nothingness' opposed to being is further developed by Sartre in *La transcendance de l'ego* (1936) and in *L'être et le néant* (1943) (Merleau-Ponty 2012: n535).
13. James Schmidt summarises Merleau-Ponty's career as an attempt to revise the idea of subjective agency – a project that begins with the body subject. Merleau-Ponty's awareness that 'the problem of agency could not be resolved simply by assuming that the Cartesian *cogito*, with suitable modifications, could be resurrected as that body-subject' leads him to refine his ideas about agency by turning to structuralism and ontology (163).
14. The term 'body schema' has been sometimes used interchangeably with 'body image', for instance by Paul Schilder in *The Image and Appearance of the Human Body* (1950: 11). Shaun Gallagher distinguishes between these terms, clarifying that body *image* designates the manner in which a body is perceived 'from without' and *schema* refers to a postural intuition of the location of the body relative to its surroundings (1986; see also Gallagher 2005).
15. In her analysis of Merleau-Ponty in relation to Beckett, Ulrika Maude highlights Merleau-Ponty's use of the term 'habit body', which coexists with the present body, informing its sense of its abilities (2009: 12–13).
16. The word 'natural' seems to distinguish the biological world from the cultural-linguistic one, but Merleau-Ponty's sense that '[t]out est

fabriqué et tout est naturel chez l'homme' (*Ph* 230) undermines any rigid distinction between nature and culture. In the *Phenomenology*, the body 'transgresses' into the domain of language, and words enter the space of the sensible.

17. Yves Thierry identifies a porousness between the sensible and linguistic worlds in his analysis of Merleau-Ponty's vexed account of the body's power to signify in language. Thierry argues that Merleau-Ponty's philosophy is devoted to the project of elucidating the notion of a 'speaking body' (*corps parlant*), which is made possible by the fact that, for Merleau-Ponty, the sensible world and the linguistic world are reversible, since the sensible constitutes itself via relations of difference (and relation) in the same way that significations develop in language. Moreover, Thierry explains, *la parole*, by instituting itself in the life of the body, moves between thoughts and sensory experiences (1987: 159–60).
18. In the *Meditations*, Descartes writes: 'I will now shut my eyes, stop my ears, and withdraw all my senses. I will eliminate from my thoughts all images of bodily things, or rather, since this is hardly possible, I will regard all such images as vacuous, false and worthless' (Descartes 1988: 86–7).
19. Two articles in a 1959 special issue of *Perspective* established the tradition of 'Cartesian Beckett': 'The Cartesian Centaur' by Hugh Kenner and 'Beckett's Murphy: A Cartesian Novel' by Samuel Mintz. Ruby Cohn points to Beckett's ambivalence, writing: 'all Beckett's work paradoxically insists upon and rebels against the Cartesian definition of man as "a thing that thinks"' (Cohn 1965: 170).
20. Beloborodova divides postcognitivism into two strands: the extended mind thesis, which argues that cognitive representations need not be restricted to the interior of the mind but can be 'externalized' via writing tools (notebooks) or other technological devices. The second strand, enactivism, rejects a representational account of cognition, claiming that cognitive processes take place as an intelligent agent interacts with its surroundings. The enactivist position draws explicitly on Merleau-Pontian phenomenology, not least in its suggestion that perceiver and world are mutually shaped by their interactions (2020: 7).
21. The 'Nothing' of this passage alludes to Democritus, whose dictum *Nothing is more real than nothing* was influential for Beckett. In *Demented Particulars*, Chris Ackerley suggests that *Murphy* 'may be seen as a would-be Occasionalist universe which is blown apart by the guffaw of the Abderite [Democritus]' (2004: 21). In his preface to *Demented Particulars*, S. E. Gontarski describes the 'grafting' technique Beckett uses in *Murphy*, borrowing phrases and ideas from his reading notes. This 'grafting' or bricolage calls attention to the complex agency of authorship, giving us a picture of Beckett

remixing the inherited fragments of Western philosophy, exercising a material agency in the domain of language and culture, rejecting a cult of originality while admitting that there may indeed be nothing new under the sun (for novelty would be the result of recombination) (Ackerley 2004: 8–9).

22. Ackerley reads 'a mote in the dark of absolute freedom' as 'a condition transcending (in Kant's sense) the state of being "sovereign and free"'. He connects it to a line from Proust (*The Guermantes Way*): 'when, after the most rigorous demonstration of determinism one discovers that, above the world of necessity, there is that of freedom' (2004: 128).

23. For a more detailed analysis of how all four nouvelles subvert Romantic tropes, see my discussion in 'Poets of their Own Acts' (Dennis 2015).

24. Beckett's antipathy to postwar humanism has been amply discussed by Andrew Gibson, who demonstrates Beckett's distaste for a Gaullist valorisation of the unity of man, of heroism and of progress in post-Liberation France – a rhetoric that tended to ignore the victims (particularly Jewish ones) (2014: 107). Shane Weller, similarly, draws upon Beckett's postwar art criticism to articulate his fraught relationship with a certain (Sartrean) brand of postwar humanism (2020). These points are further discussed in Chapter 2 and the Conclusion.

25. David Tucker's *Samuel Beckett and Arnold Geulincx* offers further discussion of Geulincx, and it includes chapters on *Murphy* and 'The End' (2012: 99–101). See also Geulincx's *Ethics* edited with Beckett's notes (Van Ruler and Uhlmann 2006).

26. This image is echoed years later in *Krapp's Last Tape* (1958), when not one but two people – in a boat, feeling the waves rocking beneath it – are united not only with each other but also with the environment.

CHAPTER 2

Short-Circuited Rationalism, or How the Body Means

As the Second World War began in France, Beckett set to work on a more methodical but no less ludic deconstruction of certain tenets of rationalism, connected to a critique of language. An obsession with how we know (and are known by) the world by means of language threads through the multiple phases of Beckett's long career (Boulter 2008: 3).[1] Early fantasies about tearing the 'veil' of language and boring holes in wordsurfaces in 1937 (LB1 518) give way by the early 1940s to a more strategic approach: juxtaposing contradictory terms generates space in which the objects of representation become visible from multiple perspectives.

This technique has a recognisable analogue in visual art – in cubism, and particularly in the paintings of Paul Cézanne, whose deconstructive approach interested both Merleau-Ponty and Beckett. In letters from the 1930s, Beckett praises Cézanne for refusing anthropomorphic representations of landscape, while Merleau-Ponty's essay 'Cézanne's Doubt', published right after the *Phenomenology of Perception* in 1945, credits Cézanne with a vision that 'penetrates right to the root of things beneath the imposed order of humanity' (CD 67). For Merleau-Ponty, Cézanne reveals objective space as a second-order construction, laid over a primary spatiality generated by the body's interests. In *Dream of Fair to Middling Women* (written in 1932), Beckett links Cézanne's exposure of representational artifice to an immanent critique of language, whereby juxtapositions create an absurdity that leads readers to intuit what escapes representation. Perhaps the young Beckett, like his protagonist Belacqua Shuah, considered himself a Cézanne of the printed page.[2] For verbal conundrums in Beckett's interwar novel *Watt*, much like Cézanne's impossibly positioned objects, comically expose representational artifice, and the novel's erratic, sonorous language, like Lucky's spirited glossolalia in *Waiting for*

Godot five years later, combine a Cézanne-like technique with a direct appeal to the body and senses. Like a Cézanne of literature, Beckett exploits the jarring of what Merleau-Ponty calls 'incompossibles' to open a zone in which language is renewed through its reintegration with the life of the body.

The admiration for Cézanne that Beckett expressed in letters from the 1930s is consistent with his postwar views on abstract painting, developed in two art-critical essays on the Van Velde brothers and in his correspondence with Georges Duthuit, published in *Transition* in 1949. In a letter from 1934, Beckett credits Cézanne with calling into question received ideas about the human in relation to its environment – ideas implicit in conventional techniques of representation in painting: 'Cézanne seems to have been the first to see landscape & state it as material of a strictly peculiar order, incommensurable with all human expressions whatsoever' (LB1 222). This incommensurability runs counter to the anthropomorphic biases that inform classical perspective. In the same letter (to Thomas McGreevy), Beckett writes:

> Perhaps it is the one bright spot in a mechanistic age – the deanthropomorphizations of the artist. Even the portrait beginning to be dehumanized as the individual feels himself more & more hermetic & alone & his neighbor a coagulum as alien as a protoplast or God, incapable of loving or hating anyone but himself or of being loved or hated by anyone but himself. (223)

This description of a rupture of relations between the human subject and its world (including other humans) finds reprise more than a decade later in 'Three Dialogues', when Beckett praises Bram Van Velde for being 'the first to desist [from] estheticised automatism' and 'submit wholly to the incoercible absence of relation' (PTD 125). This leads Beckett to his oft-quoted assertion that 'to be an artist is to fail, as no other dare fail, that failure is his world and the shrink from it desertion, art and craft, good housekeeping, living' (PTD 125). Moving into this breach (the absence of relation) is what Beckett calls the artist's 'fidelity to failure'. Yet failure may precipitate 'a new occasion, a new term of relation, and the act of which, unable to act, obliged to act, he [the artist] makes, an expressive act, even if only of itself, of its impossibility, of its obligation' (PTD 125). Consistent across this statement and Beckett's earlier reflections on Cézanne is the idea that a breakdown of conventional relations and the possibility of an absence of relation present 'new occasions' for the artist – even as the materiality of landscapes and of objects aligns them with a 'peculiar' order that slips free of attempts to domesticate them within the bounds of human expression. The human must, perhaps, adapt itself to the materiality of the landscape, not vice versa.[3]

Merleau-Ponty's understanding of Cézanne has been called incompatible with that of Beckett, though both support a stripping away of convention to discover a more volatile, vital world where relations (between subject and object, human and nonhuman) can be re-explored. Kevin Brazil, situating Beckett's art criticism in the context of postwar humanism, emphasises Beckett's mockery of valorisations of the human that were in fashion at the time.[4] In this context, Brazil argues that Cézanne's painting is 'the site of an essential difference between Beckett and Merleau-Ponty, one that is not without political implications' (2013: 91). For Brazil, Merleau-Ponty's Cézanne essay presents the 'victory of the human over the inhuman' (91).[5] Merleau-Ponty finds in Cézanne the possibility of re-establishing the subject-object dialogue central to his phenomenology, while Beckett bravely faces the breakdown of subject-object relations (91). Brazil's opposition between Merleau-Ponty and Beckett, while it does justice to the radicalness of Beckett's stated position, underestimates the human capacity to access our own material embodiment, rediscovering 'relations' with our environment of a vastly different order. Brazil's position may be, in part, attributable to his focus on Beckett's essays, since Beckett's explorations of material embodiment are, arguably, more forceful in his art than in his criticism and in his letters.

Second, while Merleau-Ponty may have endorsed humanism in a political sense, his Cézanne essay does not necessarily reinstall the hierarchy of the human as superior to its material environment. Indeed, the reversibility of human and landscape implied by Merleau-Ponty's citation of Cézanne – 'The landscape thinks itself in me [. . .] and I am its consciousness' (67) – does the opposite, attributing agentic capacities to the landscape, which uses the human to express itself. Merleau-Ponty describes Cézanne's work in terms that evoke phenomenology's efforts to access fundamental structures of experience (by means of the *épochē*) as well as Beckett's comments on the incommensurable strangeness of Cézanne's paintings:

> We live in the midst of man-made objects, among tools in houses, streets, cities, and most of the time we see them only through the human actions which put them to use. We become used to thinking that all of this exists necessarily and unshakably. Cézanne's painting suspends these habits of thought and reveals the base of inhuman nature upon which man has installed himself. This is why Cézanne's people are strange, as if viewed by a creature of another species. (CD 66)

The effect of a Cézanne painting is clearly one of defamiliarisation, a rupture of habit that reacquaints us with the bedrock of the 'inhuman' that supports it. Despite his humanist vocabulary (i.e. his fondness for words like 'expression'), Merleau-Ponty finds in Cézanne affirmation of a fundamental reciprocity between the human and the nonhuman world – a reciprocity that is necessarily at odds with humanist ideals of voluntarism.

In Chapter 1, we saw that, for Merleau-Ponty, abstract thought is founded on the body's position and perspective. '"[M]ental" or cultural life', including language, borrows its structures from the body's orientation of its physical surroundings, and 'the thinking subject must be grounded upon the embodied subject' (PP 199) (la vie «mentale» ou culturelle emprunte à la vie naturelle ses structures et [. . .] le sujet pensant doit être fondé sur le sujet incarné) (Ph 235).[6] In *Watt* and in Lucky's speech in *Waiting for Godot*, language is configured to appeal to the body, first by exposing the representational inadequacy of language, linking it to binary systems used to organise information, and second by foregrounding a rapport between the body and language. I argue that Beckett's investigation of a 'sensory poetics' begins with Sam and Watt's language-dance in the garden and comes to fruition in Lucky's speech, where ostensible movement towards impasse (humanity's decline and death) revitalises language by emphasising the body's role in the production of meaning. Lucky's monologue unveils intellection as a bodily process, and the body's jerky, machine-like qualities in both texts reveal it as passive as well as active, challenging the assumptions undergirding humanist models of agency.

Beckett's *Watt*, written in the early 1940s and published in 1953, is significant in the landscape of experimental literature because it interrogates meaning by enacting its breakdown. For critics such as Michael Robinson, the novel is a journey that 'ends in the discovery of non-meaning', where 'all that is usually assumed true disintegrates into an ill-defined series of phenomena' (1974: 112). The semantic disorientation we find in *Watt* is marked by Beckett's experience of the war – he wrote most of the novel while in hiding in Roussillon – but the novel is more than 'daily therapy' or a way for its author to keep sane, as Deirdre Bair suggests in her Beckett biography (1990: 348).[7] The novel might be said to limn the horrors of the Second World War by means of determinate negation, saying (by not saying) that historical circumstances require a renegotiation of what it means to mean.

On the page, wrestling with meaning becomes what the editors at Routledge, who rejected the novel for publication in 1945, describe as a 'wild and unintelligible' text (UoR, Routledge and Kegan Paul, MS 1489, Box 1958 as qtd in LB2: 14). We find musical notation, lists of objections and their solutions, croaking frogs, informational tables, poems, songs, inventories, series and phrases that repeat in obsessive loops. Certain repetitive passages make language appear to 'glitch', as if it were a malfunctioning computer program or electronic device. (The word 'glitch' comes from the Yiddish, *glitsh* or *glitshn*: a slippery place, to slide.) The aberrant quality of *Watt*'s prose has led Matthew Feldman to identify the novel as a pivot point in Beckett's oeuvre that heralds an increasingly experimental style (2009: 13). While Beckett's *Murphy* problematises a Cartesian split between body and mind, *Watt* shifts the emphasis to language, 'dismantling coherence through language itself rather than through concepts' (Nixon 2011: 187). In order to critique language by means of literary style, the novel develops a peculiar poetics whereby it explores and expands the category of the meaningful.

The dominant critical response to *Watt* has been to read it as a mordant critique of rationality, and especially of systems that embrace a binary logic of either-or. Frequent glitches in *Watt*'s stuttering prose undermine the idea that language is primarily a conduit for information, and its excessive verbal and non-verbal sounds reveal the limitations of language conceived as a wholly rational system (an ideal of language dear to philosophers such as Bertrand Russell and Ludwig Wittgenstein as well as to the logical positivists). Various scenes in *Watt* dramatise the trumping of semantic meaning by pure sound, and the song sung by Watt's patron, Mr Knott, is a good example. Mr Knott's song was 'either without meaning, or derived from an idiom with which *Watt*, a very fair linguist, had no acquaintance. The open a sound was predominant, and the explosives k and g.' Sensation (sound) continues to dominate sense: Mr Knott's speech is described as 'wild dim chatter, meaningless to Watt's ailing ears' (W 208). As the novel troubles familiar hierarchies – intelligibility over sensation, mind over body – a 'sensual poetics' emerges that foregrounds the importance of the physical body to the possibility of comprehension and communication. As it mocks language conceived as a rational system, *Watt* explores how language might operate differently through recourse to the body and the senses.

Six years after the novel's publication, an influential article by Jacqueline Hoefer set a precedent for reading *Watt* as a pastiche of logical positivism, which Hoefer links to Wittgenstein. Continuing in this vein, reading *Watt* as an 'anti-logical' novel, John Mood argues that *Watt* signposts the end of rationalism, calling it a 'devastating depiction of the cul-de-sac of modern Western rationalistic philosophy' (1971: 255). For Mood, *Watt*'s glitches are designed to show how easily rational systems such as logic and language can shift into their opposites, and he underscores the urgency of a critique of hyper-rationalism given the historical context of the novel's composition (259–62). The comparison Hugh Kenner draws between *Watt* and computer programming code furthers readings of *Watt* as a pastiche of rational systems (1987). Such readings convincingly demonstrate how *Watt* mocks a binary logic of either-or, and there is no doubt that criticism of hyper-rationality is necessary in the 1940s climate of fascism. But *Watt*'s critical gesture also proliferates possibilities for language, which emerge as the text disfigures and parodies predictable modes of expression.

In the late 1980s Steven Connor suggests that *Watt*'s repetitive language and logical glitches initiate alternative ways of meaning. Connor argues that the field of semantic, linguistic and sonorous possibilities grows larger in response to the dead ends and exhausted series in *Watt* (1988: 28). In a similar spirit, John Wall contends that Watt's perception that 'reality is deeply contradictory' spurs and sustains creative and imaginative activity (2002: 545). Most interesting of the attempts to elucidate how the strangeness of *Watt* constitutes an attempt to mean differently is Marjorie Perloff's suggestion that language in *Watt* is, literally, a 'language of resistance'. She derives the cryptic non-sequiturs of the novel's prose from code languages used by the members of the resistance cell Gloria SMH, for which Beckett volunteered during the war. Perloff suggests that *Watt*'s odd language alludes to the 'cut-out' system according to which agents would identify each other via code phrases – often non-sequiturs – to protect the identity of members of the resistance cell. In the context of Beckett's work for the resistance, Perloff observes, language was used to obfuscate as much as to convey information (1996: 122–5). Laura Salisbury expands this idea, arguing that in *Watt* the power of language 'to hide, to render secret, also becomes its capacity to spill, to link, to contaminate, to secrete' (2014: 166). Observing how affect 'oozes' into slippages between interference and information in *Watt*, she argues that 'entropic disorganization of a message in one system can open up meaning in another' (165).[8] Perloff compares this to poetry, citing Wittgenstein's observation that 'a poem, although it is composed in the language of information, is not used in the language-game of giving information' (qtd in Perloff 1996: 177). Perloff then draws a parallel between the non-conventional use of language among resistance operatives and the innovations of poetic language; language used for purposes *other* than to convey information becomes poetics.

Following this distinction between informational and poetic language, we may begin to distinguish a 'sensual poetics' in *Watt* by assessing the novel's critique of language as a conduit for information. For Hoefer, *Watt* is a parody of the early Wittgenstein's ambition to create an 'ideal language' that would enable one to live according to a completely rational system. Later, Jennie Skerl faults Hoefer for conflating Wittgenstein with the logical positivists, distinguishing Wittgenstein's critique of language from those of Russell, Feigl, Mach and others involved with the Vienna circle (Skerl 1974: 474). Both Skerl and Linda Ben-Zvi argue that it was neither Wittgenstein nor the logical positivists who influenced Beckett, but the Austrian philosopher Fritz Mauthner, whose major work, *Beiträge zu einer Kritik der Sprache* (1901), Beckett is known to have studied.[9] In his *Beiträge*, Mauthner draws attention to the inescapability of language – the difficulty of waging a critique of language by means of language itself. (This problem accounts for much of the hilarity we find in *Watt*.) Yet while Mauthner advocates mystic silence and the destruction of language, the critique waged in *Watt* engenders a different mode of linguistic activity: an experimentation akin to poetry (in Wittgenstein's sense).

It is easy to see how Hoefer arrived at her reading of *Watt* as a pastiche of logical positivism. The novel depicts the struggles of its hero to capture the vicissitudes of his world in language, and the failure of his enterprise, coupled with his dogged insistence, contributes to the novel's tragicomic humour. As a 'hyperrational man in the face of an irrational world' (Mood 1971: 259), Watt finds in language – specifically in the act of naming – a means to control the chaos that assails: 'Watt's need of semantic succour was at times so great that he would set to trying names on things' (W 83). Watt neutralises disturbances by turning them into words, and he longs to hear a voice 'wrapping up safe in words the kitchen space' (W 83). Further, he dreams of making 'a pillow of old words' (W 117) and attributes apotropaic powers to explanation: 'to explain had always been to exorcise, for Watt' (W 78). But the novel's anxious, exhaustive lists, series and permutations undermine the dream of a world ordered by language and advertise the inability of ordinary, logical language to order chaos, protect from danger or even to express what is or can be known.

What can be known, the text tells us, lies outside the purview of language: 'what we know partakes in no small measure of the nature of what has so happily been called the unutterable or ineffable, so that any attempt to utter or eff it is doomed to fail, doomed, doomed to fail' (W 62). The gong of the double 'doomed' seems to underwrite (or overwrite) this insistence on the failure of language by showing that language can create (rather than represent) sensory experiences for a reader. On a semantic level, the passage suggests that representational language creates order precisely because it *cannot* represent in full what can be known, which would overwhelm discursive categories. Language, since it cannot capture the complexity of what is lived, neatly reduces the chaos of living to what can be said.

It seems the young Beckett would share with Mauthner the observation that, while knowing the world through language is perhaps inevitable, language necessarily changes, freezes or obfuscates what it purports to know. For Mauthner, the only way to move beyond language and the deception to which it leads is to destroy it or shatter it. His *Beiträge* champions the critique of language as the most important business of humankind:

> He who sets out to write a book with a hunger for words, with a love of words, and with the vanity of words, in the language of yesterday

or of today or of tomorrow, in the congealed language of a certain and firm step, he cannot undertake the task of liberation from language. I must destroy language within me, in front of me, and behind me step for step if I want to ascend in the critique of language, which is the most pressing task for thinking man; I must shatter each rung of the ladder by stepping upon it. (qtd in Ben-Zvi 1980: 183)

At times, Beckett's frustration with language expresses itself in similarly violent and defeatist terms, as when Molloy laments the death of a world 'foully named' ('the icy words hail down upon me, the icy meanings') (TN 31). In his oft-cited letter to Axel Kaun, Beckett expresses the hope that language might be used to indict itself, a sentiment similar to Mauthner's.[10] But unlike Mauthner, Beckett in *Watt* finds a way of working *within* existing language (rather than destroying or shattering it) to make it mean in unexpected ways. Despite Beckett's initial idea that language could lead to nothing nobler than its own destruction, *Watt* explores the sensory dimensions of language – sonority, consonance, repetition and rhythm – rather than remaining strictly in the mode of critique.

Though Mauthner valorises silence, this valorisation is complicated by the existence of his *Beiträge*, which, far from laconic, goes on for thousands of pages. Skerl makes sense of this contradiction by characterising the Austrian philosopher as a 'supreme rational-empiricist [who becomes] a mystic by way of realizing the limitations of his philosophy' (1974: 478). In other words, Mauthner's all too rational critique of language leads him to embrace mystic silence. According to Skerl, it is in the spirit of Mauthner that *Watt* chronicles the 'inevitable failure of one who attempts to know truth through language' (478). But Skerl also rightly identifies how Beckett's hero differs from Mauthner: '[Watt] revolts and fails again and again, clinging to logic and language' (478). Watt cannot remain silent, and the novel chronicles his attempts – perhaps also those of the novel's author – to render a deeply contradictory, polyvalent experience in language. These attempts generate innovations that begin with the erratic glitches and stammering permutations of *Watt*'s odd prose.

Play with sound and rhythm distracts from narrative chronology, frustrates intelligibility and mocks rationalism's fondness for series and formulae. Exhaustive lists and permutations create patterns of sounds that establish an 'order' in the text that is other than semantic. This can occur via graphic representations of sound that resemble musical notation, as in a well-known passage consisting of frog noises:

Krak!	--	--	--	--	--	--	--
Krek!	--	--	--	--	Krek!	--	--
Krik!	--	--	Krik!	--	--	Krik!	-- [. . .] (W 137)

Nearly two pages of text are devoted to frog sounds followed by beats of rest. This interruption (or eruption) comes as Watt remembers 'a distant summer night, in a no less distant land, and Watt young and well lying all alone stone sober in the ditch, wondering if it was the time and the place and the loved one already, and the frogs croaking at one, nine, seventeen, twenty-five, etc.' (W 136). Watt's memory of the ardour he felt (for the fishwoman, Mrs Gorman) overwhelms conceptual and discursive categories. Not only does the text give way to sound and rhythm – animal noises associated with sexual desire – but Watt, given his excessively rational temperament, imposes on the frogs' mating calls the regularity of a series. He observes that the terms *Krak! Krek! Krik!* occur on the first, ninth, seventeenth and twenty-fifth beats and so on (W 136). Watt's effort to discern patterns in the auditory ejaculations of amphibian desire is comical, but the reader understands, more deeply, that it is the erratic, unknowable nature of his own desire that incites Watt, as in a compulsion, to seek regularity – a version of meaning – in pure sensation. The difficulty of rendering desire in language is made manifest by the fact that the frog sounds appear in a chart and constitute a hiatus in the regular layout of the text.

In other passages, binary systems falter on the edge of absurdity, inviting, perhaps, a return of the irrational. A parlour maid named either Ann or Mary (there is some equivocation) is described 'eating onions and peppermints turn and turn about, I mean first an onion, then a peppermint, then another onion, then another peppermint, then another onion, then another peppermint, then another onion, then another peppermint, then another onion, then another peppermint [. . .]' (51).[11] We've only to consult our bodily memory to grasp why onions (especially raw onions) and peppermints constitute the terms of an opposition. These terms, like the zero and one of binary code, or the 'yes' and the 'no', repeatedly alternate until Mary, who was dusting, forgot 'little by little the reason for her presence in that place' and the 'duster, whose burden up till now she had so bravely born, fell from her fingers, to the dust, where having at once assumed the colour (grey) of its surroundings it disappeared until the following spring' (W 51). Here, alternation between opposites, which is, incidentally, the basis for binary code, leads to a condition of grey where differentiation is difficult (the duster falls to the dust) and tasks are forgotten. Moreover, Mary's fantasies – 'Erotic cravings? Recollections of childhood? Menopausal discomfort?' (51) – are allowed to 'ravish' her from her task, thereby illustrating how a highly rational logic of binaries, taken to a humorous extreme, begets the resurgence of the irrational, or at least interferes with the *telos* of completing certain chores.

In instances such as these, repeated variously throughout the text, the language of *Watt* calls to mind the images and sounds of a machine short-circuiting. Here, the use of the word 'watt' to denote a measurement of current may be at play.[12] In the example mentioned above, a system based on binary logic (onions and peppermints) stumbles into a glitch, repeating as if it were a computer program gone haywire that keeps performing its function even after the function has lost all meaning. The necessity of controlling closed systems (circuits, but also, more broadly, social systems) links to another allusion embedded in the novel's title. As Jean-Michel Rabaté points out, the novel's title alludes not only to the metaphysical question, '*What* is,' but also to James Watt (1736–1819), inventor of the steam engine, one of the first automatic self-regulating devices (Rabaté 2005: 101).

Watt's steam engine included a feedback valve called a 'governor' (the word shares an etymological link with cybernetics, since both derive from the ancient Greek word for 'steering') that could control the speed of the engine. Cybernetic theory, which post-dates the writing of *Watt* by several years, transfers the necessity of auto-regulation into the domain of social systems, where individuals form closed feedback loops with their environments.[13] Looked at this way, aspects of *Watt* might be read as auto-regulatory devices for the communicative 'system' of language. Erratic eruptions of sound may be necessary to ensure the proper functioning of language, purging it of excess (letting off steam). The theme of auto-regulation, in the background of *Watt*, reminds us that irrational excess emerges as a byproduct of any rational, machinic order that seeks to exclude it.

The verbal aberrations we find in *Watt* also resemble the surges in current that threaten the integrity of a system (language, rationalism), except that these aberrations have a sonorous coherence and, like poetry, affect the senses. The excesses of language in *Watt*, like those in Lucky's speech in *Waiting for Godot*, are to be looked at and listened to as well as read.[14] Watt's predecessor at the house of Mr Knott, Arsene, creates sensory experiences by associating words on the basis of sound and rhythm – alliteration, rhyme and meter – in his 'brief' monologue of twenty pages: 'Not a word, not a deed, not a thought, not a need, not a grief, not a joy, not a girl, not a boy [. . .]' (W 46). In an earlier manuscript draft of *Watt*, this passage and others like it were set out in verse and only later changed to prose (Ackerley 2010: 70). The following passage was initially set out in two quatrains: 'The Tuesday scowls, the Wednesday growls, the Thursday curses, the Friday howls, the Saturday snores, the Sunday yawns, the Monday morns, the Monday morns [. . .]' (W 46). The homophonic relationship between 'morn' and 'mourn' gives those who read the passage on the basis of sound the option of anthropomorphising the days of the week. This would make a sentence with a subject and a verb (*Monday mourns* is a grammatically correct sentence; *Monday morns* is not). Reading by sound allows a duality of sense – 'mourns' and 'morns' – to coexist. More generally, by reorienting language according to sensual, aural associations, the text exposes (and perhaps unsettles) our allegiance to linguistic norms – like a sentence comprised of a subject and verb – by which we orient ourselves in language.

The 'singing alongside of' embedded in the word parody (*para + ode*) makes it appropriate that Watt's unsettling of linguistic norms comes through poetic attention to sound. However, more colloquial meanings of parody (pertaining to humour and imitation) are equally important in *Watt*, for the novel's most salient critique occurs via laughter. Mauthner, though he may aspire to absolute silence, writes that the only way to *articulate* the mystical state is through laughter: 'Basically speaking, pure critique is merely articulated laughter. Each laughter is critique, the best critique [. . .] and the danger of this book [the *Beiträge*], the daring aspect of this attempt, lies in merely having put an articulated text to this laughter' (qtd in Ben-Zvi 1980: 197). This idea resonates in *Watt*, where there is great attention to varieties of laughter:

> Haw! Haw! Haw! My laugh, [. . .] My laugh, Mr. Watt [. . .] Of all the laughs that strictly speaking are not laughs, but modes of ululation, only three I think need detain us, I mean the bitter, the hollow and the mirthless. They correspond to successive, how shall I say successive . . . suc . . . successive excoriations of the understanding. (W 48)

The laugh, as ululation or convulsion of the throat, creates eruptions of sounds that can, as the passage's stuttering 'suc' and repeated 'x' sounds (su*ccess* and e*xcor*) show, excoriate the kind of understanding that relies too heavily on presupposition. Not only does the laugh peel the skin from the understanding, it also creates staccato breaks in the prose, interrupting narrative progress.

More importantly, perhaps, the three types of laugh – the bitter, the hollow and the mirthless – correspond to and parody Aristotle's hierarchy of ethical, intellectual and dianoetic virtues, which lead to the perfection of the rational nature of man. Beckett copied out these virtues in his Philosophy Notes on Aristotle (Ackerley 2010: 75). *Watt* replaces the Aristotelian virtues with a typology of *laughter* – an involuntary bodily response born of emotion rather than reason. The highest, purest order of thought (*dianoesis*) finds its correlate in a laugh that goes 'down the snout' or through the body of the human-animal: 'the mirthless laugh is the dianoetic laugh, down the snout – Haw! – so. It is the laugh of laughs, the *risus purus*, the laugh laughing at the laugh [. . .]' (W 48). Aside from problematising the kind of dualist thinking that would distance the thinking mind from the laughing body, the idea of a dianoetic or 'pure' laugh that laughs at itself parodies the auto-critique of reason (Kant).[15] The laugh is derisive, 'mirthless', full of irony. Where reason's critique of itself becomes laughable, reason and rationality may be trumped by forces outside their domain. And if laughter, which can erupt uncontrollably from the body, becomes a pre-eminent mode of critique, this further undermines the division between rationality and its opposite. *Watt* emphasises serious faults in the foundations of rational understanding and provokes laughter at rationalism's attempts to save itself from crumbling.

Trumping (or flaying) the understanding through laughter indicates a theme of crucial importance in *Watt*: the relation between language and the body. Laughter is a convulsion of the speaking organs; it is felt in the stomach and in the face. It exemplifies one way in which language might short-circuit the understanding through an appeal to the body. Humour is an efficacious means of provoking bodily responses in one's readers; like sound and rhythm patterns, humour creates effects in excess of what the understanding can produce.

J. M. Coetzee, a reader sensitive to *Watt*'s brand of humour, studies Beckett's manuscript revisions in an effort to determine how *Watt* was revised to create stylistic patterns that would produce effects in excess of conventional meaning structures. As an example, Coetzee takes the following sentence: 'for Watt to get into Erskine's room, as they were then, Watt would have to be another man, or Erskine's room another room' (128). The crucial twist to what Coetzee calls a 'comedy of the logical impasse' is the use of the conditional (*would* rather than *will*). Coetzee situates *Watt* within the 'subgenre of logical comedy', reminding us how often humour is derived from substitutions of context (Coetzee 1972: 480). Things could be otherwise, and meanings depend upon one's position and angle of view. Comedy makes much out of meaning's context-dependence, as do poetic attempts to alter the manner in which language might mean. But humour in *Watt* also directly appeals to the bodies of its readers; it provokes affective responses by inciting us to laughter.

The role of the physical body in the transmission and comprehension of meaning is explored most explicitly late in the novel, when Watt creates a series of idioms that his interlocutor, Sam, begins, with some practice, to understand. This scene, in the grounds of a mental institution, occurs when Sam and Watt emerge from holes in their respective fences to meet in a zone between their gardens (W 60).[16] Sam observes, regarding the idioms that Watt invents to narrate his adventures in the house of Mr Knott, 'that the inversion was imperfect;/that the ellipse was frequent;/that euphony was a preoccupation' (164). Sam also points out that Watt's language, in addition to its concern with sound, involves talking just as he walked, from back to front. Watt's sentence asks to be read in reverse, following the back-to-front movement of his body: '*Day of most, night of part, Knott with now . . .*' (W 164). Reading the phrase from back to front (right to left), we understand: *Now with Knott, part of night, most of day*. Further idiomatic variations consist in Watt's inverting the order of the words in the sentence, the letters in the word, the sentences in the period or some combination of the three. Watt's penultimate idiom is as follows: '*Dis yb dis, nem owt. Yad la, tin fo trap. Skin, skin skin. Od su did ned taw? On. Taw ot klat tonk?* [. . .]' (We might hazard a translation: *Knot talk to Wat? No. Wat den did us do? Niks [Nichts], Niks, Niks. Part of nit[e], al day. Two men sid[e] by sid.*)[17] So as to better understand Watt's increasingly complex inversions, Sam mirrors Watt's way of walking: the two walk face to face, breast to breast, belly to belly, pubis to pubis, and finally 'glued together' (W 168). By fitting himself to Watt's body, Sam grows 'used to these sounds' (165). The text hints humorously that understanding may be predicated as much on the body as on the rational capacity to decode Watt's murmurings at the border of sense and nonsense.

But the correspondence of body parts does not, finally, yield complete communicative success. At first, the sounds of Watt's idiom, 'though we walked glued together, were so much Irish to me' (W 169). Given the link between emotion, irrationality and Irishness in Beckett's writing – in *Molloy*, tears and laughter are associated with the Gaelic language (TN 37) – we wonder what understanding might involve beyond the rational, informational or logical. The 'information' Watt transmits to Sam exceeds certain conventions of expression; language contorts in grotesquely comic inversions as it attempts to convey what exceeds it. We glean as much from the pathos of its failure as we do from attempts to 'translate' the idioms into comprehensible English. We know that whatever transpires between Watt and Sam is particularly relevant given that these questionably understood conversations are what generates this strange, anti-logical novel we are in the process of reading: Watt's adventures in the house of Mr Knott narrated by a certain Sam(uel Beckett). Language's appeal to the body, its poetic preoccupations (euphony and ellipsis), and the impossibility of complete linguistic accuracy constitute a commentary on the art of the novel, particularly the experimental novel we are reading – a *mise en abîme par excellence*, and not without humour.

The physical body does not operate in this passage as a 'key' that enables us to decode languages with which we are unfamiliar. Instead, the body points towards a means of communicating that surpasses the strictly logical. In *Watt*, we find a vivid example of how a parody of the binary movement of back and forth becomes the basis for movement in new directions. This parody both ridicules systems of communication that limit themselves to binary alternatives and accents the flexibility of the body to move in ways that are unpredictable. Early in the novel, a passage details how Watt's body dramatically jerks between the poles of north and south in order to move east:

> Watt's way of advancing due east, for example, was to turn his bust as far as possible towards the north and at the same time to fling out his right leg as far as possible towards the south, and then to turn his bust as far as possible towards the south and at the same time to fling his right leg as far as possible towards the north. (W 30)

We have the image of Watt as a 'headlong tardigrade', a microscopic organism moving jerkily on stubby 'legs', swinging stiff limbs. This parody comes at the expense of a version of the dialectic: why move via alternation between north and south (yes and no, affirmation and negation) when one might simply turn to the east? Jockeying back and forth will surely culminate in exhaustion, and the movement is laughable insofar as we know that this back and forth labouring is unnecessary: sideways movement is easily achieved by turning the body.

The strangeness of Watt's walk becomes an interpretive dilemma for Lady McCann, who remembers a joke from her girlhood days. In the joke, medical students speculate about the stiff walk of a gentleman on the street. When they stop him to ask whether it is piles or the clap that is responsible for his stiff walk, he replies: 'I thought it was wind myself' (W 31). The body, like language, is subject to interpretation and misinterpretation; misunderstandings in language parallel the ways in which we might 'read' the body askew, attributing false causes or motives to its movements and gestures.

Watt's mechanical walk, the 'funambulistic stagger' that Lady McCann deems too regular and dogged to be attributable to the effects of alcohol, corresponds to a definition of the comic elaborated by Henri Bergson. Bergson's theory sets up a dichotomy between the body's natural grace – a vitality we associate with intellectual and moral life – and the jerky movements or automatism we associate with mechanised systems. For Bergson, comedy occurs when the the rigidity of a machine is superimposed upon the living: 'The attitudes, gestures and movement of the human body are laughable in exact proportion as that body reminds of us of a mere machine' (2008: 21). Bergson's earlier critique of language, in *Time and Free Will*, faults language for its rigidity and describes it as a system that is inadequate to the fluid, flexible and ever-changing ideas it pretends to contain and convey. He recommends a poetic language for philosophy, which he aspires to in his own writing, and finds in the pitfalls of ordinary language a basis for comedy. Ulrika Maude, noting that Beckett read Bergson's book on laughter in or around 1930, argues that aspects of Beckett's humour and his general treatment of language, repetition and compulsion owe much to his reading of Bergson (2014: 47). She uses Bergson's definition of the comic – 'Something mechanical encrusted on the living' – to point out the extent to which the body and mind can act without the conscious control of the will, '[casting] serious doubt over received notions of subjectivity, suggesting that the automatic and the involuntary were integral to the self' (48).

In addition to Watt's jerky, mechanical walk and the tendency of language to 'glitch' in ways that remind us of a machine malfunctioning, we also find in *Watt* a curious detachment from feeling, a condition that also comes up in Bergson's writings on the comic. If we look at life as disinterested spectators, Bergson suggests, 'many a drama will turn into a comedy'. He gives the example of stopping one's ears to the sound of music in a room where people are dancing so that the dancers appear ridiculous. 'How many human actions would stand a similar test?' he asks, 'Should we not see many of them suddenly pass from grave to gay, on isolating them from the accompanying music of sentiment?' The comic is a temporary 'anesthesia of the heart', a direct appeal to intelligence (Bergson 2008: 10–11). In *Watt*, the 'music of sentiment' is transposed into an atomised language in which emotions, such as Watt's sexual longing for the fishwoman or the parlour maid's daydreams, are transformed into aberrations or glitches in language: *Krak! Krek! Krik!* or the obsessive alternation between onions and peppermints. Language in *Watt* breaks down with the first suggestion of emotion. It betrays its inadequacy in the face of the incalculable and transforms itself to comedy.

The bizarre automation of language in *Watt*, its repetitions and glitches, give us the image of a machine on the point of collapse. By parodying rational systems that operate according to a binary logic of either-or, the novel veers towards impasse, having declared it impossible that language might mean what it says. But in *Watt*, limitations of language are exhibited not only in the interest of critique. From the fragments of stalled-out rational systems, the possibility of more vital, embodied ways of inhabiting language emerge. By undoing the oppositions that structure understanding in the conventional sense – divisions between rationality and irrationality, sensation and meaning – Beckett strives, in *Watt* as in many of his works, to create a language in which form and content blend so that sense is 'forever rising to the surface of the form and becoming the form itself' (1983: 27). Such a language explicitly appeals to and involves the body – its sensitivity to sound, its possibilities for movement and its capacity for laughter.

*

The monologue delivered by Lucky in Act I of *Waiting for Godot*, written between 1948 and 1949 in French, is a highly concentrated section of experimental prose that excites expressive powers of language latent in our daily speech. While interpretations tend to characterise it as signifying the decline of humanity, logical contradictions operate, as they do in *Watt*, to spur reinventions of language. Lucky's speech privileges homophony, sonority, rhyme, rhythm, allusion and repetition and develops a poetics that works against the established meanings of words and stock phrases, especially those of academic discourse. The speech also calls into question the tyranny of semantics in linguistic practice, working to illuminate relationships between language and the physical world by uncovering the concrete foundations of abstract terms. It locates the beginnings of language in a body that moves, orients, gestures or even dances before it thinks or speaks. Innovative, poetic language can be linked to the task of expanding possibilities for bodily movement, as the comparison between thinking and dancing in *Godot* suggests.

Beckett creates situations of paradox in Lucky's speech by carefully calibrating its parts to the expectations his reader is likely to have. At several points in Lucky's monologue, Beckett avails himself of a familiar discursive convention only to undermine the abstract sense of a word with its more concrete meaning – a meaning that is disclosed, for example, through the addition of a further adjective. Beckett's prose carefully plays to our expectations – even provokes them – only to challenge them by exploiting the polysemy of certain abstract, discursive terms. In this sense, Lucky's speech works against and is thus *beyond* the *doxa* of conventional language usage. Amidst the parodied ruins of discursive rationality and its preferred modes of expression, Lucky's logorrhea forges new trajectories within language, as pathways between words multiply possibilities for linguistic expression. Lucky's speech also reminds us, provocatively, of how language may extend the concrete activity of the body, as in Merleau-Ponty's example in the *Phenomenology* of the body's sensibility extending to material prostheses, for example a cane.[18] Because this is more evident in the French version of Beckett's text, my discussion will cite the French *Godot*, followed by Beckett's translation.[19]

In Lucky's speech the activity of *thinking*, with all its serious scholarly associations, is reconceived as a performance art – a way to pass the time on par with circus acts, recitations and public singing or dance. The reduction of thinking to mere show or performance recalls charges made against the Sophists by Plato and his followers; rhetoricians were faulted for using the arts of language to manipulate or bewitch their audiences, arguing for one position or its opposite without appropriate regard for truth. The emptiness of mere 'thought' or rhetoric in Lucky's speech is suggested by a savage parody of scholarly discourse in the form of fragmented repetitions and distortions of stereotypical words used in academic discussions: *d'autre part, étant donné, attendu d'autre part, quaquaquaqua, qu'en vue des labeurs, à l'opinion contraire, en même temps et parallèlement, je reprends, considérant d'autre part, au suivant* (on the other hand, given the existence, what is more, established beyond all doubt, quaquaquaqua, in view of the labours, concurrently simultaneously, for reasons unknown, the facts are there).[20] The demotion of thinking to casual entertainment is clear from the way in which Pozzo introduces Lucky's routine: 'Que puis-je faire [. . .] pour que le temps leur semble moins long?' (*Go* 54) (is there anything I can do in my turn for these honest fellows who are having such a dull, dull time) (G 26). Pulling the cord attached to Lucky's neck, Pozzo asks Vladimir and Estragon: 'Que préférez vous ? Qu'il danse, qu'il chante, qu'il récite, qu'il pense, qu'il . . . [. . .] Alors, vous voulez qu'il nous pense quelque chose?' (*Go* 55) (What do you prefer? Shall we have him dance, or sing, or recite, or think, or – [. . .] Well, would you like him to think something for us?) (G 26). To describe 'thinking' as a performance goes against the expectation that intellectual activity is an earnest quest for truth.

The unexpected relegation of thinking to the status of a spectator sport – for ourselves as well as for Didi and Gogo – hints at a major theme of Lucky's speech: the notion of man-as-thinking-actor before the eyes of a divine spectator. Lucky begins his speech with the description of a 'Dieu personnel [. . .] qui du haut de sa divine apathie sa divine athambie sa divine aphasie nous aime bien à quelques exceptions près' (*Go* 59) (personal God [. . .] who from the heights of divine apathia divine athambia divine aphasia loves us dearly with some exceptions) (G 28). The image of Lucky as an actor before an all-powerful spectator-god has been linked by some critics to the Baroque concept of *theatrum mundi*, or the world as a stage (Cohn 1962a). Several aspects of the speech and its surrounding dialogue reinforce this idea: first, there is Lucky's sense, described by Pozzo, of being caught in a net. Pozzo explains that Lucky calls his dance 'La danse du Filet. Il se croit empêtré dans un filet' (*Go* 56) (The Net. He thinks he's entangled in a net) (G 27). We might associate a net with entrapment, but the theatre critic Toby Silverman-Zinman relates the experience of 'dancing in a net' to a proverb that describes a state of being watched while thinking oneself unobserved (1995: 311–12). This links the content of Lucky's speech – descriptions of mankind dwindling or wasting away under the gaze of an apathetic deity – with Lucky's own aphasic decline as witnessed by Pozzo, Estragon, Vladimir and ourselves. Second, the rope attached to Lucky's neck indicates his subservience to Pozzo and alludes, perhaps, to puppetry, to the marionette theatre and the circus, undermining views of the human as an agent capable of acting on his own volition. It is Pozzo, a circus ringleader of sorts,[21] who controls Lucky's movements and commands him to perform: 'Pense, porc!' (*Go* 59) (Think, pig!) (G 28). Lastly, the increasing speed of Lucky's delivery reinforces the sense that he is out of control with regard to the spectacle he produces. Though the speed of the text is not mentioned in the stage directions,[22] in many productions Lucky's speech is delivered at a breathless pace that accelerates as the monologue progresses. The text itself, a single sentence spliced with aberrant interjections, non sequiturs, loops and repetitions, creates an impression of movement towards entropy and loss of control on the part of the speaker that jars usual associations between 'thinking', rationality and order.

Rosette Lamont uses the monologue's speed to compare it to the ancient Greek dramatic convention of *pnigos*. *Pnigos*, also called the 'choker', and frequently used by Aristophanes, is a section of the *parabasis*. Because *parabasis* constitutes a break in the dramatic action of the play (the chorus directly addresses the audience), Lucky's inability to control or direct his own thought is that much more jarring: even moments of direct address are not subject to human volition. The breathless speed of the speech also refers us to its source in the body of the actor – a body that tends, in keeping with a main refrain of the speech, to 'waste and pine', to dwindle towards entropy and exhaustion. Metrical changes ensure the rapid delivery of the *pnigos*, often uttered in a single breath. Lucky's speech is almost certainly an allusion to *parabasis*, given that stage directions in both the French and English versions direct Lucky to turn towards the audience before speaking.[23] That Lucky does not seem to have control over his 'thinking' – that language flows on in loops and glitches without his volition – is reinforced by the image of Lucky as a mere player on the world's stage – an 'actor' subject to the constraints of a script and a flow towards entropy he can do little to resist.

Entropy, disarray, chaos, absurdity and apocalypse are the themes Beckett critics have most often used to describe Lucky's speech, and most agree that, in terms of content, it portrays humanity's decline: a shrinking, dwindling, wasting or pining under the gaze of an indifferent God. Such readings draw support from the following lines: '[l'homme] malgré les progrès de l'alimentation et de l'élimination des déchets est en train de maigrir [. . .] malgré l'essor de la culture physique [. . .] de rapetisser [. . .] de maigrir rétrécir' (Go 60). Beckett translates this passage as follows: '[man] in spite of the strides of alimentation and defecation wastes and pines wastes and pines and [. . .] in spite of the strides of physical culture [. . .] fades away' (G 29). This description of wasting and pining probably inspired John Fletcher to observe that the point of Lucky's monologue is to illustrate that 'humankind, notwithstanding the existence of a caring God of sorts and progress of various kinds, is in full decline' (Fletcher 2000: 70).[24]

That Lucky's soliloquy represents the decline of humanity is further reinforced by the deterioration of its language, which becomes increasingly encumbered with asyntactic loops, interjections and senseless repetitions. Jean-Claude Lieber calls it 'un discours exterminateur et terroriste' (1998: 76) (a terroristic, destructive speech) while Anselm Atkins calls Lucky a 'man babbling his way to silence' (1967: 427). Elements of chaos in the speech notwithstanding, both critics agree that the monologue is carefully structured in three parts. Atkins argues that the first two parts of Lucky's speech are fragmented parodies of rationality in the manner of Descartes and Spinoza respectively. The third section is a breakdown of rationality, evidenced by the fact that it 'lacks syntax, has many more aphasic interjections than the first two parts, and is richer in poetic imagery connotative of death, decline and pathos'.[25] Lieber divides the French version at the same joints, but organises the three sections around the themes of God (*dieu*), man (*l'homme*) and stones (*les pierres*). A coupling of organisation and dissolution in the speech hints that neat divisions between order and chaos, structure and entropy, measure and decadence (decline) no longer hold. Eruptions of physicality during the process of 'thinking' (attention to the materiality of language achieved through the repetition of certain sounds, the shaking of the actor's body or stuttering over certain words) also trouble a strict separation between mind and body – a point that is underscored by the emergence of the skull (*la tête*) as a material, bodily site of thought. Such ruptures contribute to dominant interpretations of Lucky's speech as signalling the breakdown of reason and the decline of humankind.

We might ask whether Lucky's decline, or, given the element of *theatrum mundi*, the decline of humankind in general, precipitates or coincides with the breakdown of language. The fact that Lucky is mute in the second act suggests that the erratic flows of his speech mark a crisis of language, or at least a reassessment of the manner in which it 'makes sense'. In particular, certain terms in the monologue become changed as a result of their context. Focusing on a few such polysemic terms, I'll show how at certain moments in the speech they effect transitions from abstract, academic discourse to descriptions of concrete, physical, even bodily realities. In this way, play on words has the effect of rooting or grounding a certain kind of abstract language in the physical world and in the body. Whether it qualifies as a radicalisation, renewal, dissolution or poeticisation of language, this strategy suggests modes of meaning in language that emphasise its bodily dimension, either by referencing physical activities or, in Merleau-Pontian fashion, by foregrounding the primacy of the body relative to abstract ideas.

The first term to undergo the change as I have described is the verb *jaillir*, closely followed by *travaux*. Both terms appear in the opening lines of Lucky's speech: 'Étant donné l'existence telle qu'elle jaillit des récents travaux publics de Poinçon et Wattmann d'un Dieu personnel quaquaquaqua à barbe blanche' (*Go* 59) (Given the existence as uttered forth in the public works of Puncher and Wattman of a personal God quaquaquaqua with white beard) (G 28). Conditioned as we are by Lucky's rhetorical-sounding false start ('D'autre part, pour ce qui est . . .') (On the other hand with regard to), and our knowledge that Lucky has been instructed to *think*, we could read this line as follows: Given the existence of God such as it has emerged from the recent work of two eminent scholars. But the modification of *travaux* by *publics* disrupts this scholarly reading, for while *travaux* in French is ambiguous (it can refer to intellectual or physical work), *travaux publics* conjures the image of public works projects, which can only be physical labour. The addition of the term *publics* also modifies the meaning of the verb *jaillir*, which appears earlier in the sentence. Whereas we might initially read *jaillir* in its figurative sense (the existence of God is an idea that had emerged or sprung forth), the mention of public works forces the more physical connotations of *jaillir* to surface: to gush out or spurt suddenly (as liquid), to flow (as tears), to shoot up (as flames).[26] Beckett's invented names, Poinçon and Wattmann, are also suited to public works, since they mean ticket puncher and tram driver, respectively. From its first lines, Lucky's speech promises a breakneck, terrifying ride into a zone in which rational thinking and linguistic conventions are radically destabilised. An allusion to *Watt* (what? man?), a work engaged in a similar project vis-à-vis language, is underscored by the repetitions, loops and glitches we find in the speech, as well as by the use of 'quaquaquaqua', a play on *quoi?* (what?) that achieves a denaturing of the academic jargon word 'qua'. (It repeats it to the point of senselessness, until it resembles the quacking of a duck.)

A pattern according to which academic jargon is modified to connote something more concrete, or is reduced to a play of seemingly nonsensical sounds that refer to bodily emissions (a sort of potty humour), recurs throughout the speech. The *'recherches inachevées'* (unfinished labours) of Testu and Conard (names that are variations on words for male and female genitalia) as well as those of Fartov and Belcher (gaseous emissions of the body) link academic research to procreative acts performed by the body and to physical excretions. The oft-cited 'l'Acacacacadémie d'Anthropopopométrie de Berne-en-Bresse' illustrates the manner in which abstract terms become phonetically connected to the body's activities; *caca* and *popo* designate children's words for faeces and chamber pot respectively. Anthropometry, the science of measurement, has been relegated to the fictive locale of Berne-en-Bresse, the first word of which resembles the French verb *berner* (which means to fool or to deceive). Part of Lucky's convoluted sentence reads as follows:

> qu'à la suite des recherches inachevées n'anticipons pas des recherches inachevées mais néanmoins couronnées par l'Acacacacadémie d'Anthropopopométrie de Berne-en-Bresse de Testu et Conard il est établi sans autre possibilité d'erreur que celle afférente aux calculs humains qu'à la suite des recherches inachevées inachevées de Testu et Conard il est établi tabli tabli ce qui suit qui suit qui suit [. . .] (Go 59–60)

that as a result of the labours left unfinished crowned by the Acacacademy of Anthropopopometry of Essy-in-Possy of Testew and Cunard it is established beyond all doubt all other doubt than that which clings to the labors of men that as a result of the labors unfinished of Testew and Cunard it is established hereinafter [. . .] (G 28)

Once we bracket the syntactical nesting of clauses and repetitions, the major line of the sentence emerges as follows: 'qu'à la suite des recherches inachevées [. . .] de Testu et Conard il est établi [. . .] que l'homme [. . .] est en train de maigrir [. . .]' (*Go* 59–60) (that as a result of the labors left unfinished [. . .] of Testew and Cunard it is established [. . .] that man [. . .] wastes and pines [. . .] (G 28–9). While supporting the views of critics who read the speech as symbolising decline, this simplification elides the spasmodic eruptions in the monologue's language that serve to confuse, double with doubt and thicken its prose with richness of sound. What are we to make of the recurring loops that emerge to interrupt the linearity of Lucky's thinking, either with backtracking (repetitions of earlier parts of the speech), repetitions that create eruptions of sound (*inachevés inachevés*), stuttering (*cacacaca, quaquaquaqua, tabli, tabli, tels, tels, tels le tennis*) or obsessively looping clauses (*ce qui suit qui suit qui suit*)?

Progress, development and culture (*progrès, l'essor, culture*) are the next targets of the monologue's word game. These terms, which we associate with forward movement and a flowering of the arts, become the designators of bodily rhythms: cycles of digestion and sports practices. *La culture (physique)* is modified in the same way as *travaux (publics)*. It is usual to associate progress with linear advancement, yet in the course of Lucky's tirade, *progrès* is used to describe a cyclical process of eating and excretion that contributes to man's diminishing: '[l'homme] malgré les progrès de l'alimentation et de l'élimination des déchets est en train de maigrir' ([man] in spite of the strides of alimentation and defecation wastes and pines). Similarly: 'malgré *l'essor* de la *culture* physique de la pratique des sports tels tels tels le tennis' (*Go* 60; my emphasis) (in spite of the strides of physical culture the practice of sports such as tennis) (G 29). While the development (*l'essor*) of culture might make one think of a Golden Age of Athens or of artistic and intellectual flowering more generally, here culture is *physical* and pertains to the practice of sports. The inclusion of *conation* ('conating' in the English version) in the list of sports that require physical exertion (cycling, tennis, skating, etc.) is a manner of physicalising the exercise of thought, while poking fun, perhaps, at the energetic impotence of the human will.[27] The English version of the speech contains a further connection of abstract concepts – in this case, the concept of number – to the body. Approximating a number to the nearest decimal generates 'round *figures* stark naked in the stockinged feet in Connemara' (my emphasis) (G 29). The polysemy of 'figure', which can designate numbers or bodies, is exploited to forge further connections between abstractions (culture, progress, mathematics) and the form, functions and exertions of physical bodies.

The final group of examples has to do with mutations of words based on qualities of sound. In these examples, phonic resemblances gain ascendancy over semantic connections, and words are related and ordered based on consonance (*recherches inachevées*, for example) or internal rhyme. The idea that thinking, especially towards the end of the speech, becomes an *irrational* poetics – sense-as-sound and sense-as-meaning run together, rubbing away the dichotomy between the two – coincides nicely with the climax of the speech in terms of its content: the appearance or unburying (*ressort*) of the skull (*la tête*), the material and bodily substrate of thought. This 'logic' of sound and the placement of thought in *la tête* (the skull) suggest that intellection is a bodily process. Near the beginning of his speech, Lucky plays on the homophonic relation between *dans* and *dont*, *peu* and *peut* (from *pouvoir*): 'on a le temps *dans* le tourment *dans* les feux <u>*dont*</u> les feux les flammes pour *peu* que ça dure encore un *peu* et qui <u>*peut*</u> en douter [. . .]' (Go 59). In this passage, the *dans* changes surreptitiously to *dont* and *peu* changes to *peut*. In both cases the sound repeats, but the meaning it carries is different. Because the resignification of words based on their sound-qualities is associated with the work of poetry, it is fitting that the next line alludes to a canonical work of French poetry by Verlaine: 'si bleues [. . .] et calmes si calmes' (Go 59; Fletcher 2000: 90).[28] If Lucky's speech situates itself within a poetic tradition, we might associate it, like poetics, with a remaking of language. The shifts between words based on phonic similarities tend in the direction of meanings that relate to the physical world. For instance, the *en cours* of Steinweg and Peterman's experiments becomes *cours* (currents or flows) of water and of fire. Towards the end of the speech, Lucky sputters:

> <u>ce qui est encore plus grave</u> qu'il ressort <u>ce qui est encore plus grave</u> qu'à la lumière la lumière des expériences *en cours* de Steinweg et

> Petermann il ressort <u>ce qui est encore plus grave</u> qu'il ressort <u>ce qui est encore plus grave</u> à la lumière des expériences abandonnées de Steinweg et Petermann qu'à la compagne à la montagne et au bord de la mer et des *cours* et d'eau et de feu en l'air (*Go* 61; my emphasis)

> what is more much more grave that in the light of the labors lost of Steinweg and Peterman it appears what is more much more grave that in the light the light the light of the labors lost of Steinweg and Peterman that in the plains in the mountains by the seas by the rivers running water running fire the air (G 29)

In the French, a sound loop repeats four times, each loop set off by the phrase 'ce qui est encore plus grave', and each moving away from discussion of abandoned scientific experiments in favour of references to nature (*compagne, montagne*) and the elements (*eau, feu, air*). Looping, staccato interjections of jargon words and glitches (*est établi tabli tabli ce qui suit qui suit qui suit*) segue into the assonant lines: 'l'air et la terre faits pour les pierres par les grands froids hélas au septième de leur ère l'éther la terre la mer pour les pierres par les grands fonds les grands froids sur mer sur terre et dans les airs peuchère' (*Go* 61) (the air and the earth abode of stones in the great cold alas alas in the year of their Lord six hundred and something the air the earth the sea the earth abode of stones in the great deeps the great cold on sea on land and in the air) (G 29). The internal rhyme of *air-terre-pierres-ère-éther-mer* (like the sounds loops, stuttering consonants and repetitions) calls attention to the sensuous qualities of language. This attention to the sounds of words troubles the opposition between bodily sensation and intellection, suggesting that language is material and sensuous as well as semantic. It is fitting, in relation to the rebirth of language, that Lucky's monologue, in addition to developing its own poetic lexicon (keywords recur, as do phrase-refrains), draws on French, German and English poetic traditions (Lieber mentions allusions to Shakespeare, Verlaine and Hölderlin).[29]

Throughout Lucky's speech, reminders of the relation between language, nature and the body surge with sudden violence through the stuttering fault lines of a system that tends to repress its bodily beginnings. But what does it mean to say that language is rooted in the body? While the preceding discussion has focused on wordplay that favoured sonority over semantics, it is also possible to tease out a relation between language, gesture and dance. A linkage between Lucky's monologue and the dance with which it begins is clear from the way in which Beckett exploits the phonic similarity of *pense* and *danse* (Kanelli 2010). A relation between thinking and dance is also suggested by the following exchange:

> *Pozzo* – [. . .] Alors, vous voulez qu'il nous pense quelque chose?
> *Estragon* – J'aimerais mieux qu'il danse, ce serait plus gai [. . .]
> *Estragon* – Il pourrait peut-être danser d'abord et penser ensuite? Si ce n'est pas trop lui demander.
> *Vladimir (à Pozzo)* – Est-ce possible ?
> *Pozzo* – Mais certainement, rien de plus facile. C'est d'ailleurs l'ordre naturel. *(Rire bref.)* [. . .]
> *Pozzo* – [. . .] Danse, pouacre! [. . .]
> *Lucky danse. Il s'arrête. [. . .]*
> *Pozzo* – Autrefois il dansait la farandole, l'almée, le branle, la gigue, le fandango et même le hornpipe. Il bondissait. Maintenant il ne fait plus que ça. Savez-vous comment il l'appelle?
> *Estragon* – La mort du lampiste?
> *Vladimir* – Le cancer des vieillards. (Go 55–56)

> Pozzo: Well, would you like him to think something for us?
> Estragon: I'd rather he dance, it'd be more fun. [. . .]
> Estragon: Perhaps he could dance first and think afterwards, if it isn't too much to ask him.
> Vladimir: *(to Pozzo)* Would that be possible?
> Pozzo: By all means, nothing simpler. It's the natural order.
> *He laughs briefly* [. . .]
> Pozzo: [. . .] Dance misery! [. . .]
> *(Lucky dances. He stops).* [. . .]
> Pozzo: He used to dance the farandole, the fling, the brawl, the jig, the fandango and even the hornpipe. He capered. For joy. Now that's the best he can do. Do you know what he calls it?
> Estragon: The Scapegoat's Agony.
> Vladimir: The Hard Stool. (G 26–27)[30]

That dancing first and thinking next is the natural order of things reinforces the idea that bodily orientation may be the foundation upon which the possibility of abstract language and thinking is based. Vladimir and Estragon's guesses about the title of the dance ('La mort du lampiste', 'Le cancer des vieillards') indicate that it is slow and laboured, unlike the torrential flows of Lucky's thought. Despite the parodic tenor of the scene, Lucky's dance, which precedes his thought-speech, associates the body – its gestures and movements – with modes of orientation that precede meaning in language.

The invocation of dance – especially in relation to thinking – suggests that Lucky's creative power of resistance vis-à-vis Pozzo depends upon his ability to self-orient and to organise space through the motion of his body.[31] Lucky's inability to self-orient, because of his subservience to Pozzo, may be related to his muteness, for Lucky is silent except for his monologue.[32] Like some *deus ex machina*, Lucky must be ritually prepared to perform: Pozzo instructs Vladimir to set Lucky's hat on his head, and Vladimir, having done so, jumps back in expectation: '[il] lui met le chapeau sur la tête et recule vivement'. ([He] puts the hat on his head and recoils smartly.) Pozzo then pulls the rope attached to Lucky's neck and issues the incantatory command, 'Pense, porc!' Pozzo's sobriquets for Lucky (*porc, charogne*) designate the latter as unthinking, or even inanimate (dead) flesh (*charogne*) – a mere vessel that must receive its spirit or vital energy from some external source. Given Pozzo's attempts to divest Lucky of his power for self-orientation, the self-generated vitality of Lucky's tirade increasingly disturbs Pozzo, as indicated by stage directions that describe Pozzo moving from disgust, to suffering, to audible agitation, to a forceful attempt to curb Lucky's free expression by pulling the rope. Lucky responds to this by taking control of the rope and shouting his text: 'Pozzo se lève d'un bond, tire sur la corde. Tous crient. Lucky tire sur la corde, trébuche, hurle. Tous se jettent sur Lucky qui se débat, hurle son texte' (*Go* 61) (Pozzo jumps up, pulls on the rope. General outcry. Lucky pulls on the rope, staggers, shouts his text. All three throw themselves on Lucky, who struggles and shouts his text) (G 28). The capacity for self-orientation is bound up here with the act of thinking as it is performed in language. This manifests itself concretely in the battle for control of Lucky's rope; Lucky wrenches it from Pozzo before Pozzo regains the rope and destroys the magical hat. Stomping on the hat, Pozzo says: 'Comme ça il ne pensera plus' (There's an end to his thinking!). To Vladimir's question, 'Mais va-t-il pouvoir s'orienter?' (But will he be able to walk?), Pozzo responds: 'C'est moi qui l'orienterai' (*Go* 62). (In French, Pozzo responds that he will be the one to orient Lucky, but this exchange is altered in the English to elide mention of orientation) (G 30). Thinking is linked to Lucky's ability to orient his body in space, an ability he loses insofar as he is subject to Pozzo's tyranny.

In Lucky's speech, an ostensible movement towards humanity's decline and death revitalises language by underscoring its dependence on the physical body. Lucky's fragmenting and stuttering over rational, academic language constitute resistance not only to Pozzo's dominance; his glossolalia surfaces buried connections between the body's power of orientation and language, and sound patterns and repetitions unsettle the dominance of semantic meaning and reference. We hear the ridiculousness of 'Pense, porc!' (Think, pig!) and 'Debout! Charogne!' (Stand up! Corpse!) and laugh at the idea that the power to think is conferred by a hat. But oppositions between the mental and the material are complicated by the monologue's way of revealing language as concrete and also heightening its appeal to the body and senses. The fact that the speech was written to be performed anchors language in the body as *voice*, but the text also, through its sonority and emphasis on physical culture, accents relations between linguistic sense-making and the efforts of the physical body to orient itself in space and among the fragments of culture. Lucky's unravelling of oppositions between movement and speech, dancing and thinking, suggests the body and mind as intertwined (or 'reversible' in Merleau-Ponty's sense) and joins language to the body's way of sense-making (by orientation). Rational discourse peels away to reveal a more vital, poetic language.

By pairing opposing terms and splicing rational language with sonorous glitches, Beckett's writing contorts ordinary language so that things become visible from multiple perspectives. We could say that Beckett's critique of rational language opens a dimension or grey zone in which possibilities are expanded and language renewed on the basis of bodily movement. *Watt* and Lucky's speech experiment linguistically with modes of meaning that are more bodily than intellectual. 'Speak the speech of Lucky trippingly on the tongue', one critic instructs, 'clutching through all the eschatological gibberish at the loose ends of Western philosophy' (Blau 1986: 258). A sonorous bricolage of fragments of philosophical-scholarly traditions, Lucky's speech involves less a premonition of the decline of humanity than a 'corporeal idiolect' that accents the body's role in meaning production (Kanelli 2010: 31). Syntactical deviation, decomposition of habitual speech and attention to sensory language (rhythm, assonance, sonority) become major preoccupations of Beckett's late prose, while the novels that compose Beckett's postwar trilogy, to which I now turn, unhitch meaning not only from the binary oppositions undergirding rational systems but also from dialectical progression, reconfiguring 'progress' as a wandering, with eddies, journeys and returns.

Notes

1. Boulter views Beckett's career as 'an elaborate and nuanced commentary' on a phrase from Hans-Georg Gadamer: 'Language is not just one man's possessions in the world; rather, on it depends the fact that man has a *world* at all' (*Truth and Method* as qtd in Boulter: 3).
2. In *Dream*, Belacqua imagines that he might become 'the Cézanne [. . .] of the printed page, very strong on architectonics'. S. E. Gontarski reminds us that this aesthetic is 'no sooner uttered than regretted' by Belacqua, but he claims that Beckett's constellation of impossible perspectives is nevertheless reminiscent of Cézanne (2002: 13).
3. Similarly, Jean-Michel Rabaté locates in Beckett's correspondence with Duthuit an 'ethics of non-relation' whereby the artist must face up to the disorderly, chaotic nature of experience. This requires humility on the part of the artist in front of the world, painting what is there. As Beckett puts it in *Three Dialogues*, 'what I paint is there, but it's there not as the result of my will' (qtd in Rabaté 2014: 143). For Rabaté, an ethics of non-relation opens the possibility of forming new relations as a result of recognising the difference between the artist and the world (2014: 142–3).
4. Beckett targets Sartrean humanism in 'Le peinture des Van Veldes ou le monde et le pantalon' (1946), the final section of which begins: 'parlons de l'"humain"' (1983: 131). For further discussion of Beckett's vexed relationship with postwar humanism, its valuation of unity and of heroism and its 'routine consolations', see Gibson 2014 and Weller 2020. For Gibson, Beckett's writings of the mid-to-late 1940s are a 'counterblast to the new, Gaullist, heroic moralism' (2014: 107).
5. Brazil reads 'Cézanne's Doubt' as a bridge from the *Phenomenology* to Merleau-Ponty's first work of political philosophy, *Humanism and Terror* (1947), which responds to Arthur Koestler's novel *Darkness at Noon* (90). Seeking an alternative to the binary choice Europe faced between the United States and the Soviet Union, Merleau-Ponty criticises Koestler for setting up an opposition between pure freedom and determined history. Revelations about the Gulag camps and the outbreak of the Korean War forced Merleau-Ponty to revise his position on Marxism in *Adventures of the Dialectic* (1955) (Toadvine 2019).
6. Merleau-Ponty describes language and its power to name as a way of articulating and recreating the world. The word-in-use (*la parole*)

has much in common with the subject, traditionally assigned the role of meaning creation. Merleau-Ponty cites the beliefs of 'pre-scientific' peoples for whom naming meant conjuring into existence: 'For pre-scientific thought, to name an object is to bring it into existence or to modify it: God creates beings by naming them, and magic affects objects by speaking of them' (PP 183). Language alters our experience of the world by framing its parts, bringing possibilities into being through a reorganisation of form (much like the way in which the body's tasks structure its space).

7. Paul Stewart discusses why Bair's appeal to the historical Beckett explains away confusing aspects of the novel rather than confronting them as literary devices worthy of study (2006: 84–5).

8. Salisbury's article includes a War Office report of an 1945 interview with Beckett conducted by a branch of MI5 tasked with investigating counter-espionage. Salisbury, like Perloff, compares *Watt*'s 'cryptic aesthetic' to an 'information network' that demands 'attentive forms of speaking, writing, reading and listening' and an ability to 'filter meaning from interference' (2014: 157). In illuminating contrast, Seán Kennedy reads *Watt* as Beckett's critique of the Irish Big House novel, noting how in early manuscript drafts the landlord's name is Roe (Beckett's mother's maiden name). Though the name is replaced in later drafts (becoming Knott in the published version), its early inclusion makes clear Beckett's personal complicity with Big House culture (his mother was raised in an Irish Big House in Leixlip) (225). Kennedy further suggests that insofar as the Protestant Ascendency cleaved to privilege founded on ethnicity and religion, it was distasteful to Beckett as he witnessed the rise of Nazism in Europe (232).

9. The date of Beckett's reading of Mauthner has been the subject of considerable debate. Ben-Zvi dates it to 1929 and James Knowlson agrees that Beckett read Mauthner at the request of James Joyce around 1930. John Pilling dates Beckett's reading of the *Beiträge* to 1938 and cautions that critics have overrepresented Mauthner's influence, looking for a 'key' that would explain *Watt*'s enigmas. For further discussion of Beckett's transcriptions of Mauthner in his 'Whoroscope Notebook' (1938) and his marking up of his copy of the *Beiträge*, see Van Hulle and Nixon 2013: 169.

10. Mauthner illustrates the possibility of using language to indict itself by 'placing language at the heart of the *Critique*, subsuming under it all knowledge, and then systematically denying its basic efficacy' (Ben-Zvi 1980: 183). Similarly, in his German letter, Beckett writes, 'language is best used where it is most efficiently abused' (LB1: 518).

11. The names, Mary and Ann, may be an allusion to Lewis Carroll's *Alice's Adventures in Wonderland*. The white rabbit mistakes Alice for his housemaid, Mary Ann.

12. Evelyne Grossman points out the prevalence of electrical terminology in Beckett's texts, reminding us that the title of *Come and Go* in French (*va-et-vient*) pertains to circuits and switches (88).
13. The beginning of cybernetic theory dates to Norbert Wiener's *Cybernetics, or Control and Communication in the Animal and the Machine*, first published in 1948. On the relationship between cybernetic theory and Beckett with particular emphasis on *Watt*, see Franklin (2013), 'Humans and/as machines: Beckett and cultural cybernetics'.
14. Beckett's observation about James Joyce's prose pertains to *Watt* as well: 'It is not to be read – or rather it is not only to be read. It is to be looked at and listened to. His writing is not *about* something; *it is that something itself*' (1983: 27).
15. For a reading of *Watt* as a Kantian novel, see P. J. Murphy (1994).
16. This garden scene has been read as an (in)version of Eden. Richard Begam identifies what he terms a 'lapsarian epistemology', explaining that if the garden is where 'subject and object have broken apart', it is also where the self's encounter with the 'not-I' becomes possible. He argues that the epistemological process transforms into a narrative one (1996: 73).
17. It is relevant that Watt's inversions operate upon the phonetic rather than orthographical versions of words: what we *hear* is more important than conventions of standard spelling (the German word *nichts* becomes *niks*, *Watt* becomes *Wat*, *Knott* becomes *Knot* and *then* becomes *den*). For a full translation of the inversions see Ruby Cohn (1962b: 309–10) and Chris Ackerley (2010: 47–158).
18. For discussion of this passage in the *Phenomenology*, see Chapter 1.
19. Anthony Roche draws attention to the 'strong vein of Irish and Dublin idiom which Beckett introduced into the relatively neutral French' when he translated *Godot* (2014: 199). He notes distinctive Irishisms – for instance, the substitution of the word 'blathering' for 'talking' – and pays particular attention to the Pike Theatre performance in Dublin in 1955, in which director Alan Simpson cast Pozzo to sound like an Anglo-Irish landlord. But Roche argues that it was Beckett himself and not Simpson (as is sometimes believed) who is responsible for the 'over-Hibernicized' text (2014: 206).
20. These are not exact translations but phrases in the English version that similarly imitate academic discourse. Georges Mounin argues that Beckett creates a stereotype of academic discourse through the repetition of key terms: 'hélas (deux fois), au suivant (trois fois), assavoir (trois fois), il apparaît que (quatre fois), mais n'anticipons pas (quatre fois), je reprends (sept fois), bref (huit fois), on ne sait pas pourquoi (onze fois), etc.' (1968: pp. 23–4).

21. John Fletcher, in his study of *Waiting for Godot*, notes that Jean Anouilh likened the play to Pascal's *Pensées* performed as a comedy sketch by clowns, with 'Pozzo's cracking of his ringmaster's whip lifted straight from the repertoire of the big top' (2000: 66). Consider also:

    > Vladimir – On se croirait au spectacle.
    > Estragon – Au cirque.
    > Vladimir – Au music-hall.
    > Estragon – Au cirque. (*Go* 47)

22. The only directive is '*débit monotone*', which is elided in the English version (*Go* 59).
23. '*Lucky se tourne vers le public*' (*Go* 59); '*Lucky turns towards auditorium*' (G 28).
24. Similarly, Jane Goodall calls attention to 'shrinking, dwindling, wasting and pining', noting that the speech represents an '[e]volution in reverse, as the cycle of being heads back toward stasis in an abode of stones' (2006: 190). Her version of the speech's plot event emphasises the skull mentioned towards the monologue's close: 'Lucky is trying to recount the story of the skull in Connemara, as documented by the Academy of Anthropometry, but his memory of it has disintegrated so that he succeeds only in acting out an entropic drama whose script has worn away in his mind' (189). Also emphasising decline, Jean-Claude Lieber writes: 'compte tenu de l'impuissance divine et de l'état actuel de l'homme et de la terre, l'humanité est inéluctablement voué à la disparition. La version anglaise vient butter sur l'image du crâne, *the skull*, la tête de mort, dernière trace de la présence de l'homme dans un univers désertique et pétrifié' (1998: 76).
25. Atkins argues that the breakdown of rationality in the first two sections is mirrored by their syntactic incompletion; the first section is a protasis without an apodosis (following 'given the existence of god') and the second is an apodosis without a protasis (1967: 427).
26. '*jaillir*', Centre Nationale des Ressources Textuelles et Lexicales, <www.cnrtl.fr/definition/jaillir> (last accessed 28 December 2020).
27. John Calder reads this second section of the monologue as an allusion to Nietzsche's concept of the superman and to George Bernard Shaw's 1903 play *Man and Superman*. He argues that it describes how humankind can become stronger, more intelligent and healthier because of a better diet, body development through sport, medicine and science (2002).
28. Verlaine's poem, from the volume *Sagesse*, begins: 'Le ciel est, par-dessus le toit,/Si bleu, si calme!' Beckett retains the allusion in English: 'heaven so blue still and calm so calm' (G 28).

29. The repetition of 'labors lost' in the English version evokes the title of Shakespeare's *Love's Labour's Lost* and 'wastes and pines' alludes to Holderlin's poem 'Hyperions Schicksalslied', especially the lines: 'Doch uns ist gegeben,/Auf keiner Stätte zu ruhn,/Es schwinden, es fallen/Die leidenden Menschen'. Lieber compares 'es schwinden, es fallen' not only to the English version's 'wastes and pines' but also to the French version's 'maigrir rétrécir'. He adds that references to 'Hyperions Schicksalslied' are also found in *Watt* (79).
30. The slippage between the French and English versions of these lines is particularly marked.
31. Kanelli argues that the power of self-orientation, along with originality, is necessary to dance: 'Lucky semble suivre un parcours similaire au parcours de la danse: muni jadis de diverses techniques de danse, il évolue vers un dépouillement de la forme, développe son propre mouvement, son «idiolecte corporel», se laissant aller vers le sol' (2010: 31).
32. There is something sad about Lucky, the subhuman, being pulled onto the stage by a leash and made to perform. Orientation words, or spatial directives, are issued by Pozzo: 'Arrêt' 'Arrière' 'Là' (*Go* 59). And Lucky is repeatedly compared to an animal: 'Il souffle comme un phoque' (*Go* 40), 'il porte comme un porc' (*Go* 42), 'les vieux chiens ont plus de dignité' (*Go* 43). Lucky is also compared to a buffoon and to a slave: 'Autrefois on avait des bouffons. Maintenant on a des knouks' (*Go* 46).

CHAPTER 3

From Dialectics to Infinity: Life Cycles in *Molloy*, *Malone Dies* and *Endgame*

As the first two chapters demonstrated, Beckett's pre- and interwar fiction parodies Cartesian dualism and language as a rational system. Beckett's postwar writing, however, evidences a shattering of faith in the predictable progress of thesis, antithesis, synthesis. Dialectical movement, where a position and its negation are 'sublated', shores up faith in human progress.[1] But, with reference to Theodor Adorno's claim that it is barbaric to write poetry after Auschwitz (1997: 34), one must wonder whether the inhumanity of the Holocaust makes such faith untenable. Although Hegel's attitude towards the Enlightenment was ambivalent, the dialectic favours reason and progress.[2] This chapter examines how its method is playfully subverted in Beckett's postwar writing, as tacking towards an 'elsewhere' gives way to immanent negotiations among bodies and environments.

Beckett's play with cyclicality destabilises the oppositions (such as beginning vs ending) on which dialectic rests, revealing the interdependence of extremes. Like Beckett, Merleau-Ponty – though less explicitly than the deconstructionists that succeed him – troubles oppositional thinking, not least through his search for a middle way between empiricism and a consciousness-centred intellectualism. In a document prepared in 1951 as part of his candidacy for the College de France, Merleau-Ponty describes finding 'beneath' (*en deçà de*) the pure subject and the pure object a 'third dimension where our activity and our passivity, our autonomy and our dependence, cease to be contradictory' (2000: 13; my translation).[3] Merleau-Ponty's mediation between positivist science (pure objects) and reflective philosophy (pure subjects) moves to encompass contradictions instead of transcending them. He uses '*en deçà*' (beneath) instead of '*au-delà*' (beyond) to distinguish his 'third dimension' from a Hegelian synthesis. (The 'third dimension' is not a synthesis to be achieved, but a different perspective. It exists already.) His definition of the body as perceiver and perceived, seer and seen, reinforces this, as does his insistence that bodily 'activity', insofar as it responds to stimuli in the environment, depends on 'passive' receptivity. Merleau-Ponty's unravelling of contradictions illuminates Beckett's postwar challenge to narratives of progress and to binary logic of the sort attacked in *Watt*, which gives way to exploration of a space between oppositions.

What comes to replace dialectical progress for Beckett is a circular wandering that directs attention to the journey itself. Beckett's reconceptualising of the journey and his interest in vagabondage and vagrancy inform his four nouvelles from 1946, where narrators wander through strange-familiar land- and cityscapes, and his first novel in French, *Mercier et Camier* (written in 1946 and published in 1970), which swivels around a journey described as 'unmotivated, arbitrary, directionless, full of halts, false starts, returns, revisions and indecisions' (Campbell 1993: 142). Beckett's parodies of progress coincide, appropriately, with mockery of faith in human voluntarism. Just before beginning work on *Molloy* in May of 1947, Beckett wrote *Eleutheria*, where the main character 'renounces the world of will' in favour of a 'Schopenhauerian willlessness' (Knowlson 1996: 330).[4] These first writings after the war scaffold a more concerted approach, developed in the trilogy, which recasts human agency and progress. Beckett's alternative to narrative and dialectical progress redirects attention to the physical body's rapport with its material environment (including language). Molloy sleeps in ditches, sucks stones and crawls through forests, while Malone projects himself into objects: a stick, a pencil, an exercise-book. In *Molloy* (1951) we also find a receptive passivity that mirrors the wandering and doubling of the narrative itself, as dialectical progress is abandoned in favour of more earthbound modes of negotiating space. A final aspect of Beckett's replacement of the dialectic – the discomfort of holding oppositions in the mind at once and its link to bodily endurance – will be discussed in Chapter 4 with *The Unnamable* (1953).

H. Porter Abbott argues that the novels in Beckett's trilogy have the structure of a quest, which is disrupted by a 'willful shredding of narrative linearity' in *Texts for Nothing* (1950–2) (1996: 90–3). But the doubling and infinite regress that characterise *Molloy*, *Malone Dies* (1951) and *Endgame* (1957) already undermine the quest's ideal of progress and its orientation towards an end. *Molloy*'s beginning at the end of his quest, in his mother's room, replaces destination with the idea that subject and place co-constitute each other (room as womb). Detained by Sophie Loy/Lousse, a Circe figure allied with the fleshy body, Molloy's materiality intertwines him with others and with his surroundings. *Malone Dies* toys with the creative horror of limitlessness, and in *Endgame* we find immanence joined to infinity, the discomfort of which suggests an ethics of bodily endurance. This chapter explores how Beckett's postwar writings unhinge meaning from the dialectic to incorporate it, make it bodily, such that movement towards an elsewhere gives way to the body's immanent and reciprocal shaping of landscapes, rooms, objects and language. Instead of a dialectical *Aufhebung* where contradictions are resolved, Beckett's works expand possibilities in *this* world, attentive to the meaning-making potential of the body in space.

Molloy's narrative conflation of beginning and ending replaces the idea of the body moving through space towards a destination with something more akin to gestation, where the body interacts with its surroundings to create – if not meaning more generally – then at least the work of art we're reading. The idea of the room-as-womb is made explicit at the end of *Malone Dies*, when the ceiling rises and falls, dilating and contracting to 'birth' Malone into death (TN 283). Angela Moorjani also likens the ditch into which Molloy falls to 'the womb and the tomb, the in-between realm of artistic gestation' (1991: 60). She points out that Molloy's situation at the beginning of the novel resembles Malone's, since both are in rooms writing stories.

Published first in French and translated by Beckett in collaboration with Patrick Bowles, *Molloy* is a tale of two quests: Molloy's for his mother and Moran's for Molloy. Both quests end in failure, with Molloy in a ditch and Moran in his garden listening to birdsong and a mysterious voice. The novel's beginning at the end of a quest has been rightly cited as evidence of how the novel both borrows and subverts the quest narrative (Maude 2009: 87; Moorjani 1991: 60). In his mother's room, Molloy produces pages, ostensibly those we are reading: 'Here it is. It gave me a lot of trouble. It was the beginning, do you understand? Whereas now it is nearly the end' (8). In one sense, we have a frame narrative, common enough in literature, which cues us to expect that we will discover how Molloy arrives at his mother's house. But *Molloy* frustrates this expectation in its third line – 'I don't know how I got here' (7) – and, rather than fulfilling his quest, Molloy ends up 'lapsed down' in a ditch: 'Molloy could stay, where he happened to be' (91). The frame hangs open, uncompleted. The teleological bent of the quest is further undermined by the fact that Molloy and Moran come to resemble their quest objects. Molloy says of his mother: 'I sleep in her bed. I piss and shit in her pot. I have taken her place. I must resemble her more and more' (7), and the hyperrational Moran takes on Molloy's sensual receptivity. Subject and object change places, illuminating a constitutive interdependence between antitheses that troubles (dialectical) progress.

Building on the idea that *Molloy* unravels the quest, Ulrika Maude argues that the progressive disintegration of the characters' bodies 'toys with' teleology and intentionality (Maude 2009: 87). Molloy and Moran's deteriorating bodies frustrate the forward impetus that underpins the quest, and the physical decrepitude of the quest-object – Molloy's mother '[v]eiled with hair, wrinkles, filth, slobber' (TN 19) – represents the 'decay of the journey's telos' (Maude 2009: 173).[5] Maude observes further how 'categories of self and other, subject and object, pursuer and pursued are switched around until the opposites merge into one' (87), identifying a loss of 'traditional sense-making binaries' (91) – Molloy admits: 'I confuse east and west, the poles too, I invert them readily' (TN 19). Maude goes on to read the arduous bodily movement in the novel as 'triggered by a dynamic that differs substantially from Merleau-Ponty's affirmative notion of bodily or "organic" intentionality' (93). For Molloy and Moran, an optimal relation between body and environment is unattainable. Thwarted by a landscape that persists in labyrinthine imperviousness rather than letting itself be oriented and made meaningful by his bodily projects, Molloy develops what Maude calls 'negative intentionality', fleeing at every opportunity (93). Instead of progress, we find a 'dynamics of equivocation' (93), an exhausting, meaningless movement that accounts for the bodily tics and infelicities Maude inventories in her reading. But Molloy and Moran's difficulties moving along rational trajectories are balanced by the eerie alacrity with which their bodies intertwine with the earth, attuned to animal voices and to the sound of the planet's labour. How might 'negative intentionality' account for Molloy's (albeit ironised) communion with the environment, his glee at vanishing into ditches? The body in *Molloy* seems to explore possibilities for receptivity and material agency even as it disintegrates (from the perspective of a voluntarist, action-centred rationalism).

An ecological reading of *Molloy* goes some way towards addressing these curious moments of congress between body and environment. Paul Saunders seeks to move beyond what Timothy Morton has labelled an 'ecocritical cliché' – the idea that the subject-object binary, identified by radical ecologists as the 'root' of ecological calamity, must be dissolved (Saunders 2011: 56).[6] Saunders reads Molloy's 'passiveness' as a refusal of instrumentalism that could signal a progressive ecological consciousness. The only problem is that Molloy, despite his 'privileged access to the chaos of sensations', fails to have impact on the society he challenges (58). Saunders compares him to a 'grotesque and comically ineffectual deep ecologist' (58). Molloy's privileged access to sensations is afforded by his eschewal of *habit*, which Beckett mocks vociferously in his 1930 Proust essay, calling it 'a compromise effected between the individual and his environment' and 'the guarantee of a dull inviolability' (PTD 18–19). If the world is 'a projection of the individual's consciousness (an objectivation of the individual's will, as Schopenhauer would say)', then transitions between consecutive adaptations to one's surroundings 'represent perilous zones in the life of the individual, dangerous, precarious, painful, mysterious and fertile, when for a moment the boredom of living is replaced by the suffering of being' (PTD 19). At these moments of transition, when habit must relax its grip in order to adapt to something unpredictable, raw sensations and 'enchantments of reality' are briefly accessible (PTD 22). It is in this state of continual adaptation that Molloy seems to live, free of habit and its gift of security.

For Saunders, *Molloy* challenges instrumentalism, but critique is as far as the novel goes. Any possibility of relating to the environment differently is foreclosed by Molloy's ineffectualness. Saunders uses as an example the scene in which Molloy is lost in a forest, which alludes to Descartes' advice that walking in a straight line is the surest way out of the forest (2011: 59). Molloy gets this twisted:

> having heard, or more probably read somewhere [. . .] that when a man in a forest thinks he is going forward in a straight line, in reality he is going in a circle, I did my best to go in a circle, hoping in this way to go in a straight line. (TN 85)

Molloy's 'anti-Cartesian mode of navigation' puts comical pressure on the idea of a rational subject moving through an inert landscape, but Molloy's moribund condition makes any alternative to the rational order 'inchoate' and 'impracticable' (Saunders 2011: 59). He just confuses things. Saunders reads the second part of the novel in much the same way. Moran elects to give up 'being a man' and live in the garden with wild birds and a voice associated 'with the non-human "language" he can now hear emitting from all things' (61). Saunders goes on to conclude that ecology reaches an impasse in Beckett as 'its (romantic) will to effect reconciliation is undercut by its self-reflexive (modernist) awareness of the impossibility of this project, yet somehow without losing faith in it' (71). This reading elegantly alludes to Beckett's fondness for pairing obligation and impossibility (we 'go on'), but Molloy and Moran's congress with the non-human world seems to offer more than a cautionary tale about the failure to be practically ecological (74). Their intertwining not only with nature but with objects and with the materiality of language evokes the Merleau-Pontian idea that the human subject is embedded in the material world; this challenges the divide between human and environment that underlies instrumentalism and illustrates a more receptive mode of relation to the non-human environment.

Molloy's aim of reaching his mother is continually imperilled by invitations on the part of the earth to join it (alluding perhaps to an 'earth-mother', a variation on the figure of the material feminine). He describes the 'daily longing of the earth to swallow me up' (81), and, climbing into a ditch where the grass is high, he lies down 'with outspread arms' and 'pressed about my face the long leafy stalks. Then I could smell the earth, the smell of the earth was in the grass that my hands wove round my face till I was blinded. I ate a little too, a little grass' (27). Entwined with grasses, eating them like an animal, Molloy remembers his aim but not his reasons. Reasons would enable him to 'sweep, with the clipped wings of necessity' to his mother (27), indicating *one* direction at the expense of all others. The will, the exercise of which is associated with freedom (for an autonomous subject), is presented as a constraint – as that which reduces multidirectional possibilities to a single telos. Freedom is presented not as the ability to exercise one's will unhindered but, alternatively, as having full range of access to one's sensations. Molloy may exhibit 'negative intentionality' and he is certainly ineffectual (at getting anywhere), but the optic has changed, such that a rational journey towards a destination is no longer the highest value. Molloy's comfort where he is (embedded in the earth, in a ditch) is only half ironic – 'How joyfully I would vanish there, sinking deeper and deeper under the rains' (27). The pleasure of relaxing into the earth is one of relinquishing habits and directives that cut off sensation and possibility. Bipedal movement in one direction (excluding all others) is painful to Molloy, whose imperatives set him in motion only to abandon him (TN 87).

Molloy spends long hours in the garden, hearing the noise of his life 'become the life of this garden as it rode the earth of deeps and wildernesses [. . .] I forgot not only who I was, but that I was, forgot to be' (49). Forward momentum eddies as Molloy feels himself merging with vegetal life which, coupled with amnesia (forgetting to be), suggests fusion with the natural world or, more interestingly, a capacity to recognise and assume the object side of one's being – which, for Merleau-Ponty, is the precondition of our being subjects. As Molloy reflects:

> I was no longer that sealed jar to which I owed my being so well preserved, but a wall gave way and I filled with roots and tame stems for example, stakes long since dead and ready for burning, the recess of night and the imminence of dawn, and then the labour of the planet rolling eager into winter [. . .] Or of that winter I was the precarious calm, the thaw of the snows. (49)

Rational subjectivity is figured as a sealed jar that 'preserves' against the vagaries (and decay) of the material world. In a jar, one must constantly ask oneself questions, 'for example whether you still are' – in order to 'keep you from losing the thread of the dream' (49). Rational subjectivity is figured as a dream with a thread, a story we tell. When the separation gives way, Molloy tangles with roots, feels the changing seasons and feels himself become the labour of the planet and the thaw of the snows, a part of the world. In the *Phenomenology*, Merleau-Ponty describes our usual relation to objects and surroundings relaxed at night, which 'makes us sense our contingency, that free and inexhaustible movement by which we attempt to anchor ourselves and to transcend ourselves in things' (296). When the habits that orient us are relaxed, we sense that they are provisional, and there is the possibility of a remapping. Beckett's descriptions of communion with the natural world are both comic and startlingly poetic (the former, perhaps, permitting the latter), but they nevertheless reveal rational habits as contingent, suggesting that we are, perhaps, more embedded in the world. Molloy's longest detour from his quest is his disorienting stay with Lousse, the Circe who holds him comfortably captive in her house and garden.[7] With Lousse, Molloy loses agency in the voluntarist sense, along with his capacity for rational orientation. He wakes to find himself bathed, perfumed with lavender, shaved and dressed in a nightgown 'adorned with ribands and frills and lace' (44). He tries to escape: 'I went to the door. Locked. To the window. Barred' (38). Physical barriers are complemented by subtler mechanisms of entrapment – Lousse's hypnotic language, compounded by potions mixed into Molloy's beer: 'doubtless she had poisoned my beer with something intended to mollify me, to mollify Molloy, with the result that I was nothing more than a lump of melting wax' (47). To Molloy in his softened state, Lousse enunciates her propositions, until 'nothing was left but this monotonous voice' (47–8).[8] His stay with Lousse induces a forgetting of space and time. Molloy feels himself 'in a cage out of time [. . .] and out of space too' (51).

Given that Molloy loses his powers of rational orientation, it is unsurprising that the problem of agency is raised, in terms of human freedom, upon his arrival at the house of Lousse: 'Can it be we are not free? It might be worth looking into' (36). Later, when he finally leaves Lousse's house, attempting to discover why he stayed so long, Molloy evokes Geulincx: 'I who had loved the image of old Geulincx, dead young, who left me free, on the black boat of Ulysses, to crawl towards the East, along the deck' (51). David Tucker, citing Beckett's 1954 letter to his German translator, illuminates this passage with regard to its intertexts: Geulincx's *Ethics* and the Ulysses episode in Dante's *Inferno* (2012: 119–28). The passage presents human freedom as the power of a man on a boat travelling west to walk east along the deck – that is, drastically limited. Molloy's stay with Lousse foregrounds lack of freedom, weakness, disorientation and even negative intentionality. But a lapse in rational self-direction nevertheless affords him access to other modes of being. Among the men tending the garden, Molloy 'drifted like a dead leaf on springs [. . .] they stepped gingerly over me as though I had been a bed of rare flowers' (52). The men are labouring to 'preserve the garden from apparent change' (52), and Molloy's sense of himself as a flower bed suggests susceptibility to change, his acknowledgement of his own materiality and mortality.

To Molloy's poetic sensuality – his florid descriptions of sea, sky, lavender and the smell of the earth – Moran is a rational foil. His phrases are shorter, jerkier, and his tone more conversational, filled with facts and inflected with bouts of irritation. A rational figure on a quest to capture a more sensual one presents a neat commentary on the representational dilemma of narrative. Resonances between the novel's two parts are there for the reader to notice: both characters are searching, both encounter a shepherd and flock as they set out, both suffer progressive stiffening of the legs, both have violent encounters in the woods (Molloy with the charcoal burner, Moran with his curious double) and both narratives meditate on circularity, as Moran ends where he begins (writing the report) and Molloy begins at the end of his quest (in his mother's room producing pages). Thomas Cousineau suggests that echoes between the two parts make it the reader's active role to bridge the two narratives (1999: 80), to generate a space of interpretation in which the two worlds might coexist. While differences in tone and style as well as the fact that the narratives never intersect may motivate a reader to create a third perspective to relate the two parts, Moran's story is hardly an antithesis in a dialectical progression, for a synthesis would yield some greater understanding, and the novel leaves us with nothing more than the persistence of narrative despite its impossibility. The second part of *Molloy* is less a negation than an acoustic refraction, where dissonances and assonances create effects not directly expressed in either of the two narratives.[9]

The most famous paradox in Beckett's work, aside from the one that brings *The Unnamable* to its stuttering conclusion, is the paradox that frames part two of *Molloy*. At the start of his section, Moran sits at his desk and thinks about his report: 'It is midnight. The rain is beating on the windows' (92). He muses: 'My report will be long' (92). At the end of the novel, Moran listens to a voice that tells him to write the report:

> They were the longest, loveliest days of all the year. I lived in the garden. I have spoken of a voice telling me things [. . .] It told me to write the report. Does this mean I am freer now than I was? I do not know. I shall learn. Then I went back into the house and wrote, It is midnight. The rain is beating on the windows. It was not midnight. It was not raining. (176)

Moran narrates himself going back into the house and writing the words with which part two opens – and then negates them, calling the narrative we have been reading up until this point into question. By inscribing its beginning into its end, moreover, the text plunges us into infinite regress, as we find ourselves in a fictional world that gives birth to itself. Since Moran's report describes his quest to find Molloy (part one is nested within part two), the fact that part two calls attention to its impossibility throws the first section of the novel into question also (Federman 1970: 107).

Molloy introduces a self-reflexivity that has been associated with the advent of contemporary literature (literature that no longer tells *a* story, but the story of its own telling). Raymond Federman identifies in Beckett such a move from traditional to contemporary fiction, marked by linguistic self-reflexivity. He cites a review of *Molloy* by Olga Bernal:

> If the literature of the past described reality (or believed it did), that of today realizes that what it describes is not reality, but the very language of which it is captive as soon as it begins to speak. And no doubt, this is the first time in the history of literature that language no longer situates itself opposite the world but opposite itself. (Bernal as qtd in Federman 1970: 115)

The importance of language as the material that supports discourse is foregrounded in *Molloy* by Moran's meditations on the intelligibility of the voice he hears and at numerous other moments throughout the novel. But what has been less discussed is the way that linguistic reflexivity in *Molloy* suggests a more general reflexivity, whereby what produces a system is shown to be part of that system. If our body is our means of having a world, for instance, it must inhere in the world it 'creates' through its perception.

In *How We Became Posthuman*, Kathryn Hayles defines reflexivity as 'the movement whereby that which has been used to generate a system is made, through a changed perspective, to become part of the system it generates' (1999: 8). As an example she cites Jorge Luis Borges's story 'The Circular Ruins', in which the narrator creates a student through his dreaming only to discover that he himself is being dreamed by another; 'the system generating reality is shown to be part of the reality it makes' (8). Hayles points out that reflexivity tends towards infinite regress and is subversive insofar as it 'confuses the boundaries we impose upon the world in order to make sense of that world' (8–9). Reflexivity refuses to separate agency from its effects, embedding us within the world in which we act.

Hayles's discussion of reflexivity occurs in the context of a broader argument she makes about the importance of embodiment to the posthuman. Lamenting that information has 'lost' the body – intelligence has become a 'property of the formal manipulation of symbols rather than enaction in the human lifeworld' (Hayles 1999: xi) – Hayles emphasises embodiment not because it differentiates the human from the machine but because it reveals thought as a 'broader cognitive function' dependent on the embodied form enacting it (xiv). Recognising the embodied nature of cognition, Hayles argues, is what transforms the liberal humanist subject (regarded since the Enlightenment as the model of the human) into the posthuman (xiv). The humanist subject, identified with the rational mind, is said to *have* a body rather than *be* a body, which splits it off from the material world and siloes thought within it. Hayles's model of distributed cognition, by contrast, extends agency not only to the body but also to its surroundings, such that posthumanism emphasises human life as 'embedded in a material world of great complexity, one on which we depend for our continued survival' (5).

In *Molloy*, the origin of the story we are reading emerges within that story, meeting Hayles's criteria for a reflexive system. The idea that what generates the story is necessarily *part of it* questions the humanist subject's separation from the world within which it acts. In this sense, a posthumanist reading echoes a poststructuralist one; both emphasise a dismantling of humanist subjectivity in Beckett's work. But poststructuralism applies this to language. In *Molloy*, characters' 'selves' are consolidated under the influence of a mysterious voice, as in Barthes's *S/Z*, where subjectivity is described as a plurality of other texts: 'The "I" which approaches the text is already itself a plurality of other texts, of codes which are infinite, or, more precisely, lost (whose origin is lost) [. . . Subjectivity's] deceptive plenitude is merely the wake of all the codes that constitute me' (Barthes 1974: 10). To this description posthumanist and phenomenological approaches add the experience of embodiment. Hayles views the deconstruction of the liberal subject as an opportunity to 'keep disembodiment from being rewritten, once again, into prevailing concepts of subjectivity' (Hayles 1999: 5). She also insists on the importance of the flesh. *Molloy* uses techniques of narrative reflexivity to challenge the subject-object dichotomy (without collapsing them), but Beckett's play with reflexivity also vaunts the interrelatedness of narrator and narrated, body and world.[10]

*

If the narrative structure of *Molloy* resembles an ouroboros, eating its own tail/tale, then that of *Malone Meurt/Malone Dies* is more classically metafictional, weaving between a diary-like narrative and a series of stories that comes to show curious narrative unity. We have the story Malone is telling about himself, alone in his room waiting for death, and his stories of Sapo, the Lamberts and of Sapo-Macmann's entry into an asylum (Saint John of God's) not unlike Malone's abode. That Malone may be spinning a version of autobiography, fancifully embellished, is a compelling hypothesis.[11] But Malone also seems to be using the stories (as he uses his stick) to extend into the world, to travel beyond the confines of the bed where he lies immobilised. Malone's story, for the way it hews to a life that could have been Malone's, for its dependence on the material supports of a lead pencil and exercise-book and for its inter-bleeding between frames is less the antithesis of Malone's life than that which supplements and prolongs it, Scheherazade-fashion. We note the appearance of a man with an umbrella in both tales, as a mysterious intruder in Malone's room and as an inmate – the 'thin one' – at Saint John of God's (TN 287). The story-world Malone concocts does not negate his immobilised present but embellishes it. Rather than operating dialectically (thesis/antithesis), the two tales intertwine and reverberate as we seek connections between them.

This intertwining of the layers that comprise *Malone Dies* mirrors Malone's preoccupation with endings, both temporal (narrative) and spatial (bodily). The 'end', for Malone, becomes less a goal or direction in which life is heading than the expression of a limit between body and world. In *The Unnamable*, we find anxiety about lack of limit– 'I feel no place, no place round me, there's no end to me' (TN 399) – but Malone's obsession with ends as limits is more an interrogation. He wonders where and how he ends by testing the limits of his body. He inserts himself into the body of another, that of his character, Sapo-Macmann – 'I slip into him, I suppose in the hope of learning something [. . .] But before I am done I shall find traces of what was' (TN 226). Elsewhere he speaks of trying to 'live, cause to live, be another, in myself, in another' (TN 195). Malone assumes the body of his character in the hope of learning about himself and, ultimately, of capturing in writing the end of his life. He wishes to 'live, long enough to feel, behind my closed eyes, other eyes close. What an end' (TN 195). The unstable boundary between Malone and his invented character(s) (and by extension between Beckett and Malone) is part of what 'diary fiction', with its foregrounding of the materiality of the written page, explores.[12]

In addition to his temporal ending, which he interrogates through narrative (telling the story of himself via another), Malone interrogates his spatial 'endings' by means of inventorying his possessions. He devises a definition to determine which of the things surrounding him are his: 'only those things are mine the whereabouts of which I know well enough to be able to lay hold of them, if necessary, that is the definition I have adopted, to define my possessions. For otherwise there would be no end to it' (TN 249). Malone instantly qualifies this – 'But in any case there will be no end to it' (TN 249) – for it becomes impossible for Malone, as he approaches death, to say where he and his possessions end and the world begins. He finds himself embedded in the world: 'The search for myself is ended. I am buried in the world' (TN 198). If 'end' in *Malone Dies* is not a telos but the body's edge or limit, and if the body-subject can extend without limit (endlessly) into things, adopting them as prostheses, then the idea of progress (towards an end) is unsettled, along with the promise of transcendence. Rigorous insistence on immanence (a kind of endlessness) is one of the most emotionally harrowing aspects of Beckett's work.

Malone's body-subject exteriorises itself in three main objects: the stick with which he spears things and brings them to him, his pencil and his exercise-book. Malone describes his stick as having a hook at one end – '[t]hanks to it I can control the furthest recesses of my abode' (TN 185) – and as giving him the ability to lay hold of things even in the dark: 'I would identify them by touch, the message would flow all along the stick' (TN 249). When he loses his exercise-book, he uses the stick to 'harpoon' it (TN 208), and though he complains that his stick lacks a 'prehensile proboscis like the nocturnal tapir's' (TN 222), it nevertheless expands his body's reach. In his work on Beckett and the prosthetic body, Yoshiki Tajiri observes that Malone's stick 'seems to be incorporated into the body and function like a sentient hand – a better hand, actually' (2007: 45). In general, Tajiri illuminates how, in Beckett's work, prostheses problematise the boundaries of the body, rendering them ambiguous (40). With reference to Paul Schilder, whose idea of the body image/body schema figures importantly in Merleau-Ponty's *Phenomenology*,[13] Tajiri suggests that the image we have of our body (which is different than its actual, physical dimensions) accounts for the 'extraordinary expansion of the body' in Beckett's trilogy (47). Schilder writes:

> I have many times emphasized how labile and changeable the body-image is. The body-image can shrink or expand; it can give parts to the outside world and can take other parts into itself. When we take a stick in our hands and touch an object with the end of it, we feel a sensation at the end of the stick. The stick, has, in fact, become a part of the body-image. (qtd in Tajiri 46–7)

Certainly, Malone's body-schema expands by means of the stick, which enables him to access and explore the outer limits of his (limited) abode. Through it, he extends into the world, expanding his reach. Even more effective for this purpose, arguably, are Malone's pencil and exercise-book. The novel clearly indicates the pencil and exercise-book as the material supports for the stories Malone tells (as well as for the work we are reading), for a hiatus in the story occurs in the forty-eight-hour period during which Malone loses his pencil: 'What a misfortune, the pencil must have slipped from my fingers, for I have only just succeeded in recovering it after forty-eight hours [. . .] I have spent two unforgettable days of which nothing will ever be known' (TN 222). What was lived during this period was not recorded, the 'solution and conclusion of the whole sorry business' (222), which Malone claims to have found, must be rewritten and therefore relived. When Malone tells us, '[t]his exercise-book is my life' (274), we are reminded of his status as a character who, were it not for the text we are reading, would not exist at all.[14] We find in Malone's expansion, by means of a flexible body-schema that integrates prostheses, an anticipation of the material limitlessness that befalls the body in death, as it passes over entirely into things.

Moments of death-in-life, or imbrications of the body-subject within the world of things, occur frequently in Beckett's work, as bodies appear in bins, urns, earth and jars. *Malone Dies* attaches the body to the earth, quite literally, in the scene Malone narrates of Macmann caught in a rainstorm that is both violent and enduring. The 'thingness' of the body-subject or, to use Merleau-Ponty's terminology, the body's being-as-object, which enables its being-as-subject, is figured as extreme receptivity to the environment.

Caught in the storm far from shelter, Macmann stops and lies face down on the earth, reasoning that '[t]he surface thus pressed against the ground will remain dry, whereas standing I would get uniformly wet all over' (TN 283). In one sense, the passage is akin to many we have seen in Beckett so far – a vigorous parody of rational methods applied beyond their purview. But the passage parodies not only the brittle rigidity of rationalism in the face of what is unpredictable (rain that is violent, enduring and erratic – not 'a mere matter of drops per hour, like electricity' (283) – but also the human tendency to interpret suffering, to search for its meaning and cause, which might illuminate a course of action to alleviate it. Macmann, face down on the grass, clenches his fingers 'as though in torment':

> And without knowing exactly what his sin was he felt full well that living was not a sufficient atonement for it or that this atonement was in itself a sin, calling for more atonement, and so on, as if there could be anything but life, for the living. (239)

If living offers both atonement *and* creates more sin, then desire for atonement will have no end. The passage then gallops off on a meditation on the confusion of guilt and punishment, cause and effect, for 'those who continue to think' (240). But if we pause to take the word 'atonement' literally (at-oneness) – in *Malone Meurt*, atonement is simply *'peine'* (penalty or punishment) (154) – we might read this episode (at least in Beckett's English) as a comic rapprochement between the human and its natural environment. More generally, though, suffering, associated with passivity, creates a change in the human relationship to its environment. Just as Malone's former dominance, his time-devouring 'activity', is reversed, so Macmann finds greater receptivity to the earth in his suffering position. Pausing in his narration of the Lamberts, Malone says: 'I was time, I devoured the world. Not now, any more. A man changes. As he gets on' (202). In his old age, Malone does not devour the world but is *acted upon* by time and the world as he waits for death. Feeling remorse at his decision to lie down rather than run for shelter, Malone's character, Macmann, does not change his course but rolls over to expose his underside to the rain. In addition to commentary on the maladaptive nature of regret, Macmann's odd decision affords him a receptivity to the earth available only in a position of passivity. His clenched hands relax, change position:

> And just as an hour before he had pulled up his sleeves the better to clutch the grass, so now he pulled them up again the better to feel the rain pelting down on his palms, also called the hollows of the hands. (242)

Here suffering as torment changes into passive receptivity (suffering means to endure or to allow), where Macmann (and by extension Malone) unclenches and accepts his embeddedness in the world.

Like Molloy in Lousse's garden, Macmann's humble posture (lying on the ground, close to the earth) enables him to sense things he might not in an upright, 'human' posture.[15] With his ear 'glued to the earth', he hears the 'distant roar of the earth drinking and the sighing of the soaked bowed grasses' (239). His hair is described as intertwined with the earth. On a dry, windy day, it might have 'gone romping in the grass almost like grass itself', but the 'rain glued it to the ground and churned it up with the earth and grass into a kind of muddy pulp, not a muddy pulp, a kind of muddy pulp' (242). Tongue-in-cheek, Beckett is careful not to fuse body and world. Macmann's hair is 'not a muddy pulp' (*une pâte boueuse*; 160) but 'a kind of muddy pulp' (242). While there are those who look tirelessly to locate a precise cause of suffering – 'sticklers have been met with who had no peace until they knew for certain whether their carcinoma was of the pylorus or whether on the contrary it was not rather of the duodenum', Macmann's earthiness exempts him from such queries: 'these were flights for which Macmann was not yet fledged, and indeed he was rather of the earth earthy and ill-fitted for pure reason, especially in the circumstances in which we have been fortunate enough to circumscribe him' (243). Macmann's earthiness means he is ill-equipped for the airy abstractness of pure reason. His earthbound position and aptitude for suffering make him more reptilian than bird, and more mineral than reptile:

> he was by temperament more reptile than bird and could suffer extensive mutilation and survive, happier sitting than standing and lying down than sitting [. . .] And a good half of his existence must have been spent in a motionlessness akin to that of stone. (243)

'Reptilian' survival of suffering, a preference for lying down (close to the earth) and stony motionlessness seem oddly preferable here to human verticality and 'flights' of pure reason. Macmann's opening of the hollows of his hands and his receptivity to the sounds of the earth seem more comfortable than his fingers clenched in torment, which we might associate with willing (or wanting to atone for sin so as to bring an end to suffering). Macmann, like many of Beckett's characters, reveals himself inadept at any useful job (unable to tell the difference between weeds and carrots, he razes all), but, like the narrator of 'The End', he is able to fit himself out with the trappings of nature, '[consolidating] his boots with willow bark and thongs of wicker, so that he might come and go on the earth from time to time and not wound himself' (245). Beckett's image of (Mac)Man(n) ('Mac' means 'son of') embedded in his natural environment shows the discomfort of a relation to the world based on will. Acceptance of a certain degree of passivity, by contrast, brings receptivity and awareness of the body as sentient matter, involved irremediably in the material world.

The intertwining between body and world figured in *Malone Dies* is nowhere near the harmonious, chiastic reversals between subject and object that Merleau-Ponty describes in the *Phenomenology* and in *The Visible and the Invisible* (the duality of seer-seen). For Beckett, interrogation of the body's 'ends' (its spatial and temporal limits), especially insofar as it challenges our habitual understanding of these limits, entails a certain horror, as well as comedy. Malone finds himself swelling, his body impossibly distended: 'All strains towards the nearest deeps, and notably my feet [. . .] to call them in, to be cleaned for example, would I think take me over a month' (234). Malone's sense of self has 'fled' to his head, such that his extremities – his feet – feel 'beyond the range of the most powerful telescope. Is that what is known as having a foot in the grave?' (234). This sense of the body's limitless expansion is linked to mortality, as it anticipates the body's passage into things (the total abrogation of the body's limits is the stuff of classical horror). The body extends across the globe, and Malone imagines, famously, that if he were to shit, 'the lumps would fall out in Australia' (235). And yet, Malone muses, 'in spite of my stories I continue to fit in this room, let us call it a room, that's all that matters' (235). The room becomes a figure for a body, which will eventually eject Malone, who imagines his death as a birth, his end a beginning:

> I am swelling. What if I should burst? The ceiling rises and falls, rises and falls, rhythmically, as when I was a foetus [. . .] I am being given, if I may venture the expression, birth to into death, such is my impression. The feet are clear already, of the great cunt of existence [. . .] The render rent. My story ended. I'll be living yet. Promising lag. That is the end of me. I shall say I no more. (283)

Malone's eschewal of the 'I' ends the frame narration, and the last pages of the novel tell of another character, Lemuel (as in Lemuel Gulliver, Swift's famous character), and a murderous rampage on a charitable excursion to an island for the inmates of Saint John of God's. Malone the 'render', maker of stories, is rent. 'La déchirante déchirée' in French gives us a perhaps even greater sense of Malone's feeling that his power has left him. Torn apart, he feels no longer able to fashion a coherent narrative, nor to speak of himself. The room (as womb) begins to release him from an existence he downgrades to 'subsistence': 'A few lines remind me that I too subsist' (283). Earlier, Malone describes the 'world that parts at last its labia and lets me go' (189). The worry here is that Malone has gotten too big, having expanded into stories and into things, and his expansion cannot be stopped; this expansion becomes a figure for death, this swelling to bursting, this abrogation of the boundary between body and world. This reading finds tacit support in the evocation, in the final scene of *Malone Dies*, of Dublin Bay. From the boat, the members of the excursion party see 'hot yellow bells, better known as gorse' and hear the 'hammers of the stone-cutters' (286). Though Dublin Bay is alluded to regularly in Beckett's work, it appears most notably in 'The End', just as the narrator is about to be scattered to the utmost confines of space.

Malone's playful attempts to renegotiate or capture his 'end' (a temporal and spatial limit) serve to interrogate the relation between self and world. Much as Malone jokes about fleeing to the head as the seat of the self, it is the whole body that is put into question in the pages of the novel, creating an image of subjectivity consistent with Merleau-Ponty's body-subject. Malone finds modes of expanding into the world through the prosthetic use of objects and of stories, engendering a mode of subjectivity that is inextricably intertwined with the material world and with language. Instead of straining towards a telos, Malone toys with the body's possibilities for expansion into the world (by means of objects and language), while admitting the horror of the body's limitlessness, an expansion akin to death, as fusion with the world of matter.

Rather than moving from start to finish, or from thesis to antithesis, towards something beyond, the first two volumes of the trilogy explore the space between oppositions, riveting our attention to the here and now and, I argue, to embodiment. A discussion of unravelling ends and intertwining opposites in Beckett urges attention to *Endgame*, with its overt thematisation of the impossibility of ending. Although *Fin de Partie* (1957) premiered six years after the publication of *Malone meurt* – at the Royal Court Theatre in London after the Théâtre de l'Oeuvre backed out – manuscript notebooks show that Beckett conceived of the play much earlier, at least before 1954. An early draft of 'Avant Fin de partie' (the play that grew into *Fin de partie*) appears in a notebook with part of *Malone Dies*.[16] One of *Endgame*'s most arresting effects is that it insists that art is not an escape from life but intensification of it. Beckett stressed the erosion of the life-art divide in his decision, in the Schiller Theatre production he directed, to omit curtain call, preserving the tableau at the end of the play of Clov prepared to leave, but waiting (Ackerley and Gontarski 2004: 143). Formally and thematically, *Endgame* joins immanence to infinity, opening for viewers a space of uncomfortable if not agonising suspension – a heightened awareness and passivity that is linked to recognition and acceptance of our being as bodies. The impossibility of moving forward, teleologically, accentuates awareness of an embodied present. We become aware, too, of not being fully in the here and now.

Set in a shelter between ocean and land, the play revolves around Hamm, who is blind and confined to a wheelchair, his servant, Clov, who manoeuvres stiffly about the space, looking out of two high windows, and Nagg and Nell, Hamm's parents, who are confined to ashbins, having lost their legs in the Ardennes or on the road to Sedan (sites of lost battles for the French). Apart from Nagg and Nell's reminiscences, no temporal or historical markers situate us. Like the characters, we endure an undifferentiated present in a post-apocalyptic world, a world without bicycle wheels, pap, sugarplums, painkillers, coffins or other signs of human life.

Anna McMullan persuasively links the deterioration of physical bodies in *Endgame* to the decline of their environment, claiming that the immobility and decrepitude of the characters' bodies echo the privation of their world, with its shortage of food, medication, horses, bicycles and light (2010: 42). Drawing on the *Phenomenology*, McMullan further claims that if, 'as Merleau-Ponty argues, the body is our medium for having a world [. . .], *Endgame* literalizes this proposition' (2010: 42). Without the body, there would be no world for us. Hyperbolising this, *Endgame* gives us the sense of a 'deteriorating world-body or body-world' (2010: 44). McMullan connects the play's focus on entropy and decay to Theodor Adorno's reading of *Endgame* as testifying to the 'debris of post-Holocaust atrophied culture'. He writes: 'everything is destroyed, even resurrected culture, without knowing it; humanity vegetates along, crawling, after events which even the survivors cannot really survive' (Adorno 1982 as qtd in McMullan 2010: 44).

The passivity and helplessness Adorno ascribes to postwar Europe is reflected also in McMullan's reading of prosthetic devices in the play, which accents the extreme vulnerability of bodies amalgamated with physical objects that do not improve their capacities; Nagg and Nell are no better off in their ashbins, Hamm's glasses do little for his eyesight and Clov's telescope can do nothing to help him see if there is nothing on the horizon. Rather than helping the human body surpass its limitations, prostheses in *Endgame* draw attention to bodily impotence and vulnerability. Like the chess metaphor in the play's title, they emphasise the extent to which the body is subject to forces (both internal and external) outside the control of the will. McMullan points out that prostheses 'tend to emphasize the limits of agency or perception' and become means of control in an adversarial relation: 'If Clov controls perception of the exterior spaces, Hamm attempts to control both the bodies of his subjects and history through language and narrative' (2010: 44). McMullan's reading draws attention to the fact that we, as bodies, share with the world of things a passivity and sensitivity overlooked by voluntarist theories of agency, which emphasise the importance of controlling the external world (and require that we hold ourselves separate from it). Building on McMullan's reading, I'll show how the loss of values like progress and teleology in *Endgame* restores to us a not always comfortable sense of the body's embeddedness within its physical environment.

This entails a recognition of the limits of our control and a renewed awareness of our implication in the physical world.

The only refuge on offer from the sense of decline and decay we feel so acutely in *Endgame* are the fleeting pleasures of play. *Endgame* unravels oppositions (between beginning and ending, creation and destruction) in such a way as to frustrate forward progress, leaving us no choice but to linger in the here and now – where we can play. Laura Salisbury cannily comments on the oxymoron implicit in the English title. If 'end' implies urgency, necessity and need, then 'game' is just the opposite – a play with ends and needs, which indicates a certain freedom, if only from necessity. This oxymoron presages the stalemate with which the play ends, a draw between Hamm and Clov, the latter ready to leave but hesitating, suspended (Salisbury 2012: 113). Like *Molloy*, *Endgame* ends as it begins, with Hamm's handkerchief held before him like a double of the theatre curtain – an interpretation that Beckett did not discourage (McMullan 2010: 41). *Endgame*'s metafictional elements, including its play within a play, are reinforced by Hamm's 'soliloquy' and by his chronicle, which contains facts that might explain how Clov came to live with him, gesturing towards (Hamm's) autobiography. *Endgame*'s imperfect cyclicality, its unwillingness to end, manifests also in Clov's sighting of a small boy on the horizon at the end of the play, which stirs anxiety that a cycle may begin again, albeit with other players.

Clov's opening line – 'Finished, it's finished, nearly finished, it must be nearly finished' (E 8) –famously intertwines beginnings and endings, not fusing them but highlighting their interdependence. Clov's line echoes Christ's last words on the cross: 'When Jesus therefore had received the vinegar, he said, It is finished: and he bowed his head, and gave up the ghost' (John 19:30 as qtd in Gontarski 2001: 18). This echo, along with crucifixion imagery throughout the play – Hamm has been thought to be a hammer, hammering three nails: Clov (from the French *clou*), Nagg (from the German *Nagel*) and Nell (from the English nail) – challenges the eschatology bound up with Christianity while also refusing the definitiveness of ending, since the crucifixion led to the resurrection (Gontarski 2018: 149–50). Hamm yearns for an ending he is unable to effectuate: 'it's time it ended, in the shelter too [...] And yet I hesitate, I hesitate to ... to end' (E 9). Hamm asks, 'Why don't you finish us' (45), and proclaims 'this is deadly' (36). Refrains throughout the play perform the undifferentiated tedium they describe: 'Why this farce, day after day?' (20, 40). We find ourselves, with the characters, in an indeterminate present, frozen and timeless, populated by phrases that echo and repeat: 'Then it's a day like any other day' (53). 'All life long the same inanities' (53). The weather is 'as usual' (35), the light is 'sunk', the waves are 'lead' and the sun is 'zero' (39). There is 'no more tide' (70), 'no more nature' (18), and there is nothing on the horizon (38) – no fin or sail to break the tedium. When asked about the sun, the position of which might provide some sense of temporal and spatial orientation, Clov responds that the world is grey, '[l]ight black. From pole to pole' (39). The oppositions that might support dialectical progress – even the movement from day to night, light to dark – are undone. And yet something is taking its course, time dragging on. Hamm puts it best: 'The end is in the beginning and yet you go on' (77). What remains among the ruins of dialectical meaning (the friction of thesis-antithesis dissolved) is a state of indeterminacy and non-differentiation, a state akin to waiting, a state of passivity, a state of almost unbearable being-present as something takes its course. Among the ruins of the old stories (subject-object, Christian, eschatological) is the chance that a different way of describing things might take form.

With its many references to the book of Genesis, *Endgame* is often read as a 'reversal' of the myth of creation. Hamm evokes the Biblical Ham, son of Noah (the one who was cursed), and the 'shelter' straddles ocean and earth, evoking Noah's ark and the myth of the flood. The post-apocalyptic world described outside the shelter, where nothing long survives – the small boy on the horizon at the end of the play will either 'die there or come here' (87) – evokes a purge, which could lead to the 'restarting' of humankind (Gontarski 2018: 152).[17] In an early draft of the play, a character who resembles Clov, 'B', reads aloud the story of the flood from Genesis (153). Creation and destruction are commingled in the myth of the flood, as 'de-creation' renews humankind. Like beginnings and endings, these oppositions are shown to be interdependent (though not fused). But their interdependence means that there is no possibility of synthesis, no transcendence, no forward momentum or movement. Instead there is only the here and now, tedious and terrifying.

Endgame reminds viewers or readers of states of sustained bodily discomfort, illness or pain, in which one has a heightened awareness of oneself as body, as part of a physical world determined by forces outside the control of the will, vulnerable to ageing and decay. Moribund, Hamm obsesses over the felt experience of his body – 'There's something dripping in my head' (25); 'Something dripping in my head, ever since the fontanelles' (58). The physical world of the play, too, is out of joint, no longer hospitable to human life after an unspecified calamity (flood, nuclear disaster – it is never mentioned explicitly). The characters find themselves living on, perhaps, after the point at which they feel they should have died, having missed their end. I've suggested that the impossibility of ending in the play ties immanence to infinity – or, if not infinity, then a length of time that feels like infinity because it is undetermined. This state of heightened sensitivity and awareness incites Hamm to reflect that he has failed to be truly present to his surroundings at a time when it might have mattered:

> HAMM: I was never there. [*Pause.*] Clov!
> CLOV: [*turning towards Hamm, exasperated*] What is it?
> HAMM: I was never there.
> CLOV: Lucky for you. [*He looks out of window.*]
> HAMM: Absent, always. It all happened without me. I don't know what's happened. (83)

What is the 'it' that has happened? Does it refer to the calamity? Or to Hamm's life more generally? Perhaps Hamm is saying that he was physically absent at the time of the disaster, and therefore unable to help. But his insistence that he was 'never' there incriminates him, suggesting that he was there but not truly present, irresponsible in the sense of unresponsive to what was going on around him. Hamm laments: 'All those I might have helped. Helped! Saved. Saved!' (77). And Clov reproaches him with the death of Mother Pegg: 'When old Mother Pegg asked you for oil for her lamp and you told her to get out to hell, you knew what was happening then, no? You know what she died of, Mother Pegg? Of darkness' (83–4). Having neglected to use his power and privilege to save others, Hamm now regrets having looked away. His blindness emerges as a physical embodiment of his prolonged unwillingness to see. In a different key, Clov too feels he has missed something, that he has failed to inhabit, in a sense, the time of his life. At the end of the play, he speaks of opening his cell and leaving it: 'I am so bowed I only see my feet, if I open my eyes, and between my legs a little trail of black dust. I say to myself that the earth is extinguished, though I never saw it lit' (89). This passage evokes a story Hamm tells earlier of a madman who, from his window, sees not the rising corn and the sails of the herring fleet but only ashes (52). Being unaware of what is real – unable to 'see' or to be there – is indeed akin to madness.

Far from epiphany, the transformative potential of which aligns it with transcendence, *Endgame* stages a painful acknowledgement of the inescapability of the here and now – which affords its own sense of awareness. Steven Connor describes the atmosphere of Beckett's work in terms of what Jean-Luc Nancy calls 'finite thinking', thinking that acknowledges its limitations, its inability to think what comes next or to orient itself towards a goal or end. Nancy writes that, in finitude 'there is no question of an "end", whether as a goal or as an accomplishment . . . it's merely a question of the suspension of sense, in-finite, each time replayed, re-opened, exposed, with a novelty so radical that it immediately fails' (Nancy as qtd in Connor 2014a: 193). This 'suspension' goes some way towards describing the feeling we have in *Endgame*, when our apprehension, which often 'skeeters off the actual into whatever might prolong or retard it' is left to face 'the exacting penury of the finite' (199–200). The idea that we voluntarily control our environment predisposes us to want to transcend limits and givens, to escape the finitude of the here and now by whatever means we are able. Connor speaks of how difficult – if not impossible – it is to 'apprehend the limited and finite nature of the lives we live every day, the fact that we can live only the life we can live, in such a place, in such a world' (2014a: 200). Awareness of being in a specific circumstance is also awareness of being a body, and embodiment may operate as a backstop against minor pulls towards elsewhere and otherwise, such as expecting the impossible, becoming lost in memories of the past or projections of the future. Hamm is returned from his reveries, often, by bodily sensation – his awareness of his pulse or of pain.

Our embeddedness (as bodies) in a specific time and place may lead also to greater recognition of and responsibility for our climate in crisis. Greg Garrard argues for the play's pertinence to environmental ethics. By proclaiming that nature is absent yet refusing to reveal the dimensions of its absence, *Endgame*, for Garrard, 'is paradoxically the perfect play for the era of anxiety about climate change, which eludes both sensory apprehension and generic representation' (2011: 383). Building on Garrard's argument, I suggest that *Endgame*'s unremitting immanence (its refusal to offer an otherwise or an elsewhere) stimulates a sense of awareness and interconnectedness that makes it more difficult to look away from a climate in crisis. Such heightened awareness may lead, eventually, to efforts to mitigate the harm human resource extraction continues to do on a local and global scale. Garrard applies Timothy Morton's argument that '[i]f we want ecology, we will have to trade in Nature for something that seems more meagre' (Morton 2010 as qtd in Garrard 2011: 394). The cliched idea of nature as a balm or healing salve for a damaged society is, arguably, parodied in *Endgame* in Hamm's nostalgic and pastoral asides – 'If I could sleep I might make love. I'd go into the woods. My eyes would see . . . the sky, the earth' (E 25) – such that Beckett's resistance to idealising nature is consistent with Morton's call to relinquish traditional conceptions of nature in favour of a more capacious way of conceiving of ecology. Without discounting the play's explicit references to nature – Clov's seeds that will never sprout (E 20) and the lines 'Nature has forgotten us' and 'There is no more nature' (E 18) – Garrard retreats from what he calls 'ecocritical literalism' to argue that problematising the representation of nature is important because we are in the midst of a climate crisis we cannot see (Garrard 2011: 393).[18] Gone are the days of ecological writing about nature itself or even about (explicit) cataclysm and catastrophe, for these doomsday scenarios would afford, perhaps, an almost reassuring sense of closure, and we have moved beyond thinking of ecological crisis as an event in the future (395).

Endgame plunges us, by contrast, *in medias res*, leaving us, with Hamm, to reflect on our failures to act sooner and better as well as with the strong sense that, to borrow Morton's phrase, 'we *are* the world, unfortunately' (Morton 2007 as qtd in Garrard 2011). McMullan's idea that the body and environment echo each other (that *Endgame* presents a deteriorating world-body or body world) (McMullan 2010) maps compellingly onto an ecological reading of the play, which both emphasises the body's imbrication within its material environment and foregrounds responsibility for (as well as responsivity to) its calamities. An ecological reading extends the anti-escapism of *Endgame* to our contemporary environmental crisis, through which we have no choice but to live. The play's insistence on the here and now makes us acutely aware of both the body and its place (its concrete, physical environment), since we cannot be anywhere else.

In this chapter, I've sought to show how the stalling out of the dialectic intermingles opposites, replacing progress towards an 'elsewhere' with an experience of immanence, an endurance or 'staying with' the here and now that is closely tied to the experience of embodied being. In *Molloy* this takes the form of variations on the quest narrative, where seekers become the objects sought, subject and object reveal their interdependence and dizzying self-reflexivity unsettles the oppositional thinking necessary to dialectical progress. In *Malone Dies*, waiting for death becomes an occasion for play, for metafictional layering that loosens the boundary between life and art and between the body-subject and its world. Finally, the unremitting immanence of *Endgame* blocks movement towards elsewhere, undoing the reassuring finality of closure and provoking an uncomfortable awareness of the inescapability of our embodied situation on an endangered planet.

There has been some debate about which watershed marks the transition to Beckett's middle and late work, a transition that Dirk Van Hulle and Pim Verhulst aptly characterise as a shift of attention from story to discourse (2017: 23). They place the divide two-thirds of the way through the trilogy, between *Malone Dies* and *The Unnamable*, citing stylistic as well as earlier narratological analyses to support their claim. *Malone Dies* is striking in that it brings into focus the page, discourse or language as part of the materiality of being (25). This is an effort that continues in *The Unnamable* (1953), to which I now turn. The novel's narrator, more explicitly than the characters in *Endgame*, insists on immanence – 'here is my only elsewhere' (TN 402) ('ici c'est mon seul ailleurs'; I 193) – limiting his narrative setting to a 'here' that becomes, under Beckett's pen, various, as vistas, thresholds, arenas and spiral patterns form and unform across what appears to be a limitless surface. *The Unnamable* rejects the idea that the space, early in the novel, might be a narthex, the entrance to a church, discouraging his reader from imagining a 'beyond' comparable to a religious afterlife. Instead, the presence of Malone and several other Beckett characters in the space suggests this odd, elastic setting as a site of literary creation.

Notes

1. Early Beckett scholars read Beckett in dialectical terms, arguing that the 'shape of Beckett's art is the shape of dialectic' (Hesla 1971: 16). Lance St John Butler, in a Hegelian reading of *The Unnamable*, argues that the dialectic is a motive force, though he doubts that Beckett ever reaches a synthesis (1984: 114–49), and Hans-Joachim Schulz devotes a full-length study to Beckett and Hegel (1973).
2. In *Phenomenology of Spirit*, Hegel likens Enlightenment abstraction to a 'penetrating infection' (qtd in Bates 2001: 1), and Adorno and Horkheimer invoke Hegel to claim that the universalising reason of the Enlightenment 'excises the incommensurable' (*Dialectic of Enlightenment* as qtd in Bates 2001: 1). Sven-Eric Liedman summarises Hegel's ambivalence: 'Hegel shared the Enlightenment's high regard for human reason and optimistic view of progress, whereas he approached the Romanticists' holistic and organic ideas' (Liedman and Moggach 1997: 538).
3. The passage reads: 'Il faut, d'un côté, suivre le développement spontané du savoir positif, en nous demandant s'il réduit vraiment l'homme à la condition d'objet, et par ailleurs réexaminer l'attitude réflexive et philosophique, en recherchant si elle nous autorise vraiment à nous définir comme sujet inconditionné et intemporel. Peut-être ces recherches convergentes finiront-elles par mettre en évidence un milieu commun de la philosophie et du savoir positif, et par nous révéler, en deça du sujet et de l'objet pur, comme une troisième dimension où notre activité et notre passivité, notre autonomie et notre dépendance, cesseraient d'être contradictoires' (Merleau-Ponty 2000: 13). Donald Landes points out that *The Structure of Behavior* interrogates positivist science, while the *Phenomenology* questions the reflective attitude in philosophy (2012: xxxiv).
4. James Knowlson discusses Beckett's doubts about the artistic quality of *Mercier et Camier* which, after writing the trilogy, he considered an 'apprentice work' and was reluctant to see published (326). Beckett came to see *Eleutheria*, similarly, as deeply flawed and refused to publish it in his lifetime (328–30).
5. Moorjani also reads the description of Molloy's mother as an 'indictment of bodily processes', including birth and sexuality, 'an antagonism to the body' (1991: 69).
6. Saunders builds on Paul Davies's eco-critical reading of Beckett, which calls for a move beyond 'the binary Western model of constructing reality as an inner (subjective) reacting to an outer (objective)' (2011: 67). Davies argues that Beckett's work implicitly demands new forms of social organisation and a new orientation towards nonhuman nature.

7. Thomas Cousineau connects Lousse to both Circe and Calypso, pointing out that *moly*, related to 'Molloy' and 'mollify', is a plant with narcotic effects referred to in the *Odyssey* (1999: 83). Moorjani compares Lousse to the Phrygian *Magna Mater* and to the gnostic Sophia, divine wisdom and creator in female form (1991: 59).
8. *The Unnamable* develops the sense that language and voices challenge agency: 'his voice continued to testify for me, as though woven into mine, preventing me from saying who I was, what I was [. . .] To make me think I was a free agent' (309). I discuss transmission of influence in language (related to Beckett's decision to write in French) elsewhere (Dennis 2019).
9. David Watson alludes to Julia Kristeva's account of the ways in which, in avant-garde writing, the thetic, syntactic order of the symbolic is disrupted. It is invested by a 'semiotic' process of language that works outside the field of signification, thus connecting the subversion of traditional narrative to the creation of a space for a different type of linguistic utterance. This allows the text to 'reframe' itself at a metafictional level by 'miming its own mimesis (and anti-mimesis) within its verbal articulation and structuration' (1991: 81).
10. Reversibility as opposed to fusion is emphasised in Merleau-Ponty's model of the chiasm.
11. Yoshiki Tajiri argues that Malone's 'sense of the body falling apart is mirrored by Macmann, a protagonist of his story who comes to resemble him (and by extension Molloy and Moran) in terms of physical deterioration' (2007: 44).
12. H. Porter Abbott assigns *Malone Dies* to the genre of diary fiction, and Dirk Van Hulle and Pim Verhulst use this as a starting point for their genetic analysis of the *Malone Meurt/Malone Dies* manuscripts (2017).
13. For discussion of Merleau-Ponty's adaptation of Schilder's body schema, see chapter one. Schilder translates his own German term, *Körperschema*, as 'body image', but Merleau-Ponty resists describing the *schéma corporel* as an image. His English translator follows suit, using 'body schema' (Landes 2012: xlix).
14. Van Hulle and Verhulst identify a line in a manuscript draft that likely expands the metafictional frame to reference Beckett's own writing process. Malone says he has 'wasted hours writing just 4 sentences: "j'ai mis des heures faire ces 4 dernières phrases. Je m'endormais littéralement"'. Only the last part – I fell asleep – appears in the published text. Van Hulle and Verhulst suggest that the manuscript invites us into a 'who's who' game between writer and character (2017: 26).

15. There is a critical consensus concerning the devolution of the narrators' 'humanity' in the trilogy, and animality has been said to '[symbolise] the limits of the human capacity to resist the urge towards violence' (Brazil 2013: 96). I wish to focus on what a less traditional 'humanity' affords: an active passivity that is non-agentic in the liberal humanist sense.
16. This fragment is a four-page dialogue between characters F and X and two pages of notes (Trinity MS 4662 as qtd in Ackerley and Gontarski 2004: 32–4). S. E. Gontarski's *The Intent of Undoing* contains an illuminating discussion of other early manuscript drafts (1985: 25–54).
17. Gontarski also comments on the horror Hamm and Clov feel at the prospect of humanity restarting again from a flea (2018: 152–3).
18. Carl Lavery, in the same spirit, links absurdist theatre (its anti-representationalism) to a specific historical anxiety pertaining to impending ecological crisis (2018).

CHAPTER 4

Radical Indecision: Aporia and Embodied Agency in *The Unnamable*

In the previous chapter, I argued that Beckett's postwar works are not structured dialectically. Instead of advancing *beyond* the terms of a contradiction, they create openings *between* opposed terms. Beckett's writings from the 1940s, then, unhinge meaning from the dialectic in order to incorporate it, to relocate it in the body. Like *Molloy* and *Malone Dies*, *The Unnamable* (published as *L'Innommable* in 1953 and translated by Beckett in 1958), stages the scene of writing, 'dramatising' itself as text, and mobilises paradox to question its conditions of possibility. But where *Molloy* and *Malone Dies* frustrate dialectical progress in favour of a bodily reorganisation of spatial terrain, *The Unnamable* essays something more radical. This chapter argues that *The Unnamable* not only challenges linear progress (progress in general), but also works to transform possibilities for movement, for passage. It does this by exaggerating the body-subject's coextension with its environment, our bodily imbrication within our material surroundings, both spatial and textual.

A certain amount of resistance and discomfort – even horror – is necessary to this endeavour. And where Merleau-Ponty replaces the dialectic with a model of reversibility (opposing terms may change position, subtended by his notion of the flesh), *The Unnamable* insists on impasse to renegotiate possibilities for movement, passage and transformation. For this reason, Derrida's writings on aporia afford greater insight into the novel's workings than Merleau-Ponty's conception of reversibility and the chiasm (which I discuss further in Chapter 7). *The Unnamable* also reveals, perhaps, a tendency in Merleau-Ponty's thought (where ambiguity is to be celebrated rather than endured) to shy away from situations of extreme discomfort, agonising indecision or aporia – situations that may be necessary to transformation. Though

Derrida breaks with phenomenology, his thinking is indebted to the movement, and his writings on aporia, in particular, echo Merleau-Pontian ideas about space and embodiment.[1] Reading Derrida and Merleau-Ponty with *The Unnamable*, I show how an embodied relationship to earth, rather than blocking progress by miring the subject in its materiality, may radically reconfigure surrounding space so as to expand one's possibilities for movement.

What *The Unnamable* dramatises under the sign of aporia, in other words, is a temporary imbrication within one's surroundings – a merging of self, words, earth, ground, mud and sea – that may lead to unthought possibilities for interacting with one's environment, for agency and for growth (as metamorphosis). The novel's tropes of germination, tunnelling and spiralling illustrate how being embedded in one's world (rather than merely stuck) spurs a creative endurance that entails an aesthetic of survival – a going *on* (if not forward).

In *The Unnamable*, there are no directional markers that could serve to orient the reader, as setting, character, quest, filiation, soteriology, subjectivity, pronominal grammar are systematically deconstructed. Beckett has unhinged his art from progress, or from the 'teleology of narrative', through an act of what H. Porter Abbott calls 'narratracide' (1996: 87).[2] Even as words flow with indefatigable momentum (flaunting the rhythms or 'signatures' that, according to Derrida, remain after Beckett's thematic content has been exhausted (1992: 61)), narrative ground gives way at the close of the novel, when the Unnamable wonders whether the words that will carry him to the 'threshold of his story' have been said or not.

> say words, as long as there are any, until they find me, until they say me, strange pain, strange sin, you must go on, perhaps it's done already, perhaps they have said me already, perhaps they have carried me to the threshold of my story. (407)

As readers, we're plunged into a *mise en abîme*, as we doubt – uncomfortably – whether the text we are reading can logically exist. Maurice Blanchot, in his 1953 review of *L'Innommable*, reads such radical doubt as necessary to the novel's exploration of the origins of literary creation. The creative moment, for Blanchot, is not without a certain horror, since, in his view, an artist is 'immolated to art', sacrificed and transformed into an 'empty, animated space where art's summons is heard' (1982: 199).[3]

Blanchot's reading of the novel in terms of creative possibility is something of an anomaly, since *The Unnamable* tends to be read as a terminus – or at best a false threshold, beyond which there is only impasse. Citing one of Beckett's letters from 1953 – 'Since 1950 [I] have only succeeded in writing a dozen very short abortive texts in French [collected as *Textes pour rien*] and there is nothing whatever in sight' – James Knowlson describes the 'impasse in which Beckett found himself since finishing *L'Innommable*' (1996: 397). Steven Connor writes that '[n]early all commentators have agreed with Beckett in finding *The Unnamable* a kind of terminus: the ultimate point of paradoxical intensification' (Connor 2010: xviii), and Alain Badiou links *L'Innommable* to a hiatus in Beckett's productivity in the 1950s, to a decade-long 'blockage' [*une impasse*] (Badiou 1995: 8). It is clear that *The Unnamable* challenges a certain kind of spatial politics – an Enlightenment version of progress, whereby journeys and stories advance towards an end. But to equate the work with impasse is to miss the proliferation of alternatives and spatial possibilities that grow out of periods of radical indecision. Building on Blanchot, I read the novel's radical doubt as a strategy for redesigning the limit between the subject and its surroundings. To do this, I use Derrida's reconceptualisation of aporia as a refashioning of the meaning of passage.

Merleau-Ponty does not engage explicitly with the creative possibilities of aporia, though his attempt to recuperate a version of the dialectic – a 'good dialectic' – comes closest to harnessing the friction between oppositions so as to 'open space'. The problem with Merleau-Ponty's thinking for a reading of *The Unnamable* is that the flexibility, fluidity and ambiguity necessary to his conception of being may not allow for enough resistance to spur renegotiation (as Derrida puts it) of conditions of passage. The novel's harrowing contradictions and cognitive discomfort are necessary to its project of transforming spatial conditions and possibilities for movement within them. In the second chapter of *The Visible and the Invisible*, 'Interrogation and Dialectic', Merleau-Ponty rejects the fixity of dialectical terms, insisting that 'the total relation between a term A and a term B cannot be expressed in one sole proposition, that the relation covers over several others which cannot be superimposed, which are even opposed, which define so many points of view logically incompossible and yet really united with it [. . .]' (VI 98). The idea that logically incompossible points of view are united already *within the relation* erases the opposition that dialectic works to resolve. Merleau-Ponty will eventually replace the dialectic with his conception of reversibility, but here he describes the dialectic already as 'the reversal of relationships, their solidarity throughout the reversal, the intelligible movement which is not a sum of positions or of statements such as *being is, nothingness is not* but which distributes them over several planes, integrates them into a being in depth' (VI 91) (qui les distribue sur plusieurs plans, les intègre à un être en profondeur) (*Vi* 123).[4] Dialectical exchanges, for Merleau-Ponty, induce depth *within* a given space (rather than going beyond it), finding multiple planes and levels of being.

Merleau-Ponty distinguishes his version of the dialectic by naming it the 'hyperdialectic', the 'good dialectic' or the 'dialectic without synthesis'. He describes the difference between an *ambivalent* dialectic (ambivalent being the state in which opposed, fixed terms are brought into a relation of identity) and a dialectic of *ambiguity*, in which terms continually affect each other, change each other or sustain each other in their multiple meanings and directions. Merleau-Ponty explains that the 'dialectic without synthesis' is not a lapse into relativism, but that it should not become a positive statement: 'What we reject or deny is not the idea of a surpassing that reassembles, it is the idea that it results in a new positive, a new position' (VI 95). As soon as the dialectic sets itself up into theses or significations, ambivalence re-emerges. Auto-critique is necessary in order to prevent this lapse into ambivalence, hence the *hyper*-dialectic – a version of dialectic that would be able to 'shake up' (*secouer*) 'false evidences, to denounce the significations cut off from the experience of being, emptied – and to criticize itself in the measure that it itself becomes one of them' (VI 92). When dialectic sets itself up in theses it ceases to be *moving* and reactive, thus forfeiting its relationship to being.[5]

Eventually, the notions of intertwining, chiasm, reversibility and flesh replace dialectic for Merleau-Ponty.[6] And yet, perhaps out of indebtedness to Hegel and Sartre, Merleau-Ponty retains the vocabulary of the dialectic until the last section of *The Visible and the Invisible*, when the hyperdialectic gives way to the figure of the chiasm. Who knows whether the vestigial hyperdialectic would have remained had Merleau-Ponty lived to revise the drafts he composed, but what is clear is that Merleau-Ponty eschews a teleological progression described by Hegel, saying that with every 'overcoming' (*dépassement*) there is loss as well as gain, such that a hierarchical order (i.e. each synthesis is closer to 'truth') is not viable (VI 128). Merleau-Ponty's meditations on the good and bad versions of the dialectic lead him to reject linear progress in favour of spatial and linguistic reconfiguration. Inventions *within* space and language are such that oppositions (subject vs object, active vs passive) become *reversible*.

This reversibility is precisely what Derrida finds problematic in Merleau-Ponty's ontology. In his book on Jean-Luc Nancy, *On Touching*, Derrida engages with Merleau-Ponty's late essay, 'The Philosopher and His Shadow' – an essay about Husserl that includes many of the elements of Merleau-Ponty's thinking expressed in *The Visible and the Invisible*. Though Derrida's critique is multifaceted (like Irigaray, he faults Merleau-Ponty for assuming an equivalence between sight and touch), the part that bears on the present argument is his concern that reversibility risks eradicating alterity. Derrida writes that without an 'unbridgeable abyss' between two bodies, there would 'be no handshake, nor blow or caress, nor, in general, any experience of the other's body as such' (2005: 191). He adds that while Husserl insists on such a separation, Merleau-Ponty 'runs the risk of *reappropriating* the alterity of the other more surely, more blindly, or even more violently than ever' (191). Derrida's critique regarding the preservation of alterity (as a precondition for touch and for interaction) echoes the criticism Levinas makes of Merleau-Ponty.[7] Part of the Unnamable's alterity is the suffering he undergoes, and it may be that the fluidity and reversibility so important to the hyperdialectic fail to reflect this, never arriving at an aporia devastating enough to provoke a restructuring of the possibilities of passage. In Chapter 7, I take up Merleau-Ponty's insistence on the *écart* to question some of these critiques, but for the present reading of *The Unnamable*, I draw on Derrida's discussion of aporia.

My interest in aporia as a transformation of the conditions of progress and passage – a limit situation that one might associate with gestation, germination and metamorphosis – differs somewhat from other critical discussions of aporia in *The Unnamable*. Aporia has been invoked to discuss the text's tendency to embroil itself in contradictions: the simultaneous necessity and impossibility of naming, the text's abundant paradoxes (syntactical, formal, logical) and its rhythm of positing and negation. Leslie Hill, defining aporia as a 'space of indeterminacy or radical doubt where no passage exists' (1990: 63), emphasises the fact that aporia not only describes but also challenges the impossibility of passage, enabling a 'crossing of navigable verbal territory into uncharted and disorienting non-space' (63). Hill's attention to the radicalism of aporia usefully frustrates tendencies to equate aporia with blockage, but associating aporia with 'crossing' overlooks its capacity to instigate change by its imbrication within the given world. Derval Tubridy's more recent study of aporia as a subversive and productive figure in Beckett's work further undermines the easy association between aporia and blockage. It is to emphasise aporia as immanent (rather than transcendent) that I adapt Derrida's reworking of the term.

Many discussions of aporia in *The Unnamable* invoke aspects of Derridean thought: Richard Begam, Daniel Katz and Asja Szafraniec demonstrate how aporia opens a space 'in between' terms of binary oppositions.[8] Begam reads *The Unnamable* as a literary instantiation of Derridean *différance* (a realm in which 'everything and its opposite are true') and argues that the novel operates as a *tertium quid*, classical philosophy's name for an intermediate component – something that partakes of two mutually exclusive categories without being an instance of either (e.g. subject/object, narrator/narrated) (1996: 176). For Szafraniec, too, the Unnamable fashions an 'in between space' that unsettles an either-or logic of binaries (2007: 122). Daniel Katz's Derridean reading of aporia, however, is most relevant to the present argument. Katz argues that instead of founding subjectivity on certainty, as did Descartes, Beckett's texts 'found' the self on aporia, rattling the bedrock of the Cartesian *cogito* and troubling the borders, boundaries and interiors on which subjectivity depends (1999: 100). Katz points out that it is around 'the questions of subjective and textual boundaries' that Derrida and Beckett are the closest (7).

Beckett's personal letters, written while he was composing *L'Innommable*, particularly his lengthy correspondence with George Duthuit, reveal an intense preoccupation with the border zone 'between inside and outside, and its implications for the artist' (Van Hulle 2014: 93). In March of 1949, a month before beginning work on the novel, Beckett wrote to Duthuit that the only kind of work he could imagine for himself was 'boundary work, passage work' (un travail de frontières) (LB2 132), as if foreshadowing the extent to which the novel would be concerned with a working-through or renegotiation of spatial conditions. But *The Unnamable*'s passage-work doesn't involve breaking ground in the usual sense: the onward-ness that characterises Enlightenment views of progress is replaced by tunnelling, sprouting, germinating – ways of moving *within* one's material surroundings. In addition to the earth-tunnelling activity we might ascribe to a creature named Worm, the narrator conflates himself with the earth through metaphor: he is 'accompanied by Malone, as the earth by its moon' (TN 295). The Unnamable also compares himself to vegetation or flowers: he is 'stuck like a sheaf of flowers in a deep jar' (327), surrounded by 'spinach blue rustling', and 'choking in the chlorophyll' (316). Beckett's sense that his creative process was a 'working in the dark', such that to speak of his work would be like 'an insect leaving his cocoon', inspired Porter Abbott to describe Beckett within his work as a 'small, burrowing creature ... elusive, busy, threatening, purposive, blind, trapped, buried alive' (1996: xi). Tunnelling in the dark and in the earth is an apt descriptor of the way in which aporia operates in *The Unnamable* to reconfigure conditions of passage. Instead of tacking towards an elsewhere in which contradictions would be resolved (dialectical progress), aporia in *The Unnamable* persists – literally – in the ground of this world so as to bring about its reconfiguration. The porousness of borders between self and world grants the Unnamable a horrifying capaciousness that is a source of generative potential.

The novel famously opens with the Unnamable's plucky (and paradoxical) intention to *proceed* by aporia. While the novel's opening has received much attention already, it is worth emphasising its satirical jibe at various philosophical methods. In order to shuck abstract philosophical mainstays in favour of something more earthy, muddy and murky, the narrator engages a variety of methods only to reveal them as ludicrous. Procedure-by-aporia is enacted from the novel's first line, as the questions 'Where now? Who now? When now?' are undercut by the word 'Unquestioning'. Contradictions continue: 'I say I. Unbelieving' (the *cogito* comes under more explicit attack in the French: 'Dire je. Sans le penser') (1953: 7). Invalidating echoes continue – 'I seem to speak, it is not I, about me, it is not about me' – before the narrator laments: 'what should I do, in my situation, how proceed? By aporia pure and simple? Or by affirmations and negations invalidated as uttered.' Then the aporetic situation is itself thrown into doubt: 'I say aporia without knowing what it means. Can one be ephectic otherwise than unawares? I don't know. With the yesses and noes it is different' (TN 291). Here the text engages in investigative mockery of at least four philosophical ideas: Cartesian doubt, dialectical advancement (yesses and noes), Husserl's *épochè*, and Pyrrhonian Scepticism, which calls for an 'ephectic' attitude or suspension of judgement (Cahn 2007: 337).[9] The passage cited above also makes a clear, taxonomic distinction between *pure* aporia and movement between 'yes' and 'no': the narrator might proceed by aporia *or* by 'affirmations and negations invalidated as uttered' (TN 291). Aporia is presented as an *alternative* to dialectical method (characterised by affirmation and negation, thesis and antithesis): 'with the yesses and noes it is different, they will come back to me as I go along' (291). Further description of an omniscient, bird's-eye view, from which the Unnamable can shit on top of all the yesses and noes, pokes fun at Sceptical 'suspension of judgment' (holding oneself above the world). In *Eye and Mind*, Merleau-Ponty similarly criticises 'scientific thinking' for its detachment – he claims that 'a thinking which looks on from above, and thinks of the-object-in-general, must return to the "there is" which precedes it; to the site, the soil of the sensible and humanly modified world such as it is in our lives and for our bodies' (1993: 123). But Merleau-Ponty's description of the 'soil of the sensible' shows none of the horror (or humour) of what imbrication in the world might actually feel like. It is because of the discomfort of this experience, perhaps, that *The Unnamable* yearns for a state of silence or nothingness (akin to ataraxy). Yet his existence – and *per*sistence – provokes reconfiguration, a path-breaking rather than dialectical negation or sceptical 'suspension'.

A stylistic tendency towards 'suspension' in Merleau-Ponty's writing – especially in *The Visible and the Invisible*, the most literary of his works – involves similes and self-corrections that mirror (in a different register – without parody) the Unnamable's fraught language. Similes in Merleau-Ponty pile atop one another as if to suggest that what is being described resembles but finally *exceeds* whatever it is to which it is being compared: 'It is *as though* our vision were formed in the heart of the visible, *or as though* there were between it and us an intimacy as close as between the sea and the strand' (VI 130–1; my emphasis). Images layer upon images to conjure, perhaps, an outline of what cannot be said directly. Anne Simon and Nicolas Castin have identified these overlapping similes, and the more general appearance of continual qualifications in Merleau-Ponty's writing, as instances of epanorthosis, a figure of speech associated with self-correction that abounds in *The Unnamable* ('I seem to speak, it is not I, about me, it is not about me' (29)). Continually shifting images and self-correction enable Merleau-Ponty's writing to maintain awareness of its own contingency and to avoid rigidifying into propositional truth-claims; the qualification 'as if' (*comme si*) implies that whatever is claimed might as well be otherwise (Simon and Castin 1998: 16). But maintaining this equivocation comes, as the Unnamable hints through his parody, at a certain cost.

Unlike Husserl's *épochè* and Cartesian doubt (which burrows only until it reaches the bedrock of the *cogito*), aporia enjoys a privileged status in *The Unnamable* because of its radicalism. Literally meaning 'non-passage' (from the Greek *poros*), aporia has been used since antiquity to expand one's thinking. It appears in the early dialectical method of Parmenides and his disciple Zeno and in the Socratic elenchus, where Socrates forces his interlocutors to contradict themselves in order to see the inadequacy of their positions. In her study of aporia, Sarah Kofman underscores the extent to which wit or cunning (*mêtis*) enables us to blaze a trail (*poros*) that frees us from an aporetic situation. *Poros*, she writes, 'is not be confused with *odos*, a general term designating a path or a road of any kind'. *Poros* is a passage opened 'across a chaotic expanse which it transforms', giving direction to a space 'initially devoid of all contours, of all landmarks' (Kofman 1988: 10). Kofman's paradigmatic example of a chaotic, perilous space is *Tartarus* – a realm, according to Hesiod, of 'wild swirling squalls where there are no directions, no left and no right, no up and no down'. *Poros*, then, is the 'last resort of sailors and navigators', the 'stratagem which allows them to escape the impasse and the attendant anxiety' of aporia (10). Kofman specifies that *poros* can also 'take the form of a link that binds, just as the action of linking can sometimes take on the appearance of making a traverse, of making one's way'. This suggests that the practice of ordering space, of drawing connections, is part of a creative process set in motion by situations of aporia (10). Experiences of radical uncertainty – what Kofman refers to as being '*sans voie/voix*' – can open possibilities for moving differently, and allow us to craft unexpected relationships to our environment.

The creativity called for by a non-dialectical version of aporia is also the focus of Rodolphe Gasché's essay on Derrida's reworking of the term. Gasché follows Plato and Aristotle, for whom, as for Derrida, argumentative impasse constitutes the heuristic point of departure for philosophy (2007: 344).[10] By presenting an obstacle to usual ways of thinking, aporia leaves the thinker no choice but to innovate and, as such, presents not so much a dead end as the opportunity for philosophy (330). Gasché understands the conceptual impasse of aporia (and the impossibility of dialectically solving it) as 'the very possibility of thought itself' (332).

In an essay from 1993, *Aporias*, Derrida redefines the concept in a way that aptly describes the workings of *The Unnamable*. Derrida begins by distinguishing aporia from impasse: ordinary, melancholic paralysis (impasse) is not the same as a restriction that gives way to new vistas, creations, characters or manners of thinking (aporia). Then he lists three types of aporia, which permeate and overlap: the first type is associated with closed borders (as in wartime). Free passage is impeded and movement restricted in a conventional sense. The second type of aporia, associated with peacetime, comes from a sense of limitlessness caused by too *few* lines of demarcation (*il n'y a plus de chez-soi ni de chez-l'autre*). (This, according to Derrida's critique, is as far as Merleau-Ponty can take us.) But Derrida goes on to describe a third type of aporia, where radically changing spatial conditions make it so that passage – the idea of '*trans*' – no longer exists as such. Derrida describes this third type of aporia as

> a non-passage because its elementary milieu does not allow for something that could be called passage, step, walk, gait, displacement, or replacement, a kinesis in general. There is no more path [. . .] No more movement or trajectory, no more *trans*- (transport, transposition, transgression, translation, and even transcendence). (1993: 21)

This third type of aporia develops out of spatial conditions so radically unfamiliar that there is no longer the possibility of experiencing a limit or edge. The notion of the limit itself must be redefined. This type of aporia makes possible a certain receptivity to events to come that have no plausible relation to whatever has come before – unimaginable events, for instance, one's own death. The distinction Derrida draws between impasse, which ends in blockage, and a version of aporia that conditions receptivity to events effectively redefines aporia as a site that supports the possibility of newness. Derrida describes 'trying to move not against the impasse but in another manner, according to another thought, perhaps more enduring – that of aporia' (1993: 32). He links aporia to the possibility of moving *differently*.

Aporia and the ways of moving it incites must be distinguished from dialectical advancement. If dialectical progress culminates in a synthesis that requires the invention of an 'elsewhere', aporia leads to reconfigurations of space *from within*. 'Without ceding to any dialectic', Derrida suggests a relation between aporia and what he calls a 'non passive' endurance associated with experience. This becomes the condition for responsibility and decision-making (37). Derrida goes on to distinguish aporia from dialectics of the Hegelian, Marxist or Kantian type, calling it *l'expérience interminable* (37). Unlike philosophical method, aporia cannot be anticipated. Insofar as it operates outside what it is possible to expect, it is endless, limitless and blind. Without knowing where it is going, it emerges from the contradictions of living, of experience.

The idea of aporia as endurance makes one think, perhaps, of physical endurance, which invites us to consider the relation between aporia and the lived experience of our bodies. Embodied experience provides a concrete example of how the contradictions of aporia can be endured (lived), as a passage from *The Unnamable* illustrates with particular clarity. Late in the novel, Worm finds himself in an arena surrounded by others who carry long lamps and watch him through holes they've made in a surrounding screen (TN 364). When the group departs, the narrator says that the holes they made in the screen have been filled in *and* not filled in: 'commanded to say whether yes or no they filled up the holes, have you filled up the holes, they will say yes and no ... both are defendable, both yes and no' (TN 365). The text helps us with the riddle by explaining that the holes have been plugged with lamps, prevented from closing but not left open and gaping. The lamps, 'lit and trained on the within', 'make [Worm] think they are still there', 'that the grey is natural' (365). The position of the lamps creates the effect of simultaneous presence and absence, light and dark, and permeability and impermeability (of the screen). The text's refusal to abide by the logic of exclusion (implied by a choice between binary alternatives) leads us to imagine a space in which contradictory terms coexist. And yet Worm suffers from this indeterminacy, unable to know whether he is being watched or not, and we understand, as readers, the extent to which innovation may grow out of contexts marked by a radical uncertainty. Worm's endurance means that he will eventually undergo some change of circumstance.

This idea of aporia as endurance discourages Badiou's reading of *The Unnamable* as a dead end in Beckett's aesthetic, as the exhaustion of a certain line of thinking. Instead, *The Unnamable* inaugurates a period of gestation, whereby images sketched verbally in its pages find concrete form in later works. For instance, the Unnamable's description of time piling up around the body is actualised, physically and literally, in the predicament of Nagg and Nell, embedded in bins of sand (389). The same passage is literalised in *Happy Days*, where Winnie finds herself buried to her neck in a mound of earth. *The Unnamable* does not dead-end in paradox but rather incubates (or germinates) the formal innovations and distinctive image repertoire that distinguish Beckett's late style. As David Watson argues, 'the paradoxical impasse of the unnamable becomes the very basis of the continuance of Beckett's later fiction' (1991: 56). Self-reference in Beckett's late work, moreover, makes it difficult to imagine a break of the kind Badiou proposes.[11] So instead of impasse, we might envisage *The Unnamable* as a space of gestation – as a chrysalis of sorts – in which Beckett's most striking images germinate. *The Unnamable* is a 'travail de frontières' that frays passages between Beckett's works, enabling scenes and images to carry over so as to constitute a distinctive signature or style.

The Unnamable moves away from methodological advancement by means of affirmations and negations (dialectic) in favour of an *endurance* related to the lived experience of the body. The Unnamable's oft-discussed description of himself as the tympanum (both inside and outside the body as the membrane that separates the two) is just one example of how recourse to physiology shows that it is possible to be both inside *and* outside, thus troubling the integrity of the limit or boundary. This idea of *becoming* a limit is, of course, taken up by Derrida, whose discussion of the 'paradoxical *limitrophy* of the "Tympan"' (1993: 35) may have been inspired by Beckett.[12] Extending a related aspect of Derrida's thought (the idea of a supplement necessary to self-presence), Yoshiki Tajiri addresses the problem of the boundary between self and world, as we have seen, through his discussion of prosthetic bodies in Beckett. The prosthesis, at once alien to and integral to the body, unsettles clear distinctions between the body and technology and body and world. In *The Unnamable*, Tajiri argues, the voice becomes prosthesis; it is the speaker's own *and* it has been foisted upon him from outside (Tajiri 2007). Similarly, Paul Stewart points to the undecidability between the Unnamable as (narrating) subject and (narrated) object. Does the Unnamable create suffering in fiction or does he, as passive object, suffer fiction (Stewart 2014b: 173)? Stewart writes that 'at times the Unnamable is clearly wielding the power of the novelist, at other times he is the victim of narration' as, for example, when he is made to 'swallow words and voices' (174–5). Stewart argues that, though the Unnamable may try to escape embodiment, the materiality of language within which he exists ensures his passive, bodily suffering.[13] This, again, is close to Merleau-Ponty's assertion that in order to see we must be visible, in order to touch we must be touchable. *The Unnamable* extends this principle to the field of language by inventing a narrator who anticipates his being narrated. Stewart identifies an aporetics of agency (who is doing the telling – the Unnamable or language itself?) that blurs the border between the materiality of the body (as subject) and the materiality of words.

The Unnamable continually blurs distinctions between the narrator and the world of words in which we encounter him. The Unnamable calls repeated attention to his condition of possibility in language, insisting that words say him into being – 'perhaps they have said me already, perhaps they have carried me to the threshold of my story' (414) – and lamenting that he both constitut*es* and is constitut*ed by* the words he utters: 'I'm in words, made of words, others' words, what others, the place too, the air, the walls, the floor, the ceiling, all words, the whole world is here with me, I'm the air, the walls, the walled-in one' (386). The Unnamable, like the place around him, is made of words, and to the extent that language – specifically the printed text of the book we're reading – conditions his existence, the Unnamable is walled-in (*emmuré*) by words. He complains of being trapped in

> an empty place, a hard shut dry cold black place [. . .] like a caged beast born of caged beasts born of caged beasts born of caged beasts born in a cage and dead in a cage, born and then dead [. . .] (386–7)

With the narrator enclosed in a shut black space where nothing moves – fixed in typeset perhaps – the text stumbles into a repetitive glitch, illustrating how language can act as closed space (cage) in which humanity is reduced to a cycle of births and deaths. Even the possibilities at the narrator's disposal to describe his situation have been inherited from others; 'in one of their words' he must say what he is. Similarly, the Unnamable remarks that his text is composed from a finite palette of existing linguistic conditions: 'ce sont des mots blancs, mais je m'en sers' (202). Visually, the reader understands that the narrator makes use of existing language 'je m'en sers' (I *use* them, the blank words), but a phonetic echo in French gives us 'je m'insère' or 'I insert myself into language.' By using language, the Unnamable enters the text, expanding it, forcing it to mean differently, but also enclosing his limitlessness in its space. But the Unnamable also feels himself extending in all directions, unable to stop because he lacks a *place*. He feels the borders of his body melt into the space around him: 'I feel no place, no place round me, there's no end to me' (399). The French, 'Je n'arrête pas', which Beckett translates as 'there's no end to me', signals the body's lack of outer limit as the Unnamable blends into text and world. The Unnamable's inability to stop speaking is related to his sense that he is bleeding into things. This limitless expansion is part of the Unnamable's experience of aporia; his self-extension is not volitional, and yet the fact that he is made of the words he utters affords him modes of navigating within them – 'agency' enough to arrange them into a novel.

The sinking of the Unnamable's voice into the surrounding text of the novel is related to the work's abrogation of another limit – one between the non-fictional world (represented by material traces of Beckett's writing process) and the novel's fictional content. In their genetic study of *L'Innommable* and *The Unnamable*, Dirk Van Hulle and Sean Weller write that it is fitting that the novel's compositional process reflects a working out of where the text is going – an *écriture de processus*. Van Hulle and Weller adapt Louis Hay's distinction between *écriture de processus* (exemplified by Proust's meandering mode of composing *À la recherche du temps perdu*) and *écriture de programme* (exemplified by the advanced planning of a writer like Zola). They observe that the manuscript (of *L'Innommable*) and the material traces of the writing process it bears suggest that the text finds its way – its *poros*, perhaps – in the act of being written (Van Hulle and Weller 2014:

168). They further claim that the text is meant to be transparent about its genesis, one fraught with cul-de-sacs and new departures (2014: 31).

Van Hulle and Weller show that Beckett's writing process leaves traces on the novel's content, which softens divisions between the material world (in this case Beckett's writing notebook) and the textual world of Mahood, Worm and the Unnamable. Beckett's preoccupation with the border between art and life manifests itself in a sustained play with the material boundaries of *L'Innommable* as a piece of writing. Van Hulle and Weller point out that the work comes to its breathless close on the final page of Beckett's (second) manuscript notebook. They wonder whether Beckett terminated the text where he did because he had come to the end of his notebook, thereby allowing the spatial limits of the notebook to determine the story (2014: 31). Similarly, between consecutive lines of the manuscript – 'je serai bien enfin' and 'c'est comme ça ce matin' (overleaf) – Van Hulle and Weller observe differing shades of ink. They assume that Beckett broke off writing at night and began again the next morning with the line involving 'ce matin'. Here a trace of the time of writing is embedded in the language of the story (*ce matin*) and in the manuscript (its different ink shades). Van Hulle and Weller's analysis shows the extent to which the material conditions of the writing process – ink, writing implements, notebooks – can affect the story, thinning the boundary between art and life.

The novel's way of placing literary creation within the confines of *this* world further troubles boundaries between inside and outside, foreign and familiar. As if to underscore the importance of immanence, the Unnamable quips, 'Here is my only elsewhere', refusing the lure of transcendence and limiting the narrative setting to a 'here' that becomes, under Beckett's pen, various (402). The first pages of the novel present an elastic setting: 'The place may well be vast, as it may well measure twelve feet in diameter. It comes to the same thing as far as discerning limits is concerned' (295). The Unnamable wonders, 'Are there other places set aside for us?' and concludes: 'No, no, we have all been here forever, we shall all be here forever' (293). This indeterminacy of location in the novel's opening pages creates a 'vertigo from which the text will have to emerge' (Van Hulle 2012: 100), and the apparitions of characters (Murphys, Molloys and Malones) make evident the novel's preoccupation with authorship as a form of world creation.[14] Van Hulle and Weller cite a manuscript revision to *L'Innommable* that reveals the extent to which, in Beckett's view, world creation is linked to the (re)organisation of space – an idea germane to Merleau-Ponty's thinking. Beckett replaces the word *cosmology* with *topography*: 'c'est là où on est . . . si je pouvais le décrire, moi qui réussi[s] si bien dans la ~~cosmologie~~ topographie' (FN2 61v–62 as qtd in Van Hulle and Weller: 179). Van Hulle and Weller note that cosmology becomes cosmo*graphy*, 'with the emphasis on the act of writing, or a topo*graphy*, since the autographic project is, from the start (*Où maintenant?*), linked to the search for a place' (2014: 109). With reference to Porter Abbott's idea that Beckett's oeuvre carries out a writing of self, eventuating in a style particular to Beckett (an 'autograph' revealed in the text), it is possible to interpret Beckett's revision as insisting on the immanence of literary world creation and its link to writing place.

Writing, then, may be understood as a negotiation of uncertain terrain, as a working 'with' or 'along' aporia – a point that is further emphasised by the novel's revision of narrative structure as a being embedded (or tunnelling) in the earth. Late in the novel, we are warned against a relapse into the picaresque, though it is equally impossible to read *The Unnamable* as depicting a journey, as travel towards a destination. Rejecting linear narrative (and the teleology and soteriology associated with it), the novel ends not in resolution but in paradox. Its privileged trajectory is not the '*right line*, – the path-way for Christians to walk in' – but the spiral.[15] At one stage in the novel, the Unnamable finds himself embroiled in an 'inverted spiral', 'one of the coils of which, instead of widening more and more, grew narrower and narrower' (316). The narrator, here Worm, decides to change direction:

> Faced then with the material impossibility of going any further I should no doubt have had to stop, unless of course I elected to set off again at once in the opposite direction, to unscrew myself as it were, after having screwed myself to a standstill, which would have been an experience rich in interest and fertile in surprises if I am to believe what I once was told, in spite of my protests, namely that there is no road so dull, on the way out [. . .] (316–17)

'Screwed' into an aporetic situation in which forward movement is impossible, Worm takes the opposite direction. And, contrary to Enlightenment ideals of progress, this move backwards, Worm has been told, will yield a new vista, since the path, on the way out, presents 'a different aspect, quite a different dullness' (317). The Unnamable's remark that such screwing and unscrewing would be 'fertile in surprises' mobilises the paradox of the spiral: repetitive because it circles round, but also layered, weaving in difference.

The importance of the figure of the spiral to modernity in general and to Beckett in particular is the subject of an article by Nico Israel that traces the influence of *The Unnamable* on what is perhaps the best-known artistic meditation on the spiral, Robert Smithson's 1969 'Earthwork', *Spiral Jetty*. Israel argues that both works draw on and revise the spiral's way of critiquing 'the idea of teleological history and the experience of global modernity' (2011: 2–5). If the figure of the spiral challenges enlightenment ideals of unfettered, unidirectional progress – the very ideals it has been evoked in other contexts to sustain – it might also suggest alternative forms of historical movement, a radical demarcating along the lines of Derrida's redefinition of aporia. Made of mud, rocks, salt crystals and water at the edge of the Great Salt Lake in Utah, *Spiral Jetty* is 'written' into the earth. Insofar as it literally transforms the landscape, one could argue that it enacts the crafting of *poros*, a reconfiguration of terrain.[16] The Unnamable's 'world tour', similarly, presents a situation of aporia that provokes alternative modes of moving: the narrator wanders the globe only to reach the equator and turn back – the world being finite – to the rotunda from which he set out. As he nears the centre, he suspects that, 'by virtue of a supreme spasm', he will be 'catapulted in the opposite direction' and begin his journey over (321). The notion of the spasm is telling, since part of Israel's argument is that the spiral expresses modernism's paradoxical anxieties about globalisation.[17] In modernism's 'morbidly hilarious tales of globetrotting and homecoming', he writes, 'globalization comes to signify both the anxiety of spinning out of control and the anxiety of perpetual imprisonment' (22). The Unnamable's travels to the edges of the known world end in cul-de-sacs (caged beasts born of caged beasts) that beget expansions without end. The unpredictability of terrain and the impossibility of controlling one's movement render *forward* progress – troubled after the horrors of the Second World War – impossible, as the spiral springs the Unnamable back and forth between the rotunda of home and family and the outer limits of the world.

The experience of aporia, then, undermines the opposition between captivity (paralysis) and limitless expansion ('trans' can no longer exist as such). Again, we might look to the human body to find a figure for a space that is both restrictive (it permits gestation) and generative (infinitely open). It is telling, perhaps, that both Aristotle and Plato invoke the womb as a metaphor to discuss aporia. Aristotle describes the wisdom of the midwife as the 'kind of knowledge that one assimilates during a long journey across a desert where no path is marked, where one must guess one's way and . . . take devious roundabout paths' (Kofman 1988: 24). Plato describes Socrates as '[l]ike a midwife', who 'can tell at a glance when someone is going into labour, when someone whose soul is about to give birth begins to experience aporetic pains'. Unlike the midwife, the philosopher delivers the soul from aporia at 'precisely the moment when it is emptiest', but in both cases a 'dizzying emptiness' 'awakens the tormenting desire to know' 'that brings on labor pains' (24). From the discomfort and disorientation of aporia, other configurations gestate and emerge.

In *The Unnamable*, situations of impossibility give way to radical reassessments of the possible and passable. This process, like Derrida's third version of aporia, requires a remaking of the idea of the limit. Transcendence and forward progress give way to a model that resembles gestation – change *within* or *immanent to* a place or body. Linguistic space and narrative form in *The Unnamable* expand to nourish what was previously unthinkable, which comes to fruition in Beckett's later works. We find echoes of the novel's closing line, 'I can't go on, I'll go on', for instance, in the opening of *Texts for Nothing*, 'I couldn't any more, I couldn't go on', and in the opening of *Worstward Ho*, a piece that further revises ideas about onwardness and progress: 'On. Say on. Be said on. Somehow on. Till nohow on' (NH 89). The horrifyingly generative space of aporia changes both the shape of space and the make-up of the physical body that journeys there, such that, like the enigmatic narrator in Blanchot's *La folie du jour*, what emerges from the groundlessness of aporia has been formed and transformed: 'One day they buried me in the ground, and the doctors covered me with mud [. . .] I emerged from the muddy ditch with the vigour of maturity' (1995: 42).

Notes

1. On the relationship between Merleau-Ponty and Derrida, see in particular Jack Reynolds, *Merleau-Ponty and Derrida: Intertwining Embodiment and Alterity*.
2. Porter Abbott claims that Beckett abandons the quest narrative with *Texts for Nothing*, which he reads as a companion piece to *How It Is*. He argues that *The Unnamable* still conforms to the quest narrative insofar as movement towards an end 'organizes our perception of its structure and gives the various parts a kind of belonging' (1996: 94). I argue that *The Unnamable* splinters directionality such that the newness Porter Abbott ascribes to *Texts for Nothing* can already be found in its pages.
3. Daniel Katz's discussion of 'neutrality' in Blanchot (*le neutre*) describes how subjectivity is overcome during the artistic process (1999: 24–7).
4. Renaud Barbaras situates Merleau-Ponty's hyperdialectic as a critique of Sartre (more than of Hegel) (2004: 136–9). Merleau-Ponty contemplates the dialectic as described in the history of philosophy, wondering if he should even use the name dialectic: 'it is because the dialectic is unstable (in the sense that the chemists give to the word), it is even essentially and by definition unstable, so that it has never been able to formulate itself into theses without denaturing itself, and because if no one wishes to maintain its spirit it is perhaps necessary to not even name it' (VI 92).
5. Diana Coole argues that this necessity of continual auto-critique links phenomenology to critical theory (2007: 93–123).
6. This is Hiroshi Kojima's argument in 'From Dialectic to Reversibility: A Critical Change of Subject-Object Relation in Merleau-Ponty's Thought'. Of Merleau-Ponty's ontology, he writes: 'the synthesis of subject and object is now undoubtedly denied, with their chiasmatic antithesis in reversibility introduced instead' (2002: 112).
7. Jack Reynolds and Jon Roffe discuss Merleau-Ponty's reception by Levinas (as well as Lacan, Irigaray, Derrida and Deleuze) in 'Neither/Nor: Merleau-Ponty's Ontology in "The Intertwining/The Chiasm"' in Mildenberg (ed.), *Understanding Merleau-Ponty, Understanding Modernism* (2018: 100–14).
8. Yoshiki Tajiri has noted the tendency of Beckett critics to focus on Derrida's critique of self-presence in *Speech and Phenomena* (1967), especially Thomas Tresize in *Into the Breach* (2007: 140–1).
9. Badiou emphasises *The Unnamable*'s fraught deference to Cartesian and Husserlian methodologies, which he calls Beckett's 'methodological ascesis' (*ascèse méthodique*) (1995: 19). He argues that Beckett's text brackets or suspends certain functions so as to explore others more deeply: for instance, the speaking head in a jar blocks

the function of movement to explore that of language (21). Badiou reads in Beckett a 'protocole de l'expérience, qu'il faut comparer au doute par lequel Descartes ramène le sujet à la vacuité de sa pure énonciation, ou à l'*épochè* de Husserl, qui réduit l'évidence du monde à celle des flux intentionnels de la conscience' (19).

10. For Plato, aporia is the situation in which one who is ignorant becomes aware of his ignorance and is 'set on the path to truth'. Aristotle uses aporia as a methodological starting point at which the thinker, confronted with conflicting but equally valid arguments, 'is compelled to sharpen his understanding of the problem and to explore various routes (*diaporia*) so as to work out a solution (*euporia*) to what appeared to be an unsolvable dilemma' (Gasché 2007: 332).
11. Badiou attributes the impasse of *The Unnamable* to solipsism. He argues that with *How It Is* Beckett overcomes an obsession with self-investigation and learns (as a writer of fiction) to encounter the other, which entails imaginative projection into experiences different from one's own (1995: 47–54).
12. Richard Begam notes the importance of Beckettian terms such as *unnamable* and *tympan* to Derrida's critical vocabulary (1996: 153).
13. Paul Stewart distinguishes his position from Pascale Casanova's idea that Beckett achieves an abstract literature: 'Beckett's art . . . cannot stop the word becoming suffering flesh' (Stewart 2014b: 176).
14. Early in the novel, the Unnamable hopes there is no connection between himself and Prometheus, a 'miscreant who mocked the gods' and 'denatured clay' (297). The mention of Prometheus alongside the narrator's creations (Murphys, Molloys, Malones) leads Van Hulle and Weller to suggest a relationship between the Unnamable-as-author and Prometheus *plasticator*. Beckett learned by heart Goethe's *Prometheus*, which focuses on the Ovidian version of the myth, in which Prometheus moulds human beings from clay (116).
15. The line is taken from Laurence Sterne's *Tristram Shandy*.
16. Smithson declared that he was in favour of a view of language as 'a terrain, a patch of ground within the page that you could extract various meanings from' (Baker 1972: 154 as qtd in Israel 2011: 24).
17. Israel points out that the Unnamable's 'world tour', with its duration of two or three hundred years, coincides roughly with the duration of philosophical modernity (2011: 16).

CHAPTER 5

Style and the Violence of Passivity: *How It Is*

An emphasis on endurance in *The Unnamable*, emblematised by the body's embeddedness in earth, gets transmogrified in Beckett's last novel, *Comment c'est* (1961), translated by Beckett as *How It Is* (1964). More than any of the prose works, *How It Is* exaggerates the body's inherence within its material environment. Mud is ingested and excreted as the 'I' crawls through it, carrying a jute sack with tins and a tin opener, towards his semblable, Pim, whom he tortures into speech and song. Beckett's 'epic of mud' is the apotheosis of a sustained preoccupation with muck and slime throughout his work; 'Echo's Bones', written in 1933, begins 'with shafts and manholes back into the muck' (3), Molloy dwells 'somewhere between the mud and the scum' (14), the narrator of 'First Love' lies flat on his face 'in the mud under the moon' (1995: 34) and that of *Texts for Nothing* 'on the dark earth sodden with the creeping saffron waters it slowly drinks' (1995: 101).[1] Bodies in the ground evoke the grave, but also, especially if the ground is mud, the 'primal chaos' from which forms emerge in Ovid – 'it was unstable land, swimmable water, air needing light. Nothing has retained its shape' (9) – and God's creation of humankind in Genesis, as readers of *How It Is* have noted.

Much as it has been linked to myths of creation, *How It Is* has also been read as expressing a lack of agency, especially given the excruciating slowness through which 'I' crawls, prostrate, in the muck. Critics have focused on the body's literal embeddedness in the material world (mud), pointing out the object-like qualities of the mud crawlers and comparing their movements to those of automatic, visceral processes of the body (Connor 2014a; Maude 2020). Their half-submergence in the novel's slimy material setting also evokes Dante's sullen mud gurglers in Canto 7 of the *Inferno*, making it only reasonable to interpret the novel as testifying to the impossibility of acting meaningfully within the world. As Beckett was writing *Comment c'est* he wrote to Barbara Bray about 'trying to find the rhythm and syntax of extreme weakness' (LB3 211) – which would seem to support this view, but with respect to the novel's stylistic oddities: truncated phrases, absence of punctuation and block-like strophes. The novel's coupling of broken syntax with difficulty of movement – 'syntactic' violence paired with bodily violence – frames the question of material agency in terms of language, figured in the novel as the muddy matter through which the bodies crawl. An offshoot from an early draft, published as '*L'Image*' in *A Quarterly Review*, opens with a description of the tongue clogged with mud: 'La langue se charge de boue . . .' (1998: 9).[2] The meaning of tongue (*langue*) extends metonymically from the mouth's organ to language more broadly, such that the novel's interrogation of processes of signification sits uncomfortably with the body's struggle to differentiate itself from and create meaning within its environment.

The novel's image of human bodies crawling through exaggeratedly material surroundings – which are also arguably linguistic – challenges modernity's strict separation between the human and its environment, checking the power of a humanist subject to dominate and control its surroundings. The image finds a correlate, perhaps, in Rosi Braidotti's *The Posthuman* (2013), which recognises the inherence of the human within its material surroundings, thereby revealing the insufficiency of a 'social constructivist and hence dualistic theory of the subject which disavows the ecological dimension' (83). This leads Braidotti to call for 'recompositions of both subjectivity and community' (83), a call that echoes (inadvertently) Leo Bersani's reading of *How It Is* as laying the groundwork for a renegotiation of community, subjectivity and sociality (1993; see also Bixby 2012: 243). It is consonant, too, with a tradition of reading *How It Is* as exploring its own signifying process, breaking down structures of narrative and grammar to suggest new possibilities for meaning (Blanchot 1993: 326–31). Anthony Cordingley, excavating the novel's intertextual allusions from its manuscript drafts, has presented *How It Is* as a late modernist bricolage of Pythagoras, Socrates, Christian mysticism, ancient stoicism, seventeenth-century rationalism and other 'ancient voices'. He argues that the novel 'incubates' new poetic forms in the dissolved 'excreta' of the humanist tradition (Cordingley 2018: 4–11).

The disarticulation of language in the novel (its eschewal of punctuation and sentence structure) and the dissolution of the world into mud suggest a relation between the work of signification (in language) and the physical body's orientation of its surroundings, a process that Merleau-Ponty defines as 'style'. Traditionally, style signals humanist values; its link to artistry and form implies power over nature, and insistences like de Buffon's – 'le style, c'est l'homme même' (style is the man) – link it to individuality. But Beckett subverts this ideal, portraying the human as joined in sadistic dependence, a move that reveals the violence underpinning desire for individuation. Style, as Merleau-Ponty redefines it, is not active, nor is it a flourish, nor is it intentional. Rather, style describes the bodily process of making articulations within a system, carving it into perspectives, making cuts. Merleau-Ponty's emphasis on a material 'kinship' between bodies reveals in Beckett's novel the possibility – perhaps still latent – of recognition based on awareness of style as a provisional differentiation from a common element. I argue that *How It Is* interrogates the work of signification as style in Merleau-Ponty's sense, where our initiation as speaking subjects is predicated on our material belonging to our (spatial and linguistic) surroundings, transforming agency from an act of will into a question of how we negotiate our embodiment. Yet while Merleau-Ponty's vision of intersubjectivity mediated through style is largely harmonious, Beckett's is more painful, flickering between tenderness and horror.

How It Is takes place in mud described alternately as shit, vomit, slime and as something elemental: 'warmth of primeval mud impenetrable dark' (11) (*boue originelle* in the French) (16). If the novel's 'I' has been returned to a *prima materia* where meanings first arise, he also inhabits a purgatorial underworld – 'how I got here no question not known not said' (7) – cut off from life above in the light: 'life life the other above in the light said to have been mine on and off no going back up there no question' (8). It is swiftly established that the narrator is also narrat*ed*; he hears an 'ancient voice in me not mine' which he murmurs to the mud: 'passing time is told to me and time past vast tracts of time the panting stops and scraps of an enormous tale as heard so murmured to this mud which is told to me' (27).[3] The novel announces its three-part structure – before Pim, with Pim, after Pim – only to undermine it, revealing this division of time as a narrative construction. Anticipating *Worstward Ho*'s 'No once in pastless now', the narrator reminds us: 'part three, it's there I have my life' and quips: 'divide into three a single eternity for the sake of clarity' (24). Part two, with Pim, tells of the narrator/narrated's encounter with Pim, to whom he gives 'lessons' in the form of tortures organised in a 'table of basic stimuli' (69). These tortures, which cause Pim to sing into the mud, include carving in the skin of Pim's back (70). In part three the narrator/narrated imagines a cosmology (perhaps based on the mechanistic universe of seventeenth-century rationalism), a massive circular chain where everyone passes eternally through four stages (travelling alone, torturing another, being abandoned and being tortured by another). He throws the existence of the novel's world into question in its last pages: 'all these calculations yes explanations yes the whole story from beginning to end yes completely false yes' (144).

In contrast to the hard, baked earth of *Happy Days* (1961), written just after *Comment c'est*, which similarly features a body embedded in earth – 'the earth is very tight today, can it be I have put on flesh, I trust not' (28) – the ground of *How It Is* is malleable: 'the mud never cold never dry it doesn't dry on me the air laden with warm vapour of water or some other liquid' (25). As in earlier texts (such as 'The End' – 'To contrive a little kingdom, in the midst of the universal muck, then shit on it, ah that was me all over' (98)), mud is linked to the body as excrement: 'here when you shit it's the mud that wipes' (37). But more curiously, the mud in *How It Is* is also connected to language and to the residue of culture. Drawing attention to the aural similarity between '*quaqua* on all sides', one of the novel's refrains, and *caca*, Anthony Cordingley takes the mud to represent the detritus of learning in the humanist tradition. He describes the mud as the I's 'discharged ancient voice', 'the voice of past experience and learning materialized into excremental residue (*quaqua/caca*)' (2018: 204). Jean-Michel Rabaté reminds us that Beckett is developing Leopardi's line, *e fango è mondo* (and the world is filth), to make mud and slime the substances of 'an excremental world that extends to verbal matter' (2016: 55). Rabaté writes: 'if the world is mud and if language is slime, one can barely distinguish them' (55).[4] The mud, both material and linguistic, moves through the narrator's body as he through it, a point most strikingly apparent when the narrator/narrated lolls his tongue in the mud to quench his thirst: 'the mud in the mouth thirst abating humanity regained' (27). The idea that humanity is regained by imbibing the muddy refuse of humanist learning parodically alludes to our dependence on our environment to sustain us, both physically and linguistically.

While recent readings of *How It Is* have registered the political context of the novel and its intertextuality, including colonial violence (Beckett's reading of Roger Casement's *Black Diaries*)[5], the Algerian War of Independence and the influence of Dante, Stoicism, Sade and a wealth of other philosophical, literary and theological texts and traditions (Bixby 2012; Caselli 2005; Cordingley 2018; Morin 2017; Rabaté 2016), my focus here is on how the novel represents the body as imbricated within its material-linguistic environment. The divide between the linguistic realm of 'culture' and the material realm of the body is unsettled by the novel's anchoring of speech to the body: 'brief movements of the lower face' (26) and 'a fart fraught with meaning issuing through the mouth' (26). This emphasis on the physiology of speech inspires Ulrika Maude's claim that the novel links intentional acts (like speech) to involuntary or non-agential processes of the body (Maude 2020). In her earlier work, Maude invokes the mud crawlers' horizontal position (close to the earth) in a discussion of the abject, writing that Beckett's characters 'fail to observe the otherness of the abject' (Maude 2009: 99). For Maude, incorporating the abject (failing to recognise it as other) 'demolishes clear lines of demarcation between the subject and its world' (99).[6] But though the abject breaks down received categories, it risks collapsing body and world altogether. Merleau-Ponty's body-subject, in order to orient within its linguistic-material environment, cannot fuse with it entirely.

There is a tendency among critics who write about the body in *How It Is* to find in the novel a non-agential materialism, such that the body blends with its surroundings, having little effect on them. Steven Connor describes the text as 'a metabolic amalgam of mud, body, mouth and murmured words, past, present and future, churning and percolating into each other' (2014a: 40). He identifies a 'slow oozing together of things, the body sinking into the mud, alimentation and excretion becoming simply phases of each other, everything slowly subsiding into everything else' (2014a: 40). Connor admits that the body's sinking into undifferentiated materiality is countered by an 'opposite condition' composed of 'sudden "existings", accesses of image and miracle' (2014a: 40). But this opposing force that promises to offset encroaching chaos – a sack of tins that has kept its shape, for instance – seems to come from elsewhere (a *deus ex machina*), leaving the body little chance to adjust its rapport with its world.⁷ In a similar vein, Ulrika Maude inventories bodily organs mentioned in the text – kidney, heart, brain, eye, ear, navel, bladder, urethra, rectum, anus, skin, blood, arse, testicle, genitals (2020: 265) – to claim, with reference to William James, that the thoughts and feelings we associate with intentional subjectivity originate in the body, independent of will and consciousness. She argues that *How It Is* 'insists on representing what is considered intentional action – here speech – as involuntary, non-agential' (266).⁸ Maude's analysis does not foreclose the possibility of material agency, but her characterisation of bodily organs as 'stupid' in the etymological sense, nonhuman insofar as they are insensate and incapable of controlling their activity, does seem, in this context, to indicate the body's lack of power to effect change within its environment. Maude's reading of *How It Is* rightly undermines a voluntarist model of agency, but, in achieving this, she must constrain her analysis to the insensate interior of the body – the viscera – rather than the body's holistic rapport with its environment. Building on Connor and Maude's attention to embodiment, I draw on Merleau-Ponty's theory of style, developed in the 1950s, to examine more closely the body's interaction within its material-linguistic setting and to investigate the body's agentic possibilities.

A strictly materialist interpretation also sits in uncomfortable tension with readings that associate *How It Is* with possibilities for creative novelty. Blanchot, for instance, attending to how the novel interrogates the work of signification, argues that the open-endedness of the narrator's voice overwhelms a reader's usual hermeneutic processes, causing a crisis in reading, a *désoeuvrement* or 'un-working' that creates space in which other forms may take shape. The voice in the novel could be 'the voice of all of us, the impersonal, errant, continuous, simultaneous and alternating speech in which each of us, under the false identity we attribute to ourselves, cuts out or projects the part that falls to him or her' (1993: 330). Blanchot further describes how the novel brings together author and reader, 'each nearly merged with the other' (329), such that discrete identities are held in abeyance, enabling new relations to take shape. Anthony Cordingley suggests that Blanchot's metatextual focus has discouraged scholars from piecing together Beckett's source material. His own study impressively fills this gap, identifying the novel's buried intertexts, but he also calls *How It Is* a 'fragmenting of Western philosophy's grand narrative, which inhibits the "I" from transmitting a fiction of the Enlightenment but frees him to arrange its fragments anew' (2018: 5). I find this a convincing proposition, but note its similarity to Blanchot's initial one. Cordingley further describes the mud as 'signifying *boue*' and writes of the genesis of 'new poetic relations from inherited sense' as the narrator delivers himself into 'new fictions of the present' (2018: 11).

Still other critics, inspired by Alain Badiou's claim that *How It Is* achieves an exit from solipsism and an encounter with the Other, situate Beckett within a framework of postmodern ethics based on the work of Emmanuel Levinas (Gibson 2006; Weller 2006; Smith 2008).[9] Patrick Bixby, drawing also on Leo Bersani's ideas about anti-communal modes of connectedness, calls *How It Is* a 'penetrating work of utopian writing' and the key to an 'ethico-politics' based on a 'fundamental reorientation of sociality' (2012: 243). Bersani's reading (as opposed to Badiou's) hews closer to the emotional tenor of Beckett's work, with its discomfort if not horror, in its suggestion that *How It Is* reveals the deep structure of 'reciprocal torment that originally made the social possible' (1993: 63). Bersani connects this to language, explaining that 'the torture consists in the fact that as soon as we begin to listen to voices we can't help hearing an injunction to speak' (62). For Bersani, Beckett's novel exposes the violence at the heart of sociality, implicitly critiquing the status quo (how it is) by laying bare the brutal mechanisms of subject formation. But resistance is possible: 'to be lost or disseminated in a space that cannot be dominated, and to register attentively *how relations are affected* by a shattered ego's displacements within that space' may open the way towards renegotiating relations between the human and its environment, 'a joyful self-dismissal giving birth to a new kind of power' (9).[10]

In an effort to reconcile the novel's evocations of non-agential materialism with its suggestions of radical possibilities for renegotiating signification, community and sociality, let us turn to Merleau-Ponty's theory of style, which founds the possibility of meaning (*sens*) on the body's orientation of space. A Merleau-Pontian optic emphasises that the mud of *How It Is* is not only the repository of tired, used-up forms (excrescence or waste) but also the mineral element from which forms arise in the first place. The 'primeval' mud never dries; it remains, in a sense, plastic. As a substrate on which style acts (passively), mud represents both language – its raw possibilities at our disposal – and the surrounding space that responds to a body's movement. A parallel between language and space suggests that the field of existing significations (language) might be revitalised by the body's work of style. Before discussing this, it is necessary to review briefly Merleau-Ponty's theory of style.

Style, for Merleau-Ponty, is not a personal flourish – still less affectation or artifice. It is, rather, an 'exigency of perception', a body's way of interacting with its (physical or linguistic) surroundings (IL 91).[11] Already in his first major work, *The Structure of Behavior* (1942), Merleau-Ponty describes the way an organism's vital needs structure its perception: 'each organism, in the presence of a given milieu, has its optimal conditions of activity and its proper manner of realizing equilibrium' (148). Then, in *Phenomenology of Perception*, style and expression come to characterise the perceptual exchange between an organism and its surroundings. But it isn't until 1952, in the essay 'Indirect Language and the Voices of Silence', that Merleau-Ponty extends his theory of the body-subject, laid out in the *Phenomenology*, to describe embodied agency explicitly in terms of style.

Merleau-Ponty's engagement with structuralism in the 1950s – particularly the work of Claude Levi-Strauss and Ferdinand de Saussure – resulted in two published essays and the abandoned manuscript *The Prose of the World*. The 'Indirect Language' essay was a chapter of *The Prose of the World* which Merleau-Ponty excerpted and revised for publication in *Les Temps modernes*.[12] Dedicated to Sartre, the essay responds to Sartre's 'What is Literature?' and to André Malraux's 'The Voices of Silence', and it performs the difficult theoretical task of welding elements of structuralism, which challenges the existence of a willing subject, to more humanist ideas about subjectivity derived from Husserl.[13] Merleau-Ponty theorises style as both passive (an effect of the body's perception) and active (an expressive variation on its surroundings), such that the body's manner of interacting within its environment becomes the foundation of meaning (*sens*).

Style, understood in a different sense, is what the young Beckett sought to escape, associating it as he did with the involuntary transmission of influence through language, and viewing it as a threat to self-determination and the possibility of novelty. S. E. Gontarski describes how Beckett, encumbered by his extensive education, 'launches an assault not only against a particular style, but against style itself' (2002: 12). In *Dream of Fair to Middling Women*, Belacqua extols the power of the French to write 'without style', inspiring critics to attribute Beckett's decision to write in French after the Second World War to a desire to rid himself of (English) style as well as the powerful literary influence of James Joyce.[14] In a letter to Hans Naumann, Beckett suggests that he writes in French out of 'the need to be ill equipped' (*le besoin d'etre mal armé*), famously punning on Mallarmé, who made impotence central to his poetic oeuvre (LB2 lxxxvix, 462). But Merleau-Ponty's conception of style as an effect of a body's being in the world (an 'exigency of perception') differs radically from what Beckett abhors; it resembles more the simplicity he courts as he wriggles free from the learned flourishes of high modernism. If style is what imperils agency for the early Beckett, it is, for Merleau-Ponty, the manifestation of a deeper, more passive kind of 'agency' and the engine of creative variation. It is style in this second sense that operates so forcefully in *How It Is* and in Beckett's later prose.

Merleau-Ponty begins his 'Indirect Language' essay by applying Saussure's idea of linguistic difference: 'To speak is not to put a word under each thought', he writes (IL 81). Rather, signs gather meaning in relation to other signs, such that language is 'more like a sort of being than a means' (80), signifying by a negotiation of its parts. When a child begins to speak, 'the whole of the spoken language [*la parole parlée*] surrounding the child snaps him up like a whirlwind, tempts him by its internal articulations' (78). The idea that signs draw their meaning from surrounding signs leads Merleau-Ponty to describe language not only as a 'sort of being' (*quelque chose comme un être*) (1960: 69) but also as a fabric (*tissu*) that supports folds: '[speech] is always only a fold in the immense fabric of language' (79) (*[la parole] n'est jamais qu'un pli dans l'immense tissu du parler*) (68). In his study of style in Nietzsche, Derrida similarly develops the idea that style draws meaning from its surroundings: 'the spurring style [. . .] derives its apotropaic power from the taut, resistant tissues, webs, sails and veils which are erected, furled and unfurled around it (1979: 41). This image of style gathering its force from taut, resistant tissues emphasises style's simultaneous difference from and belonging to its surroundings, and the erotic tone of the passage playfully suggests the creative, seminal power of style to expand the structure of which it is a part.

In 'Indirect Language and the Voices of Silence', Merleau-Ponty describes style as involuntary, automatic and at the same time expressive. Style is 'a mode of formulation that is just as recognizable for others and just as little visible to [the artist] as his silhouette or his everyday gestures' (IL 90). To describe style as a 'mode of formulation' implies its expressivity, but style is also 'born' without the artist's awareness (91) (*un style qui naît comme à son insu*) (87). It emerges 'in the hollows of the painter's perception as a painter; style is an exigency that has issued from that perception' (91). Style's paradox, the fact that it is at once an involuntary effect of the body *and* a legible expression of a body's rapport with the world, is related to its capacity to create meaning, or to 'found' signification.

Beckett also links creative activity to involuntary, often spastic processes of the body. While Merleau-Ponty describes style as '[living] within each painter like his heartbeat' (99), Beckett, in an earthier register, likens the urgency and lack of control bound up with artistic creation to orgasm and defecation. A pair of poems after a spell of writerly unproductivity is a 'double-yoked orgasm in months of aspermatic nights & days' (2009: 87; see also xciv). By far Beckett's preferred bodily metaphor for writing is defecation. In his introduction to Beckett's letters, Dan Gunn observes that 'Writing and shitting [. . .] share for Beckett an all-important intimacy, an urgency, a necessity even, just as they share a difficulty and delight in emission and transmission' (LB1 xcv). Even as the tendency towards scatological metaphors attenuates over Beckett's career, '[t]he correlation between the necessity of art and involuntary physical processes, especially the spasm of defecation or ejaculation, still occasionally appears' (LB2 lxvii). In 1949, Beckett writes to Georges Duthuit about finishing his play in progress, *En attendant Godot*: 'I must make sure the anus is clear' (LB2 117). Merleau-Ponty and Beckett both liken artistic expression to involuntary processes of the body, implying the work of a complex, 'passive agency'.

Much as style derives from the body, for Merleau-Ponty, it is not synonymous with it. He describes with derision childish painters (*peintre-enfants*)

> who have not learned their own gesture and who believe, under the pretext that a painter is no more than a hand, that it suffices to have a hand in order to paint. They extract petty wonders from their body

as a morose young man who observes his body with sufficient complacency can always find some little peculiarity in it to nourish his private religion. (IL 89)

Merleau-Ponty mocks those who confuse style with the body as morose adolescents, too inward-looking to sense that style, as an exchange between body and world, requires, above all, attention to the world. He praises, by contrast, 'the improvisation of the artist who has turned towards the world that he wants to express and (each word calling for another) has finally composed for himself an acquired voice that is more his than his original cry' (89). The fact that style must be honed, composed – even 'acquired' – complicates a view of it as strictly involuntary. Merleau-Ponty captures the paradox at the heart of style, its passive activity, by citing Malraux: 'How long it takes, Malraux writes, before a writer learns to speak with his own voice' (89).

Merleau-Ponty's 'Indirect Language' essay is, appropriately, animated by a tension between metaphors that characterise style as a natural or bodily process – a gravitational force, germination or a heartbeat – and those that describe it as expressive – a language, 'coherent deformation' or a consistent voice or vision. Merleau-Ponty describes a 'fecund' moment when style 'germinated at the surface of an artist's experience, and when an operant and latent meaning found the emblems which were going to disengage it and make it manageable for the artist and at the same time accessible to others' (90). Here, in the same sentence, style is at once a spontaneous process (germination) and a pictorial language of emblems that signify. Elsewhere in the essay, style is a 'system of equivalences' and a '"coherent deformation" by which [the painter] concentrates the still scattered meaning of his perception and makes it exist expressly' (91). These metaphorical crosscurrents reveal that it is style's passivity or inherence that makes possible its signifying activity.[15]

In Merleau-Ponty's thinking, style is what enables signification as well as the possibility of novelty.[16] 'There is meaning', Merleau-Ponty writes, 'when we submit the givens of the world to a "coherent deformation"' (91; translation modified). This is a more precise, refined version of a stronger claim Merleau-Ponty makes in *La Prose du monde*, where style is described as the foundation of signification (*le style est ce qui rend possible toute signification*, 81). Style as 'coherent deformation' locates its power to reorient existing structures in the consistency of its modulations, a consistency that derives from a body's perspective. No matter how radical or innovative it might appear to others, style for the artist seems to come directly from the world. He thinks he is merely 'spelling out nature at the moment he is recreating it' (IL 93) (*il croit épeler la nature au moment où il la recrée*) (1960: 90). It is in this way that style, inextricable from the perception of a particular body, rearticulates space and language to create meaning (*sens*).[17]

In the *Phenomenology*, Merleau-Ponty identifies two kinds of space: geometric (Cartesian) and corporeal. He describes geometric space as a second-order construction founded on a 'corporeal space' created by a body's interests and desires, a 'gearing of the subject into his world that is the origin of space' (262). Objective space – the space described by Descartes in *Dioptrics* with which Merleau-Ponty takes issue in *Eye and Mind* (1961) – is constructed upon a reserve of corporeal space that is always prior.[18] Merleau-Ponty describes 'a primordial spatiality of which objective space is but the envelope and which merges with the very being of the body' (PP 149). Initially, the body orders space in relation to its tasks, needs and desires: 'the mere presence of a living being transforms the physical world, makes "food" appear over here and a "hiding place" over there, and gives to "stimuli" a sense that they did not have' (PP 195). Space gains significance (*sens*) insofar as it affords the body possibilities. Merleau-Ponty calls the space around the human body, fashioned and made familiar by its movements, tastes and desires, its *habitus*, a concept developed by Pierre Bourdieu in the 1970s.[19]

Merleau-Ponty describes how the signifying activity of the body in space applies also to signification in language, for just as geometrical space is constructed upon corporeal space, so is ready-made language constructed upon an expressive or 'operant language'. In the *Phenomenology*, Merleau-Ponty distinguishes between 'a *speaking speech* [*parole parlante*] and a *spoken speech* [*parole parlée*]' (202; Ph 224). This distinction between conventional and expressive language is familiar. We find it, for instance, in Mallarmé, to whom Merleau-Ponty refers to support the idea that the empirical use of already established language should be distinguished from its creative use: 'Empirical language can only be the result of creative language' (IL 82). Merleau-Ponty describes ready-made language as 'the opportune recollection of a preestablished sign [. . .] It is, as Mallarmé said, the worn coin placed silently in my hand' (82). True speech, by contrast, 'frees the meaning captive in the thing', expressing what hasn't yet been put into words (82). Just as space is oriented by the presence of a body, so is language reconfigured by speech (*la parole*). In the *Phenomenology*, Merleau-Ponty describes 'the subject's taking up of a position in the world of his significations' (199) such that 'the phonetic gesture produces a certain structuring of experience, a certain modulation of existence, just as a behavior of my body invests [. . .] the objects that surround me with a certain signification' (199). In the same way that the body structures and organises its surroundings, expressive or operant language (*la parole parlante*) reconfigures existing language to accommodate what hasn't before been said.

Style emerges as an 'agent' of reconfiguration, restoring to already-established language and space an initial power of expression. Within empirical language, style emerges as gaps or expressive silences, an oblique meaning running between words or 'another way of shaking the linguistic or narrative apparatus in order to tear a new sound from it' (83). Style's power to modulate existing language (or space) derives from its inherence in what it modifies. Its gesture is always ambivalent: distinction and belonging. A certain way of speaking (*la parole*) may stretch the expressive possibilities of language (*la langue*), evolving it. In a 1951 lecture, 'On the Phenomenology of Language', Merleau-Ponty describes such speech (*la parole*) as the moment when a significative intention transforms 'the meaning of cultural instruments'. It 'gives us the illusion that it was contained in the already available significations, whereas by a sort of *ruse* it espoused them only in order to infuse them with new life' (1964b: 92).[20] Creative novelty, for Merleau-Ponty, is not a rupture but a variation spurred by the complex agency of style.

Merleau-Ponty's philosophical prose has been read as performing the style he describes. His distinctive lexicon of images – hollow (*creux*), wave (*vague*), wake (*sillage*), trace (*trace*), fabric (*tissu*), fold (*pli*), gap (*écart*), grafting (*enté*), flesh (*chair*) – builds a linguistic world cut out of language (*monde linguistique découpé de langage*), and his highly allusive writing borrows freely from Malraux, Sartre, Saussure, Hegel, Husserl and others, stitching them together (Simon and Castin 1998: 15–16).[21] Merleau-Ponty never mentions Beckett as exemplary of the indirect language he describes, and Beckett's most radical experiments did not occur until after Merleau-Ponty's death in 1961.[22] But style's way of recombining givens to produce new meaning certainly applies to Beckett, who, long before *How It Is*, availed himself of pastiche as a strategy for purging anxiety of influence, 'taking up' and recontextualising philosophical and literary traditions.[23] The early Beckett adopted the technique of 'grafting' his extensive reading into his own literary work, such that '[i]ntertext or assemblage or pastiche allowed Beckett to assault the idea of style and so (or thereby) develop his own', making possible his highly distinctive late minimalism (Gontarski 2012: 19–20). This is consistent with Anthony Cordingley's claim, on the basis of manuscript notebooks, that Beckett revised *Comment c'est* by paring away explicit references, '[stripping] it of information that might orient the discourse' (2018: 2). This strategy of recycling and recontextualising past learning resembles Merleau-Ponty's description of an artist 'advancing the line of the already opened furrow', without being able to say '(since the distinction has no meaning) what comes from him and what comes from things [. . .] or what he has taken from others as opposed to what is his own' (IL 95). Style plays on an interchangeability between writer and reader, listener and speaker: 'to the extent that I understand', Merleau-Ponty writes, 'I no longer know who is speaking and who is listening' (97). *How It Is*, more dramatically, joins speaker and listener, as the narrator/narrated enacts the complex agency of style.

Style 'disengages' only to rework the whole of which it remains a part. This aspect of Merleau-Ponty's theory of style anticipates his later notion of a 'flesh' that binds together physical space, material bodies and the tissue of language. I argue that a Merleau-Pontian reading reveals a material agency in Beckett's prose – innovation by 'taking up' and reworking 'what is'. But *How It Is* also explores the intimacy and violence associated with style, which Merleau-Ponty does not address. Style is born from our body's perspective, yet we impose our articulations on others as we speak and write, and we submit to others' styles in turn.

In *How It Is*, aberrant syntax unstitches ready-made meanings, returning language to an expressive, malleable state. As Merleau-Ponty writes: 'it is in the name of a *truer* relation between things that their ordinary ties are broken' (IL 93). The text makes its own articulations and teaches us where they lie. Word-groups become familiar through repetition, emerging as units of meaning that enable us to orient within the text. As we read, we come to recognise markers in the prose-scape that enable us to make the correct cut. As Steven Connor observes, 'the work of the reader becomes progressively easier, as the text starts to organize itself from the inside out through patterns of repetition and redundancy' (2014b: 279). A line from early in the novel may serve as an example: 'Voice once without quaqua on all sides then in me when the panting stops tell me again finish telling me invocation' (H 7). We don't know at first how to group these words. But as we read on, we start to recognise groupings of words as units of meaning, such as 'voice once without' and 'quaqua on all sides'. We make the following cuts: '[Voice once without] [quaqua on all sides] [then in me when the panting stops] [tell me again] [finish telling me] [invocation]'. Throughout the novel we are aware at least subliminally of our learning process, as the text teaches us how to read it by repeating its refrains. We witness the emergence of signification in language that is both malleable and material, and which 'means' not at the behest of a speaker or author, but by a self-articulating process of repetition and variation.

But any poststructuralist attribution of agency to a system (language) rather than to a subject is complicated by the novel's insistence on the body's role in shaping language. The sentence as unit of meaning is rejected in favour of fragments or 'strophes', which Beckett added late, in the fourth full-length version of the *Comment c'est* manuscript (Magessa O'Reilly 2001: xv). Edouard Magessa O'Reilly calls these 'narrative units of breath', places where a speaker might pause for air. He notes that the strophes, despite their separation on the page, don't maintain their discreteness as ideas extend across them (Magessa O'Reilly 2009: ix). In other ways, too, the novel's language is organised less according to the rational logic of the sentence and more according to bodily rhythms: 'in me a murmur scarce a breath then from mouth to mud brief kiss brush of lips faint kiss' (H 136). The prose rushes on, careering comma-less towards its end, a 'panting without pause the animal in want of air' (136). In the passage above, lips direct speech to the mud: 'murmur to the mud' 'mouth to mud' (136) (the consonance is more marked in the French text: 'la bouche à la boue bref baiser du bout des lèvres faible baiser' (1961: 211)). This image of language directing itself to the mud, kiss-like, links the body's interaction with its material environment to signification. Steven Connor, meditating on the absence of punctuation in *How It Is*, describes how the narrator/narrated struggles to set up partitions in the 'indivisible, assimilative mud' (2014b: 278). Connor connects this partitioning work to bodily articulation (at the joints), making explicit the text's insistent, provocative conflation of the body and language. 'In place of punctuation' Connor writes, 'we have arthropoetics, the articulation of joints' (2014b: 279). Reminding us that punctuation terms derive from Greek words for body parts (*colon* means limb), Connor suggests that in *How It Is* '[t]he body becomes the means of keeping one's place [. . .]' (2014b: 279). That is, the body's patterns and strategies of articulation are mapped onto language in order to 'make sense', as the text 'generate[s] its partita endogenously from the subject matter at its disposal' (2014b: 279).[24] Other passages in the novel are studded with propulsive words like 'still' (*encore*) or 'yes' (*oui*): 'yes so that was true yes the panting yes the murmur yes in the dark yes in the mud yes to the mud yes' (145). In a likely parody of Molly Bloom's soliloquy in *Ulysses* (Friedman 2017: 44), this passage uses phatic repetition to syncopate its prose, calling attention to how emotion and breath (which are both bodily) can create meaningful 'cuts' in language. The novel dramatises the physical body as crucial to the work of style.

Style, for Merleau-Ponty, is both inherited and honed – a 'mode' of expression based on the body's inherence within its material environment, its 'take' (*prise*) on the world. This version of agency, both enabled and limited by the materiality of the body, finds expression in *How It Is* through the complex ontology of the narrator's voice, as well as through the text's insistence on the physicality of language. The narrator/narrated ingests and secretes language, much as he ingests and secretes his environment (mud). Cordingley reads *How It Is* as mocking the Ancient Greek tradition of broad cultural learning, *paideia*, excavating buried references to Pythagoras, Ancient Stoicism, Platonism etc. by a subject 'worn down by the "humanities"' (2018: 140). Cordingley's 'worn down' subject both 'relinquishes the desire to remake the tradition within which it has been formed' *and* '[enacts] Beckett's later vision of consciousness as the incessant patterning of a culture's *ancient voice*' (2018: 140). Patterning an 'ancient' or inherited voice (the French '*ancien*' is more muted) – taking it apart, rendering it expressive – may indeed remake tradition, casting novelty as a 'taking up' (*reprise*) in Merleau-Ponty's sense. But what conception of agency underwrites this 'repatterning' of an inherited voice, especially if the worn-down subject is too exhausted to carry it out himself? In *How It Is*, neither language nor movement can be said to be willed. In part three, the procession of bodies advances 'in jerks or spasms like shit in the guts' (124). Similarly, the narrator/narrated is endowed with a voice – 'the voice of us all' – to which he listens and repeats. Elizabeth Barry has written persuasively about the grammatical 'middle voice' that situates itself between active and passive. She argues that Beckett's use of this tense questions agency as an expression of will and emphasises the importance of 'being seen' in order to 'be', a phenomenological theme we find elsewhere in Beckett's work, for example in *Film* (1965). Barry notes that the middle voice is often used to describe bodily experience in Beckett, and that its grammar is also that of 'senseless' material processes in nature. Beckett's characters 'watch from the sidelines as their bodies undergo experiences that they cannot control or even understand as their own' (2008: 117).

Writing explicitly about *How It Is*, Ulrika Maude similarly evokes the body to challenge the idea of agency as an expression of will. She interprets the novel's many references to viscera and its allusions to behaviourism (Pavlov, Bechterev, Watson) to suggest that 'everything over which we have agential control is premised on "deeper vegetative" or physiological processes' (2020: 261). For Maude, *How It Is* demonstrates the extent to which our intentional actions are made possible by involuntary processes of the body. This challenges a voluntarist idea of the subject that would devalue the body or treat it as a hindrance. But it isn't clear from Maude's reading how the body's materiality might affect its environment, for to the extent that the 'human' is associated with will and reason, the narrator/narrated's association with the 'stupid' or automatic functioning of the viscera suggests his affinity with the nonhuman, with dumb matter. Maude shows how the novel's allusions to the non-agential activity of the internal organs give us 'a creature whose subjectivity appears in a much starker, minimally-agential hue' (2020: 269). I'm suggesting here that a loss of voluntarist agency does not necessarily entail the loss of agency altogether. Merleau-Ponty's theory of style suggests the possibility of material agency, whereby the narrator/narrated, though he lacks agency in the voluntarist sense, participates in the shaping of his language-environment by his reception and transmission of the 'ancient voice'.

The novel's opening lines announce it as a citation or imperfect regurgitation – 'I say it as I hear it' – of a voice that is within the narrator/narrated yet not his. The refrain, 'scraps of an ancient voice in me not mine', indicates how we as speaking subjects inherit a language not of our making and perpetuate the social order through the act of speech. The idea that one's voice is one's own is further challenged by the rotation of roles and contagion of voices in the novel. Even as he extorts speech from Pim, the narrator/narrated recognises that he has been and will again be in the position of victim – Pim's position – and that a torturer, Bem or Bom, will elicit from him speech and memory: 'Bem come to cleave to me where I lay abandoned to give me a name his name to give me a life make me talk of a life said to have been mine' (109). The narrator/narrated toys with using Bem to name his torturer before part one and Bom to name his torturer to come, but admits they are one and the same (113). Following the narrator/narrated, 'let us say Bom, it's preferable' (114). When the narrator/narrated speaks of his life for Bom, Pim will assume the role of torturer, though he will torture another. In part three we find an infinite chain of bodies alternating between torturing and suffering, abandoning and being abandoned (112). The voice with its fables travels from victim to torturer, so that the narrator/narrated is influenced by Pim's voice: 'I talk like him I do we're talking of me like him little blurts midget grammar' (76) (*petits paquets grammaire d'oiseau*) (120). Just as the narrator/narrated takes on Pim's voice, he imagines that Bom will talk like him:

> I talk like him Bom will talk like me only one kind of talk here one after another the voice said so it talks like us the voice of us all quaqua on all sides then in us when the panting stops bits and scraps that's where we get it our old talk each his own way each his needs the best he can it stops ours starts starts again no knowing. (76)

Not only is there increased legibility and influence among voices – at first Pim was said to speak like a foreigner; 'I can't make out the words the mud muffles or perhaps a foreign tongue' (56) – but each voice is a variation on 'the voice of us all' (*la nôtre à tous*, 120). The 'voice of us all' is 'where we get our old talk', though 'each his own way' (76). The voice is 'ours' (*la nôtre*) but not known. The idea that we inherit a language we do not fully master is expressed often in Beckett, as in *Endgame*: 'I use the words you taught me. If they don't mean anything any more, teach me others' (51). But in *How It Is*, the transmission of language is bodily, words presented as both cause and consequence of bodily movement: 'brief movements of the lower face no sound it's my words cause them it's they cause my words it's one or the other I'll fall asleep within humanity again just barely' (44). The reception and reproduction of language makes the narrator/narrated 'fall asleep within humanity', or participate unconsciously in the transmission of culture. The voice in *How It Is*, inherited and honed ('each his own way each his needs'), modifies what has come before.

This complex agency of the voice in *How It Is* performs the double gesture of distinction and belonging that characterises Merleau-Ponty's view of style. Voices and bodies in the novel inhere within and detach provisionally from a common element: language's materiality literalised as mud. The 'invocation' of the muse at the start of the novel evokes the dependence of the poet on forces outside her, situating *How It Is* parodically within a literary tradition – of epic 'travestied' (Porter Abbott 1996: 101) – and suggesting a porosity between inside and outside. The voice in the novel is 'without' (*dehors*) and then *in* the narrator/narrated, as if to suggest that it is only by swallowing voices in the form of received language that we say anything at all. Cordingley's work on the novel's sources shows that the voice is not merely that of the story's other (the voice of Pim) but also the residue of learning in the humanist tradition, fragmented and recombined in a bricolage of style (2018: 10).

The idea that the speaker-subject is more medium or conduit than producer of language is discernible in any number of Beckett's works. In *Texts for Nothing*, language is presented as more powerful than the speaker: 'I seem to speak, it is not I' (1995: 291). But in *How It Is*, we find the speaker-subject imbricated in his material environment. As the narrator/narrated murmurs to the mud, the image of the sullen gurglers from Dante's *Inferno* Canto 7 is evoked, fighting in the mud or sunk beneath it, their laments bubbling to the surface. Daniella Caselli discusses the role of Canto 7 in *Comment c'est*'s 'painfully detailed exploration of the materiality of speech' (2005: 156). She describes the frustration of 'extorting' meaning from the materiality of the language mud (156), to say nothing of the materiality of Pim's body. Language and the body are portrayed as part of a material element from which they are forever negotiating their difference, their separation as style, given the always-imminent possibility of being swallowed up by the mud: 'signal for the mud to open under me and then close again' (39). Similarly, flashes of memory, bright images from life above in the light, gleam for a moment and are gone, returning to the dark. The piercing brevity of these images evokes the fragility of memory against a background of oblivion and perhaps also the passage of human life as a temporary emergence from unfeeling materiality – as Merleau-Ponty puts it, a 'fold' in being 'that was made and that can be unmade' (PP 223) ('un creux, un pli qui s'est fait et qui peut se défaire') (160). The novel's image of bodies half-submerged in mud suggests forms being shaped from an elemental substance – mud, dust or clay – revealing and re-enacting how meaning or signification may arise from the body's entanglement with its environment.

The body's belonging to its material environment enables reciprocity and exchange between bodies, much as part three's description of bodies joined 'one and all from the unthinkable first to the no less unthinkable last glued together in a vast imbrication of flesh without breach or fissure' (140) makes Merleau-Ponty's harmonious idea of the 'flesh of the world' look grim. As the narrator/narrated is torturing Pim, extorting speech, he bends his ear to Pim's mouth to create 'a slight overlapping of flesh' (140). This 'overlapping' of flesh underscores, by its reference to common materiality, the contingency, if not interchangeability, of their positions: 'linked thus bodily together each one of us is at the same time Bom and Pim tormentor and tormented pedant and dunce wooer and wooed speechless and reafflicted with speech' (140).[25] For Merleau-Ponty, belonging to a common flesh affords a reversibility between subject and object positions, a reversibility that conditions subjectivity. The 'overlapping' flesh in *How It Is* similarly founds a reversibility that enables bodies to alternate between the roles of tormentor and tormented.

The (ex)changing of positions in the novel is regulated by a force that emerges under the ominous heading of 'justice'. The narrator knows that the torture he visits upon Pim will be visited upon him in (re)turn, not by Pim but by Bom. Part three imagines an infinite community of Boms and Pims kept in movement by a 'justice' that ensures the cycle of torture and victimhood will have no end. Justice keeps the wheel turning because, if the procession were stopped, 'the traveler to whom life owes a victim will never have another and never another tormentor the abandoned to whom life owes one' (141). Jean-Michel Rabaté describes how Dante's *contrapasso* inflects Beckett's disturbing description of a 'justice' indistinguishable from Injustice (2016: 56). Rabaté argues that the allegory of human relations as an attempt to even scores echoes Adorno's reading of Kantian reason in *Dialectic of Enlightenment*: 'For Adorno, Kantian reason leads to the calculating rationality of a totalitarian order. Its counterpart is the systematic mechanization of pleasures in Sade's perverse utopias' (2016: 114). This idea would have had particular resonance in postwar Europe; rationalism taken to an extreme becomes so deferential to its own laws that it not only ignores the human but perpetuates human suffering to serve these laws. For Adorno, Sade's ritualisation of suffering pushes Kantian reason to its logical, horrific extreme. Jonathan Boulter reads the novel's 'justice' alternatively as a melancholic response to loss, including 'loss of species'. As unthinking repetition, the movement of 'justice' marks the subject's unwillingness to overcome this loss (Boulter 2012: 190). Different as they are, both readings find in the novel's 'justice' an evacuation of agency, implying, for different reasons, the complicity of the human in its loss.

'Justice', a rational force that directs the movement of bodies, operates in tension with an alternative cosmology in the novel. Bodies 'glued together in a vast imbrication of flesh without breach or fissure' most likely derives from Beckett's reading of the ancient Stoics, for whom there existed 'one material and cosmic body' (Cordingley 2018: 99). It would seem that agency is compromised just as much by subsumption in a 'world body' as by submission to a rational system. Beckett's pastiche of Aristotelian rationalism and Stoic materialism – which Cordingley argues are pitted against each other in the novel – reveals contradictions in both worldviews (2018: 76–109). But if we allow ourselves to read the flesh in Merleau-Ponty's sense – later applied by Christian phenomenologists to union in the body of Christ – we find that it supports the possibility of recognition, a possibility imperilled by the threat of forgetting. The narrator/narrated pauses his torture of Pim to speculate about what Pim is thinking: 'but this man is no fool he must say to himself I would if I were he what does he require of me or better still what is required of me that I am tormented thus' (63). Empathy in this instance seems perversely instrumental, used to boost the efficacy of the narrator's torture teaching. Pim learns the 'basic simuli', singing when clawed in the armpit, speaking when he feels a blade in his arse, falling silent when thumped on the head and so on. He also responds to volume controls: pestle in the kidney for louder, a finger in the arse for softer. It is only later, presumably looking back on his torture of Pim, that the narrator/narrated seems to regret a lost opportunity: 'Pim to speak he turns his head tears in the eyes my tears my eyes if I had any it was then I needed them not now' (75). 'Tears in the eyes' seems to apply first to Pim's body, then to the body of the 'I', establishing rapport by way of embodiment. The narrator questions whether he had eyes at the moment he was torturer, whether he saw what he was doing. Yet this wish that he had recognised Pim's humanity when it mattered suggests that fellow feeling comes too late for the narrator/narrated. Regret fixes him to that earlier moment: 'his mouth to my ear our narrow shoulders overlapping his hairs in mine human breath shrill murmur if too loud finger in arse I'll stir no more from this place I'm still there' (75). The narrator fixes himself in time in part so as not to forget. For, according to the rules of the novel's cosmology, 'one knows one's tormentor only as long as it takes to suffer him and one's victim only as long as it takes to enjoy him if as long' (121). The mud, then, is like the river Lethe; all is forgotten in its materiality.

The tension between memory (linked with meaning) and forgetting (unfeeling materiality) also animates one of the strangest and most unsettling aspects of the torture episode: the narrator/narrated's tenderness for Pim. He wonders 'if Pim loved me a little yes or no if I loved him a little in the dark the mud in spite of all a little affection' (74). The narrator/narrator then issues a surprising imperative: 'find someone at last someone find you at last live together glued together love each other a little love a little without being loved be loved a little without loving answer that leave it vague leave it dark' (74). However parodic this exhortation might be ('live together glued together'), it seems to suggest an alternative to 'justice' insofar as it flaunts a rationalist ideal of fairness ('love a little without being loved be loved a little without loving'). An association between 'love' and what is vague and dark also contrasts with the brutal exposure of eliciting speech from Pim and with the bright lamps held up by Krim and Kram, fantasised witness and scribe, who take note of the narrator/narrated's doings.[26] Love is presented in opposition to an automatic 'justice', its vagueness an embodied respite from the harsh light of rationalised sociality.

But the novel's horrific vision of 'Stoic love' sits in uneasy tension with a material agency derived from the body's movements and perspective:

> no other goal than the next mortal cleave to him give him a name train him up bloody him all over with Roman capitals gorge on his fables unite for life in stoic love to the last shrimp and a little longer. (62)

The novel parodies philosophical positions involving 'submission' to a higher order. 'No other goal' seems to mock Aristotelian teleology – 'a rationalist cosmic vision unfurling towards its final ends' – as much as it does a Stoic acceptance of one's humility in the face of a materialist eternity (Cordingley 2018: 104; 33). But the Ancient Stoic path to virtue deserves slightly more attention here, a path that Diogenes Laërtius describes as living in accordance with nature, where 'nature' is at once a human and a cosmic order. Cordingley describes how Beckett parodies this logic, insofar as the 'I' hopes to learn the natural order through will-less listening ('I say it as I hear it natural order') (Beckett as qtd in Cordingley 2018: 115). Cordingley demonstrates Beckett's mixed allegiance to the Stoic 'world body'. Even though the I's 'immobility and tongue in the mud may suggest a final triumph of his Stoicism', his 'withdrawal into the self and liberation from will [. . .] will never manifest a divine natural order of *Logos*' (2018: 120). The will-less submission of the Stoics to a higher body is *not* ultimately embodied agency, which manifests itself much more violently in Beckett, as 'cuts' in the flesh. Meaning or signification, in Beckett, is made through a torturous process of differentiation.

The horror of sociality in the novel reaches its apex in the same moment that language and the body are coupled in yet a different way, as the narrator uses his nails to carve writing onto Pim's back, 'intact at the outset' (70): 'from left to right and top to bottom as in our civilization I carve my Roman capitals/arduous beginnings then less he is no fool merely slow in the end he understands almost all' (70). This writing on the body is similar to that in Kafka's 1914 story 'In the Penal Colony', in which a prisoner's sentence is written over and over on his body by a harrow in a slow process of execution. The idea is that the criminal will come to understand in the moment just before his death the meaning of his sentence (the double meaning of sentence as condemnation and semantic unit cannot have escaped Beckett). The inscriptions on Pim's back are names, YOU PIM, directives to speak about YOUR LIFE ABOVE or YOUR LIFE HERE BEFORE ME and disturbing couplings of love and violence: DO YOU LOVE ME CUNT. This writing on the body, situated within a torturous pedagogical setting that calls itself 'civilization', not only underscores the necessity of the body to the work of style but demonstrates the closeness between style, desire and violence. *How It Is* interrogates the work of style, which, at the most fundamental level, demonstrates how relations and meanings arise. Style, as the passive activity of partitioning surroundings, is far sharper and more violent here than according to Merleau-Ponty's idea of it as a bricolage of other styles, harmoniously reassembled in each iteration, repetition with a difference.

In Beckett, the transmission of language, Enlightenment values, culture and learning entails violence, and we find in *How It Is* a critique of social institutions that perpetuate violence and subordination of others in the name of progress. I have suggested that *How It Is* goes deeper even than this critique of Enlightenment values; it interrogates the work of signification as an effect of style, a highly creative, bodily process which, if understood in its radical sense, implicates us (as bodies) within our material environment and within language, which, according to Merleau-Ponty, can be reconfigured like physical space. In other words, style reveals the extent to which culture and sociality are founded by means of articulations within a substance that encompasses the human and the nonhuman, and that our initiation as speaking subjects is founded on our material belonging to our environment. This environment is not just the mud of the earth but systems of language and culture that, having rigidified, are softened in the novel, so as to open possibilities for renewal.

Notes

1. Didier Anzieu discusses the prevalence of mud in Beckett, suggesting its role in an allegory of creation (1999: 12). Mud across Beckett's oeuvre is also catalogued by Leland de la Durantaye (2016: 93–7).
2. I refer to Edith Fournier's English translation in *The Complete Short Prose, 1929–1989*, 165.
3. Beckett describes the 'narrator/narrated' in a letter to Hugh Kenner dated 8 April 1960 (1973: 94–5).
4. Rabaté also notes Beckett's allusion to *Finnegans Wake*, where Shem the Penman pens his text with ink made from his own excrement, scrawling the lines on his own body (2016: 55).

5. Roger Casement was an Irishman who, on consular missions to Africa and South America, documented the atrocities of colonial violence in private diaries, which also included accounts of his sexual encounters with native men. Casement was executed by the British for his involvement in the 1916 Easter Rising and the diaries were used against him. Beckett read the diaries in 1959, as he was beginning work on *How It Is* (Bixby 2012).
6. This parallels Julia Kristeva's description of the cause of the abject as 'what disturbs identity [. . .] What does not respect borders, positions, rules' (Kristeva 1982: 4 as qtd in Maude 2009: 100). It should be noted that Maude's discussion of the abject focuses less on *How It Is* than on *The Unnamable*. She notes that the body's resistance to preconceived categories both conditions sovereign subjectivity and threatens its autonomy (2009: 98–103).
7. In an essay published the same year in *The Edinburgh Companion to Samuel Beckett and the Arts*, Connor observes a 'partitioning' within *How it Is* connected to the segmentation and articulation of the body. I discuss this essay later in the chapter (Connor 2014b: 278–9).
8. Elsewhere, with reference to *Not I* (1972) and its linguistic automatism, Maude argues that language, often 'conceived as the expression of agency and intentionality', reveals itself as an 'intention-less and agent-less performance, an uncanny absence and evacuation of the self' (2014: 51).
9. For Levinas, ethical action is grounded in the recognition of an absolute Other, 'who issues an *a priori* demand for responsibility that structures all sociality' (Bixby 2012: 245).
10. Paul Stewart argues that the absence of sexual pleasure in Beckett's fiction casts doubt upon Bersani's idea that the 'unrelated subject' can usher in new forms of relation, sexual and social (2014: 69). For Stewart, Beckett's characters remain more obstinately, uncomfortably in non-relation, refusing both the neatness of norms governing sexual activity and the impulse to reconstruct fixed social relations in their wake.
11. Linda Singer, arguing for style's centrality to Merleau-Ponty's philosophy, writes that 'style provides a way of characterizing the kind of significance that perception reveals, and a way of describing the qualitative impact of the phenomenon' (1993: 234).
12. This was Merleau-Ponty's last essay published in *Les Temps modernes*, prior to his break with Sartre and his resignation from the journal. 'Le langage indirect et les voix du silence' and 'Sur la phénoménologie du langage', were reprinted in *Signes* (1960). *La Prose du monde* (1969) was edited and published by Claude Lefort after Merleau-Ponty's death.

13. For further discussion of the tension between structuralism and phenomenology in Merleau-Ponty's work, see James Schmidt's *Maurice Merleau-Ponty: Between Phenomenology and Structuralism* (1984).
14. Ackerley and Gontarski describe Beckett's linguistic expatriatism as an attempt 'to recast his literary lineage, to father himself, as it were, by sloughing off the heritage of an English style' (2004: 207). I discuss Beckett's linguistic expatriatism in relation to his mistrust of style in greater depth in elsewhere (Dennis 2019).
15. Donald Landes identifies a 'paradox of expression' that animates Merleau-Ponty's entire oeuvre, '[from] his initial understanding of the paradox of expression as action between pure repetition and pure creation, to his deepening of this structure to the ontological register by which expressive gestures create and sustain structures that paradoxically transcend them and solicit them' (2013: 4).
16. Hugh Silverman describes style in Merleau-Ponty as '[announcing] the arrival of the "new"'; 'Style is the tendency toward signification in the lived language' (1980: 139).
17. Linda Singer describes how style's expressive potential requires its embodied point of view: '[Style] functions as the qualitative correlate of the perspectivalism that is at the heart of Merleau-Ponty's ontology. Style is the affective or modal consequence of being an embodied point of view.' She adds that '[t]he body image has the coherence of a style because, like the work of art, it is the expressive vehicle of a point of view' (1993: 240).
18. In *Eye and Mind*, Merleau-Ponty writes: 'Space is not what it was in the *Dioptrics*, a network of relations between objects such as would be seen by a third party [. . .] looking over it and reconstructing it from outside. It is, rather, a space reckoned starting from me as the null point or degree zero of spatiality' (138).
19. The term *habitus* comes from Aristotle and was adapted by Marcel Mauss in 'Techniques du Corps' (1934). There is not space here to do full justice to Bourdieu's later development of the term, but it is worth noting that he describes taste and style in terms of their paradoxical belonging *to* and difference *from* a structure. Taylor Carman and Mark B. N. Hansen describe Bourdieu's 'enormous debt to Merleau-Ponty's account of the ubiquity of style in human behavior and cultural practices' (Carman and Hansen 2005: 24).
20. The passage plays on the distinction between *langue* and *parole*: 'La parole en tant que distincte de la langue, est ce moment où l'intention significative encore muette et tout en acte s'avère capable de s'incorporer à la culture, la mienne et celle d'autrui, de me former et de le former en transformant le sens des instruments culturels. Elle devient «disponible» à son tour parce qu'elle nous donne après coup l'illusion qu'elle était contenue dans les significations déjà

disponibles, alors que, par une sorte de ruse, elle ne les a épousées que pour leur infuser une nouvelle vie' (1960: 149).
21. Simon and Castin also point out a complex use of internal focalisation, whereby Merleau-Ponty adopts the point of view of Sartre or Husserl in such an involved way that a reader forgets that Merleau-Ponty is merely retracing the philosophical views with and against which he is working (1998: 15–16).
22. In *La Prose du monde*, Merleau-Ponty focuses on five 'perceptions littéraires': Montaigne, Stendhal, Proust, Breton, Artaud.
23. Beckett shares this strategy with Proust, who expresses anxiety of influence in his essay on Flaubert's style, where style is an involuntary inheritance that must be 'purged' through deliberate imitation and parody. Proust describes 'l'intoxication flaubertienne' and 'la vertu purgative, exorcisant du pastiche'. He advocates a 'pastiche volontaire pour pouvoir, après cela, redevenir original, ne pas faire toute sa vie du pastiche involontaire' (1920: 83).
24. Connor writes: 'in the absence of any means of external punctuation, the text seems driven to generate its partita endogenously from the subject matter at its disposal, such as the division into the three temporal dispensations, before Pim, with Pim and after Pim, and in the composition of the body through its segmented parts, the cardinal points of legs, hands, knees, mouth. In place of punctuation we have arthropoetics, the articulation of joints: "I turn on my side which side the left it's preferable throw the right hand forward bend the right knee these joints are working the fingers sink the toes sink in the slime these are my holds too strong slime is too strong holds is too strong I say it as I hear it" (Beckett 1977: 21). Atomisation becomes anatomy' (2014b: 279).
25. In French, 'reafflicted with speech' is 'théâtre d'une parole retrouvée' (1961: 127). A theatre of rediscovered speech emphasises the 'taking up' of a given language – an active-passive repetition – where 'reafflicted' connotes pain and passivity.
26. In French, 'braquées sur le dedans' is also used to describe the lamps of 'they' who observe Worm in *L'Innommable*. The phrase suggests that the lights held by the witness and scribe are intrusive.

CHAPTER 6

Compulsive Bodies, Creative Bodies: *Quad* and Agency

Beckett's sustained interrogation of agency in language in the novels of the trilogy and *How It Is* gave way to a new focus: non-linguistic modes of depicting the rapport between an embodied subject and its environment. We find Winnie embedded in a mound of earth (1961) and heads intoning from urns in *Play* (1963) – among the vivid and arresting scenes in Beckett's image repertoire. At the same time, 'closed spaces' of measured dimensions emerge in Beckett's prose, particularly in the *faux départs* that culminate in *All Strange Away* (1963–4) and *Imagine Dead Imagine* (1965): 'Five foot square, six high' (169); 'Diameter three feet, three feet from ground to summit of the vault' (182).[1] Interest in closed, limited spaces also coincides with Beckett's forays into new media. *Film*, Beckett's only film, and *Eh Joe*, his first play for television, date from 1965.[2] Television, in particular, affords Beckett a new way of exploring the body in space.

Wedged in earth, crawling in mud, roaming in cylinders and peering out of ash bins, urns, jars and ditches, Beckett's personae seem to ask what possibilities exist for acting within a world in which we are inextricably embedded. Like the severed mouth in *Not I* (1972), Beckettian bodies and their parts *go on* speaking or moving in the absence of recognisable signs of subjective intention, self-mastery or rational control. *Quad* (1981), Beckett's 'ballet' for television, shows how the physical body, by means of repetition of the sort found in certain rites and rituals, may disturb the comfortable opposition between compulsion and creative invention. Bodies in *Quad* appear evacuated of conscious intent, driven to perpetuate a pattern. The liveliness of this pattern, in which bodies participate compulsively, suggests an expansion of agency (the socio-culturally mediated capacity to act; Ahearn 2001: 112). Rather than assimilating agency to conscious intention (and restricting it to the strictly human), *Quad* demonstrates how a compulsive repetition of bodily movement, despite its uncomfortable closeness to addiction, may harness a loss of individual control that demands a more capacious understanding of agency, human and otherwise.

As we've seen, in place of an esoteric rational consciousness of the sort parodied in *Endgame*, Merleau-Ponty's body-subject acts only in collaboration with its environment, such that 'meaning' is less the decree of a willing subject than an effect of a physical body's interaction with its material surroundings. Agency, then, comes into being as a collaboration between bodies and their situational environments.[3] As Diana Coole has shown, Merleau-Ponty's thought has been important to the development of twenty-first century 'new materialisms', which situate the human within a 'natural environment whose material forces themselves manifest certain agentic capacities', extending agency beyond the human (2010: 10). If we include technology and abstract systems among the self-organising matter that manifests 'agentic capacity', we might read *Quad* as unsettling the classical divide between the human as active and agential on the one hand and matter as passive and inert on the other, expanding received ideas about what agency is and how it operates.

Insofar as this questioning of the Enlightenment subject – a subject endowed with interiority and the power to do and act volitionally – participates in a broader interrogation of subjecthood in twentieth-century French thought (carried out in the work of Roland Barthes, Georges Bataille, Michel Foucault, Gilles Deleuze, Jacques Derrida, Maurice Blanchot and others), Beckett and Merleau-Ponty are of their time also.[4] It is in a mid-twentieth-century context, too, that Beckett's bodies, often driven by mechanical movements, often confined, ask insistently, by means of different image-configurations, how possibilities for agency might be expanded by recourse to its opposite, a passivity that can look like compulsion: bodies speaking or moving, driven by forces outside their conscious intention or control.

Jean-Luc Nancy calls the twentieth century's critique of subjectivity 'one of the great motifs of contemporary philosophical work in France' for its 'deconstruction of interiority, of self-presence, of consciousness, of mastery' (Cadava et al. 1991: 4). But if a subject emerges *within* social structures (such as language), patterns of interaction or implicit or explicit codes that regulate our living together, then its possibilities for acting back on the environment that shaped it – its possibilities for agency – must be rethought. Poststructuralist theory poses this problem of agency as a problem of language. Foucault's 'What is an Author' famously asks: 'What matter who's speaking, someone said, what matter who's speaking?' (1977: 115). In reply, the text suggests that even though we are brought into being by 'structures' (patterns, such as language, that organise human relationships), we still bear responsibility for our words. But where does this responsibility lie? Who is the 'we' to whom responsibility might attach itself? As a reader of Beckett, Foucault is sensitive to the problem of who is speaking, where boundaries between subject and object, world and human, have been vertiginously unsettled.

It is fitting that Foucault takes his phrase, 'What matter who's speaking, someone said what matter who's speaking', from *Texts for Nothing* (1950–2) (CP 109). Anxieties about the impossibility of acting meaningfully within one's environment (or the impossibility of novelty against the texture of repetition and sameness) recur throughout Beckett's canon. The opening of *Murphy* – 'The sun shone, having no alternative, on the nothing new' (1) – segues into questions of freedom and determinism in *Molloy*: 'Can it be we are not free? It might be worth looking into' (51) and develops into an eternal repetition of the same in *Worstward Ho*: 'All of old. Nothing else ever' (91).[5] Similar lines throughout the corpus seem to suggest that Beckett's work bravely confronts the frightening possibility of a loss of the human power to act. Representations of embodiment in Beckett would seem to support this idea, as bodies are often embedded, quite literally, in earth or in objects. According to the stage directions for *Play*, for instance, the speakers have 'faces so lost to age and aspect as to seem almost part of urns' (2006: 307). The stage directions further describe humans gripped by (lightly anthropomorphised) objects, rather than vice versa: '*From each [urn] a head protrudes, the neck held fast in the urn's mouth*' (307). And yet if we shift our focus from the diminished possibilities for movement on the part of Beckett's personae to their imbrication within objects and environments, a different story emerges. Rather than dramatising the impossibility of action, Beckett's work sketches plans for a more ecological, posthuman 'agency', a more collaborative mode of 'acting' that eases the divide not only between active and passive but between the human, the world of inanimate objects and the earth.[6]

Quad, one of the few non-verbal works in Beckett's canon, rivets attention on the physical body's interaction with its surrounding space. *Quad* is the fourth of five television plays Beckett composed between 1965 and 1982, and it is typically read, along with its companion piece, *Quad II*, as dramatising a lack of agency. In 2007, the Centre Pompidou in Paris held an exhibit devoted to Beckett that featured the colourful *Quad*. The exhibition literature attributed to *Quad* a nihilism that would come to typify descriptions of Beckett's late style: a resignation to passivity, reduction to bare essentials and a move towards abstraction. The curators focused on reduction and abstraction probably to suggest rapprochement between Beckett's late work and minimalism in the visual arts (the work of Sol LeWitt, Robert Ryman and Richard Serra), yet their reading echoes a more general sense that *Quad* is a grim testimony to human powerlessness and passivity.[7]

While these two short television plays do upset a familiar version of subjective agency, they also explore the manner in which passivity and repetition can exert positive pressure on a system or structure. In *Bodies That Matter*, Judith Butler puts the matter succinctly – and in terms of language – when she writes: 'The force of repetition in language may be the paradoxical condition by which a certain agency – not linked to a fiction of the ego as master of circumstance – is derived from the *impossibility* of choice' (1993: 84). Butler writes this in the context of a discussion about the compulsion to repeat an injury. One doesn't necessarily want to repeat the injury in the same way or stay in the 'traumatic orbit of that injury', she explains, suggesting that, in the texture of repetition, some system-change will produce itself, thereby allowing the subject to make peace with traumatic effects outside its control (1993: 84).

In *Quad*, bodies communicate in a non-verbal language that 'means' via systemic repetition. The repetition we witness in *Quad* creates an interface between body and world, cultivating receptivity to meanings (and ways of meaning-making) that are outside the control of a human will. *Quad*, as Mary Bryden writes, gives us 'no meaning other than the bodies before us, their sound and their interaction, or its avoidance. These are clearly human beings before us, and thinking beings, whose position statements are made by their bodies' (2002: 90). Bryden goes on to argue, citing Deleuze, that these 'position statements' given by bodies provoke thought, making space for what might not have been previously thinkable

(Deleuze 1985: 246 as qtd in Bryden 2002: 91).[8] We find an unexpected form of agency in the gesture of *repeating* an existing social condition in a different context – in this case, an aesthetic one. The act of repetition can, in some cases, introduce the possibility for reinscription, re-marking or variation within the texture of the same. Compulsive repetition in this piece differs from the helplessness of addiction in that innovation comes from the aesthetic, unexpected and colourful manner in which the repetition is portrayed. *Quad* exploits a version of passivity which, insofar as it repeats the status quo – performing it, reinscribing it in a different context – creates space not only for critical reflection but for a subtle form of agency. This 'passive agency' in Beckett, predicated on embodiment, reveals itself with startling poignancy in *Quad*.

First broadcast in 1981 by the German television company Süddeutscher Rundfunk, *Quad* is an energetic pattern of colour, movement and sound. Four bodies in hooded gowns pace a white square, their footsteps audible in the silences between beats of percussion instruments. The four bodies, 'players' in Beckett's text, were to be as 'alike in build as possible. Short and slight for preference. Some ballet training desirable. Adolescents a possibility. Sex indifferent' (Beckett 2006: 453). Each player is assigned a particular course, and each player completes his course four times, either in solo or in combination with other players, so that all possible combinations are given. The bodies make jerky turns to the left on their diagonal trajectories to avoid a centre point labeled 'E', the 'danger zone' (453). Beckett insists on unbroken movement, and he stipulates that the lights fade out at the end of the piece with figure one pacing the square as it did in the beginning, conveying a sense of cyclicality and endlessness (453). When Beckett saw technicians replaying *Quad* in slow motion on a black and white monitor, he is said to have remarked, 'marvellous, it's 100,000 years later', and named the differently styled and truncated piece *Quad II* (Brater 1987a: 107).

I've suggested that *Quad* and *Quad II* are often read as testifying to a lack of human agency. The players walk courses laid out in advance, never deviating, in series that will continue, ostensibly, forever, their movements perpetuating the structures or systems that constrain them to move that way. Beckett's cameraman at Süddeutscher Rundfunk, Jim Lewis, described the players as hunched forward as if bracing against a cold wind (qtd in Fehsenfeld 1982: 360) and as 'chained' to a quadrangle (Lewis 1990: 371), while others have likened the square to a prison yard (punning on *quod*, slang for prison).[9] Steven Connor likens the players to planets in gravitational orbit (1988: 144), and, citing a letter in which Beckett notes that 'Dante and Virgil in Hell always go to the left (the damned direction)', James Knowlson compares the players' turns around the centre point to the 'sinistral turns' of the damned in Dante's *Inferno*, repeating what Beckett himself had said (Knowlson 1996: 592; Gontarski 1985: 179–80). In early drafts, Beckett calls the trajectories of the players 'circuits' ('courses' appears in the published version), a term that suggests not only cyclicality, a looping *ad infinitum*, but also the sense that the players are part of a larger system, driven by forces other than their own volition to move. As an illustration of human compulsion, *Quad* maintains an uncomfortable balance between hyper-rationality and manic abandon. It has been called a 'choreographed madness' that evokes the origins of Western theatre in the dithyramb (Brater 1987: 107) and has been said to leave viewers 'half-concussed, dazed, bereft of critical tools' (Bryden 1995: 109). Others have found 'an element of the Pythagorean irrational' in the triangles made by the players' courses (Ackerley 2009: 151) and references to the alchemical dances that fascinated W. B. Yeats (Okamuro 2003). The piece has also been read as a paradigm of a Foucauldian surveillance state in which the body's range of movement is regulated and controlled (McTighe) and as a depiction of human passivity under late capitalism (Wall 2009).[10]

These readings, which cohere insofar as they suggest that *Quad* portrays a lack of agency, are complicated by readings focused on embodiment. Anna McMullan, for example, argues that *Quad* demonstrates a 'bodily "excess" or cost of subjecting human bodies to such a formal regime and its relentless permutations' (2010: 109). She refers to the fatigue spectators feel while watching *Quad*, but she also notes that the appearance of starkly human elements beneath the long robes of the players charge the piece with dramatic tension, reminding us of the possibility of error (a form of bodily action that exceeds will or intention). The robes worn by the dancers are supple enough to reveal aspects of the bodies beneath (the contours of a knee, a shoulder), and, though the players keep to their courses and rhythms with the aid of beats played on headphones under their hoods, this doesn't eradicate the possibility of error. Mary Bryden, after musing that *Quad* might be better executed by 'computer-or laser-controlled simulation', rejects this idea on the grounds that 'live impulses towards an ever-potential asymmetry' and 'hints at precariousness' are what make the play so hypnotic (1995: 111). Similarly, the human scratching of footsteps mixes acoustic traces of the body with the metallic beat of the percussion instruments. There is something bodily, too, about the crescendo and quickening of percussion which, 'heart-like, thumps more insistently' as the players circle the centre point, the 'danger zone' (1995: 111). A threat of collision occurs each time the bodies approach the centre, and the live potential for disruption is ever-present in the mind of the viewer. The TV camera's high angle, furthermore, the same angle that is used for surveillance footage, reinforces the sense that something *might* happen – some fortuitous or calamitous mutation – on the scene of systemic repetition. *Quad* provocatively muddles a divide between mechanical, agentless formalism and a humanism that restricts agency to the will of individuals or characters.[11]

Deleuze's essay 'The Exhausted', published in 1992 with the French translation of Beckett's television plays, has shaped much existing scholarship on *Quad*, particularly the idea that it depicts a lack of agency. Deleuze describes both physiological and logical exhaustion as well as the intersection between the two. He cites the tendency of many of Beckett's works to exhaust the possible by means of a combinatorial: he mentions the permutations of biscuits in *Murphy*, the sucking stones in *Molloy* and numerous examples of combinatorial sequences in *Watt* (1995: 4). For Deleuze, *Quad* is an extension of this move: all possible combinations (of solos and combinations of players) are exhausted. 'Beckett's text is perfectly clear', Deleuze writes, 'it is concerned with exhausting space' (13). The very idea of the possible is exhausted, and Deleuze makes this exhaustion of the possible a necessary condition for the advent of a new kind of language: one of spaces and images (10). In *Quad*, therefore, exhausting the possible has a constructive aspect, ushering in something un-anticipatable: a new language in addition to novelty of form. Deleuze's interest in a new kind of language calls attention to a performative contradiction between the obsessive regularity of the players' courses and the idiosyncratic novelty of *Quad's* form: part image, part dance, part soundscape. Insofar as *Quad* inaugurates a new 'language' of images, its players signify by means of their spatial positions. Deleuze calls the players 'unaffected protagonists in an unaffectable space' (12), suggesting that they have been evacuated of interiority (and of intention). Accordingly, *Quad* substitutes 'a "gestus" as a logic of postures and positions for all story or narrative' (13–14) – an idea on which Deleuze elaborates by discussing how the players' absolute avoidance of a centre point exhausts the potentiality of the space.[12]

This replacing of narrative, intention and interiority with the work of exhausting the possible can be generative insofar as it spurs the emergence of what is un-anticipatable. Readers of Deleuze have described *Quad*'s combinatorial method as dramatising a 'constructive function of exhaustion' (Wasser 2012: 129) – which Deleuze links to language. Deleuze lays out three types of language, each of which exhausts the possible in a different way: language I is an 'atomic' language that exhausts the possible with words, naming it. Language II is a language of voices and flows that exhausts the possible by exhausting words themselves, drying up the flow (7). Language III, which Deleuze associates with *Quad* and the television plays, is a new kind of language that no longer relates to 'objects that can be enumerated' or to 'transmitting voices', but to 'immanent limits that never cease to move about – hiatuses, holes or tears you couldn't account for, attributing them to simple tiredness, if they didn't expand suddenly to welcome something coming from outside or elsewhere' (1995: 8). This something 'from outside or elsewhere' is what Deleuze calls the Image, 'liberated from the chains it was kept in by the other two languages' (8). Language III is therefore composed of images and spaces (rather than words or voices), freed from the encumbrances of history – 'purged of semantico-historical memory' (Bryden 1996: 89). The Image retains nothing of the personal nor of the rational, Deleuze explains, and it is defined not by its content but through its *form*, its 'internal tension' or 'the force it gathers to make the void or to bore holes, to loosen the grip of words, to dry up the oozing of voices, so as to disengage itself from memory and reason' (1995: 9). Language III, then, concerned with form and process (rather than personal memory), both ruptures and renews the idea of language in ways that are at once destructive, invigorating and innovative. Deleuze reads *Quad* as a performance of a process-based language (or counter-language) – one that unmakes and remakes possibilities for communication. Bryden aptly observes the depersonalisation at the heart of such a 'language', noting that language III can emerge only 'from the exhaustion (*l'épuisement*) of combinatory possibilities [. . .] a stripping-away, a depersonalisation of desire' (1996: 91).

The emergence of a language of images and spaces, for Deleuze, is also bound up with a depersonalisation of the subject. In her analysis of 'The Exhausted', Bryden turns to *Anti-Oedipus* (1972) for context, emphasising how Deleuze and Guattari draw upon Beckett's earlier fiction (*The Unnamable*, *Murphy*, *Watt* and *Mercier and Camier*) to describe a subject without fixed identity, always decentred, defined by the states through which it passes – a 'nomad subject' (1996: 88; cf. Deleuze 1983: 20). In *Quad*, the bodies of the players are stripped of personal characteristics; their faces are covered and bodies made androgynous by long gowns (Beckett 2006: 453).[13] Further, *Quad*'s minimalism achieves a stripping away of personhood as the players, exhausting their courses and combinations, create moving tableaux or *Images* that become the raw material of Deleuze's language III. They are Images detached from 'prescriptive patterning' (1996: 91). Instead of a speaking subject, in *Quad* there is an 'assembly of silence, space, or gesture, in constant negotiation with each other and with the observer' that 'demands its own right to mean and to modulate' (Bryden 1996: 91). What Bryden's reading of Deleuze makes plain is the extent to which *Quad* both unsettles habitual versions of subjectivity (and the theories of agency that attach to them) and inaugurates a language that 'means' or 'modulates' differently.

Deleuze credits Beckett for linking logical exhaustion to physiological or bodily exhaustion, noting that 'only the exhausted can exhaust the possible, because he has renounced all need, preference, goal or signification' (1995: 5). The fact that *Quad* was initially conceived as a mime speaks to its role in Beckett's development of a 'decidedly corporeal aesthetic' (Tadashi Naito 2008: 398). The players in *Quad*, instructed by the stage directions in an early draft to move 'as one organism' (MSS Drama/Qua 01 MS 219, RUL), plod on in such a driven, tireless way as to evoke the Leibnizian concept of *appetition*. For Leibniz, the life of the monad consists in the unceasing desire to pass from representation to representation without hope of ever 'clarifying its own content' (Tonning 2007: 241). The passage from representation to representation evokes the slippery nature of words (which fall just short of what they seek to express) and the inability of language to reach a mythic 'centre' at which something could be said without excess, poverty or inexactitude. It is this, perhaps, that makes it necessary to keep speaking (or writing) – a point that links the players' avoidance of the centre of the square to an impossible, tireless desire to say the 'thing itself'.[14] Appetition, related to both appetite and sexual desire, suggests, in Beckettian fashion, that the efforts of language may mirror physiological drives or needs that can lead to compulsion. In his notebooks, Beckett copies a section from Windelband's *A History of Philosophy* that describes appetition as the impulse that moves the monad from passive to active (TCD 10967/191v.192 as qtd in Tonning 2007: 208). The passivity of the players in *Quad* – their dogged and repetitive movement – may, like the compulsion of desire, transmute into expression, a striving towards the unachievable (a variation of agency). Each narrowly avoided collision around the danger zone, E, temporarily diffuses tension, but the impossibility of reaching the centre becomes a motor, driving the piece to repeat itself eternally, compulsively, as if that which *could* occur to allow the piece to come to a close is ceaselessly deferred.

The endless cycling of figures in *Quad*, who can neither stop nor direct their movements, has also influenced Brian Wall's suggestion that *Quad* dramatises the alienation experienced under late capitalism. Though problematic in some ways – the suggestion of allegory affixes 'meaning' to a work that strives to question that category – Wall's interpretation suggests that repetition and compulsion in *Quad* call for a reconceptualisation of passivity, thus troubling the link between agency and subjective will and intention. Wall begins by arguing that *Quad*'s abstraction consists in its substitution of 'mere motion' for freedom, 'as if giving form to the numbing repetition and identity that characterize life under late capitalism' (Wall 2009: 93). Wall points to *Quad II* as a symptom of the fact that this system cannot end: 'once the system has been set in motion there evidently can be no end to this closed circuit of repetition, duration and identity, with the ever-same persisting' (94). Wall's analysis underscores the *passivity* of the figures relative to the continued movement that drives them: the oppressed move on predetermined tracks, not by their own will, but in a manic tarantella that, once in motion, cannot stop. But Wall goes on to argue that the 'over-determined passivity' he finds in both late capitalism and in *Quad* calls for a reconceptualisation of passivity (101). His account suggests that there is a kind of passivity endowed with the possibility of inducing *variations* within the very structures responsible for its powerlessness. *Quad* troubles the rigid dichotomy between active and passive, since the players and their patterns are active insofar as their patterns organise the space of the white square and passive insofar as they move on predetermined tracks. This active passivity is a means by which alternatives to ready-made meaning may be forged. The hooded figures, driven to follow their preordained courses, do more than simply exhaust their combinatorial potential. *Quad*'s stylised repetition – its pattern and exchange of positions – reveals a link between repetition and its opposite: difference. If language operates through the play of repetition and difference, then *Quad* dramatises both entrapment in a loop (repetition *ad infinitum*) *and* the possibility of meaning differently via variation.

This shift in the way that the body might interact with and affect its environment – a shift that demands a broader conceptualisation of agency – aligns with Merleau-Ponty's idea of creative novelty as a variation on existing structures. Merleau-Ponty associates creative novelty with the idea of a *reprise* – a 'taking up' that involves variation of the structures (or recurring patterns) that organise human relationships. In the last chapter, we saw how *style*, which can operate without a subject's awareness and control, 'acts', according to Merleau-Ponty, as the effect or imprint of one's bodily perspective. Though style can be honed, it is also involuntary; it happens without our awareness. (One's gait while walking is a good example of this Merleau-Pontian idea of style – it's something we do without thinking about it.) In 1954–5, Merleau-Ponty gave two contemporaneous courses at the Collège de France, one on the idea of 'institution' and the other on 'passivity'. Notes to these lectures suggest that, for Merleau-Ponty, the possibility of creative novelty is associated not with *rupture* but with the resumption and variation of existing traditions. It is interesting that Merleau-Ponty should associate the idea of institution with that of passivity, for just as the 'institution' (of meaning) involves assuming what is given (like *style*), so does passivity entail a situatedness within an existing structure that, if 'assumed' or 'taken up', instantiates a non-voluntarist version of agency. This 'taking up' of tradition is a way of acting from within or, better, in concert with one's situation and surroundings.[15]

Despite its abstraction, *Quad*'s manner of staging the uncomfortable relationship between passivity – often linked to the physical body – and activity is not without political significance. According to the non-voluntarist form of agency that *Quad* suggests, possibilities for empowerment, change and innovation exist even in conditions of restricted freedom, where more direct activity would be ineffectual or merely reactive. In 1982, a year after *Quad*, Beckett wrote the play *Catastrophe*, dedicated to the Czech dissident Vaclav Havel, then in prison for his political activities (defending unjustly persecuted persons and advocating for free speech). In *Catastrophe*, Beckett further explores ties between the body's limited possibilities for free movement and the possibility of reconfiguring the structures that make such conditions possible. This is part of the significance of the final gesture made by P (the silent Protagonist) at the end of the play. Though he has been poked, prodded, whitened and stood on a pedestal like a statue, P lifts his head to look at the audience in the play's closing moments (Beckett 2006: 461).[16] The players in *Quad*, like P, reveal within passivity a version of agency, but, unlike in *Catastrophe*, the agency in *Quad* does not depend upon any one gesture. It is given in the continual possibilities for variation and in the way in which the players pattern or style the space of their 'playing field'.

Bodies in Beckett, like the figures on a chessboard at the close of a game, often find themselves with diminishing possibilities for action; their range of movement narrows as they reach the endgame. But bodily constraint, abjection and limitation in Beckett, as I have sought to show, may signal more than resignation to forces of fate or to the power of systems outside the control of the individual will. The lively turn and torque of bodies in *Quad*, for instance, the energetic irregularity of percussion and the kaleidoscopic re-forming of *tableaux vivants* across the square, allow the rudiments of an alternative version of agency to suggest themselves – not the agency of willing and intention we might attribute to a humanist subject, but an agency that develops from the capacity of a physical body or collaboration of bodies to fashion space and organise an environment. This agency would be posthuman in the sense that its effects would be more capacious and far harder to predict than the intentional projects of a willing, humanist subject. This more passive version of agency would – reminiscent of the patterning of space in *Quad* – derive from a more integral relationship between our physical bodies and the world we inhabit.

Notes

1. S. E. Gontarski describes a turn in Beckett's fiction away from the motif of the journey – the compulsion to or solace in motion that characterises Beckett's fiction up to *How It Is* – towards the stillness and 'closed space' that characterise his late prose (1996: viii–xi).
2. Beckett's interest in new media extends also to radio. He composes seven radio plays (six original scripts and one translation) between 1956 and 1963. In her chapter 'Hearing Beckett', Ulrika Maude reads the radio plays with the stage play *Krapp's Last Tape* (1958) to argue that Beckett exploits the acoustic's transgression of space and time to emphasise the materially grounded nature of subjectivity (2009: 47–69).
3. Hubert Dreyfus describes how, in Merleau-Ponty's thinking, bodily movement can be 'purposive without the agent entertaining a purpose'. He writes: 'One does not need a goal or intention to act. One's body is simply solicited by the situation to get into equilibrium with it' (1996, as qtd in Maude 2009: 85).
4. 2 Jean-Michel Rabaté situates Beckett's challenge to the humanist subject in relation to Derrida, Agamben, Bataille and Blanchot, arguing that '[w]hat Beckett attacks [. . .] is anthropomorphism, in which he recognises humanism pure and simple. To achieve his program, he decides to stay on the fence between the human and the inorganic' (2016: 46).
5. *Worstward Ho* also challenges the subject of utterance, diminishing a human 'him' to a depersonalised 'it': 'Whose words? Ask in vain. Or not in vain if say no knowing. No saying. No words for him whose words. Him? One. No words for one whose words. One? It. No words for it whose words' (NH 98).
6. Diana Coole and Samantha Frost show how certain movements locate 'generative powers (or agentic capacities) even within inorganic matter, and [. . .] generally eschew the distinction between organic and inorganic, animate and inanimate, at the ontological level' (2010: 9).
7. The exhibition literature at the Centre Pompidou describes *Quad* as a 'recherche prononcée de l'abstraction': 'Le carré abstrait, les figures analogues, l'absence totale de parole, le mouvement de sortie des danseurs à la lumière et de retour à l'obscurité, sont propres à la dernière esthétique de Beckett, de plus en plus réduite à des idées essentielles. Le retour aux ténèbres, après le bref intervalle sur la scène, est un mouvement qui peut traduire celui de la vie' (Léoni-Figini 2007).
8. Bryden contends that while 'many viewers experience the demotion of subjectivity and narrative form in *Quad* as a diminishment [. . .] [f]or Deleuze, it is these factors which constitute the uncanny strength of Beckett's writing' (2002: 91).

9. Rosemary Pountney emphasises the pun on 'quod', noting that Beckett's apartment on the Rue Saint Jacques overlooked the Santé Prison, which may have made him more aware of the rhythms of prison life (1998: 210).
10. McTighe argues that bodies in *Quad* are 'visualized as objects or parts of mechanisms being ordered by various systems of surveillance and control [. . .] the reiterative retracing of firmly inscribed pathways in *Quad* reveals a lack of autonomy and agency that may be only marginally offset by the possibilities offered by performance' (128).
11. James Knowlson refuses to link Beckett's formalism to 'arid antihumanism', arguing that the 'formal, almost mathematical patterning' works not away from human feeling but 'draws one towards it' (2003: 95). His objection also wisely cautions us against eclipsing aspects of the human in discussions of posthumanism.
12. Deleuze defines potentiality in this instance as the possibility that the four moving bodies will collide: 'their collision, is not an event among others, but the only possibility of event – the potentiality of the corresponding space. To exhaust space is to extenuate its potentiality through rendering any meeting impossible' (1995: 13).
13. Deleuze's schizophrenic subject also spans binary oppositions: it is not so much intersexual as 'transsexual. He is trans-alivedead, trans-parentchild' (Deleuze 1983: 77). The following passage from *Anti-Oedipus* – with obvious parallels to *Quad* – describes processes through which the subject may come into being: 'This subject itself is not at the center, which is occupied by the machine, but on the periphery, with no fixed identity, forever decentered, defined by the states through which it passes [. . .] the subject is born of each state in the series, is continually reborn of the following state that determines him at a given moment, consuming-consummating all these states that cause him to be born and reborn (the lived state coming first, in relation to the subject that lives it)' (20).
14. Martin Esslin argues that desire for intimacy coupled with its impossibility serves as a 'motor' that keeps *Quad*'s players in orbit around an empty centre: 'the center that the hooded wanderers have so fearfully to avoid is obviously the point at which real communication, a real "encounter", would be potentially possible but inevitably proves – by the very nature of existence itself – impossible' (66–7).
15. These lecture notes were compiled and made available in French in a volume edited by Dominique Darmaillacq, Stéphanie Ménasé and Claude Lefort (2003a). An English translation by Leonard Lawlor and Heath Massey appeared in 2010. The first course was titled 'Institution in Personal and Public History' and the second 'The Problem of Passivity: Sleep, the Unconscious, Memory'. Part of the

significance of these lecture notes is that they make evident the development of Merleau-Ponty's thinking in the years before he wrote *The Visible and the Invisible*.

16. In *Beckett's Political Imagination*, Emilie Morin provides further political context, detailing the play's inclusion in 'Une nuit pour Václav Havel', conceived for the Avignon theatre festival by AIDA (*Association Internationale de Défense des Artistes victimes de la répression dans le monde*). Morin points out that *Catastrophe* 'exposes what little becomes of theatre when those who write and enact it are silenced', but she admits that the play's political dimension evades consensus; 'it has been read as a solipsistic reflection upon the dispossessed body; as a rumination on the mechanics of theatrical spectacle; as an exposition of the tyranny practised by Soviet Communism; as an examination of the enduring power of dissent in the face of oppression'. Morin emphasises that Beckett's dedication does homage to Havel, even as the Protagonist evokes 'the many political prisoners who remained anonymous and beyond the reach of the spotlight' (239–44).

CHAPTER 7

The Body and Creation: *Worstward Ho*

Beckett jotted down the first paragraphs of *Worstward Ho* in August 1981, a few months after returning from Stuttgart, where he was overseeing the production of *Quad*. In contrast to the wordless television play, *Worstward Ho* addresses itself to the materiality of language, setting itself the goal of 'worsening' words. We find an echo of the parody of teleology that animates the first trilogy, since its title evokes direction – westward – while adjusting, horrendously, the meaning of the final frontier: not only progress and discovery but also nothingness, death. *Worstward Ho* has been called a self-negating text, in which language diminishes and self-cannibalises. Its 'worsening' does not stop at language but targets bodies also, removing limbs and distinguishing features from the three 'shades' that populate its pages. As it aspires to the 'worst' (which it defines as 'less'), *Worstward Ho* also probes the relation between saying and being.

In Beckett's later prose, diminishing capacities of the body, including the capacity for self-directed movement, are paired with syntactical 'impoverishment' of the sort that distinguishes not only *How it Is* but also the novellas that constitute a second 'trilogy': *Company* (1979), *Mal vu mal dit* (1981), translated as *Ill Seen Ill Said* in 1982, and *Worstward Ho*, which, more so than its predecessors, explicitly pairs the physical body with language, worsening them together in the dim void.

Worstward Ho could be read as a bold staging (in prose) of diminishing agency, both bodily and linguistic. Beckett's own words on the subject – his articulation of an aesthetic of impotence and his description of an art weary of 'being able' – could be mustered in support of this view.[1] Months before his death, Beckett reiterated these ideas, contrasting his own work to the additive maximalism and mastery of his mentor: 'I realized that Joyce had gone as far as one could go in the direction of knowing more [. . .] I realized that my own way was in impoverishment, in lack of knowledge and in taking away, in subtracting rather than adding' (Knowlson 1996: 319). Yet methodical subtraction (not unlike the phenomenological reduction, which brackets perception to investigate its underlying structures) does not negate agency so much as explore its foundations. Or, as S. E. Gontarski writes, with respect to a vital current in Beckett's poetics that encompasses both disintegraton and regeneration, 'the theme of the imagination's dying yet conscious of its own decline, its own demise, is itself regenerative' (2015: 4). This remark about *Imagination Dead Imagine* might apply to *Worstward Ho*, which also explores the 'possibilities of imagination at points of extinction and renewal' (4). In the last chapter, I discouraged reading *Quad* exclusively in terms of exhaustion, minimalism and despair, arguing that it exploits a passivity which, by repeating the status quo (reinscribing it in a different context), creates not only space for critical reflection but also limited agency. Such 'passive agency' (of the body) has a correlate in language. As we saw in Chapter 5, Merleau-Ponty compares the way in which speech (*la parole*) can refigure existing language to the way in which the body's interaction with its surroundings makes them meaningful. (This is different than finding the origins of language in gesture, as it has to do with how entire bodies orient spaces.) *Worstward Ho* also explores the rudiments of linguistic meaning, in part by shifting focus away from representation towards the internal articulations in the surface of language that create '*sens*' (which encompasses both meaning and spatial direction).

In *Worstward Ho*, shades fade and reappear in a dim void, losing their bodily characteristics as we adapt to the strange idiom of the prose – a syntax so particular that Beckett claimed the text was untranslatable, though Edith Fournier rendered it in French as *Cap au pire* (1991).[2] Language in *Worstward Ho* is often described as 'unmaking' itself, 'undoing' itself or as self-effacing, and the content of the work does little to discourage readings of it as self-cancelling: three shades appear, disappear, reappear and are 'worsened' (from the standpoint of representation). First, there is a female shade, standing or kneeling. The second shade is a double shade: an old man and child holding hands as they plod on together in the void. The third shade is a '[h]ead sunk on crippled hands' that worsens into a skull with staring eyes (NH 102). The work begins, as is often noted, by announcing its trajectory as an inverted telos (towards nohow on): 'On. Say on. Be said on.

Somehow on. Till nohow on. Said nohow on' (89). In addition to announcing a movement from 'somehow on' to 'nohow on', these opening lines point to a reversibility between subject and object ('say' and 'be said'). With its highly self-referential idiom *Worstward Ho* explores how meanings come into being, rather than pointing to what pre-exists or exists outside of the domain of saying.

Though its language has been described as an 'anti-language' that 'assaults the foundations of verbal communication' (Finney 1987: 78), as infantile or 'midget grammar' (Brienza 1987: 254), other critics of *Worstward Ho* have found in this stubbornly obscure text innovative, creative and even revolutionary potential. Its stop-and-start prose has been called 'a stuttering of failure and renewal towards a possibility of language yet to be born' (Gontarski 2015: 66). *Worstward Ho* has also been said to spur radical rethinking of representation and the subject-object relation (Bersani and Dutoit 1993) and to overturn the historical edifice of literature in a 'literary revolution' (Casanova 2006: 12). By undermining the assumptions on which our habitual narratives and modes of relation are founded, *Worstward Ho* suggests, implicitly, that alternatives are possible. Casanova, for instance, argues that Beckett's work questions, one by one, the 'conditions of possibility of literature – the subject, memory, imagination, narration, character, psychology, space and time' (12). While she rescues *Worstward Ho* from being understood as 'the evocation of a nihilistic stance or the representation of ontological tragedy', her sense of *Worstward Ho* as 'a kind of ultimate poetic art' (26) relies on her reading of its combinatorial method and her sense that Beckett creates an abstract text while systematically and masterfully elaborating how he writes it (26).[3] Bersani's reading of *Worstward Ho* leaves more room to ascribe creative potential to the text itself. He writes that relations between representer and representee are 'severed and replaced by a sort of exercise in relationality itself' (Bersani and Dutoit 1993: 84). Gontarski finds alternations of disintegration and regeneration in a propulsive, creative force – akin to Bergson's *élan vital* – in Beckett (2015). Building on readings that identify creative and subversive potential in *Worstward Ho*, I read its attention to linguistic creation and destruction alongside two features of Merleau-Ponty's ontology: the chiasm or intertwining (*l'entrelacs*) and the flesh (*la chair*), an element that moves between our bodies, space and the 'tissue' of language. Merleau-Ponty's sense of the body and language as intertwined illuminates a reading of *Worstward Ho* – a work that dramatises language's way of affecting and even 'creating' being.

Specifically, I argue that the self-referential language of *Worstward Ho* (where phrases vary their precedents according to a pattern) shares the self-reflexive structure of the 'flesh' described by Merleau-Ponty. *Worstward Ho*'s stubborn self-reference is what enables its language to acquire a version of self-consciousness or 'sentience' as it unmakes and remakes meaning. Just as the physical body orders its space by means of its interests and projects, so does a particular way of speaking (*la parole*) navigate among existing significations to configure meaning. In French, Merleau-Ponty is able to distinguish between the equivalent of a body in the field of language (*la parole*) and the existing field of significations (*la langue*). Just as the 'flesh' of the world coils over itself to make a sentient body (such that the body and space are akin, formed from the same element), so does *langue* or the field of available significations fold over itself to create speech (*la parole*). In *Worstward Ho*, the text's way of speaking (*la parole*) takes on the properties of a sentient body, reconfiguring linguistic 'terrain'. This suggests that 'meaning' is not the work of a subject who wills, but emerges, rather, in the interaction of a body with its surroundings (physical and linguistic). Before turning to *Worstward Ho*, I'll give an overview of the two defining figures in Merleau-Ponty's ontology: the chiasm and the flesh.[4]

The 1950s and early 1960s mark an 'ontological turn' in Merleau-Ponty's thinking.[5] His posthumously published work, *The Visible and the Invisible*, edited by his friend and student Claude Lefort, presents an ontology composed of figures which, Merleau-Ponty tells us, are not metaphors, since they convey some literal truth. The most dominant of these figures designates the relation between the visible and the invisible, which Lefort adopts as the work's title. The 'visible' refers to partial perspectives on being that are given to our bodies (our senses) or expressed in language. The invisible, Merleau-Ponty claims, is the membrane or inner lining of the visible: 'Between the alleged colors and visibles, we would find anew the tissue that lines them, sustains them, nourishes them, and which for its part is not a thing, but a possibility, a latency, and a *flesh* of things' (VI 132). The seeing body and the visible body belong to one 'flesh'. Their relation is not one of consubstantiality, strictly speaking, because the flesh is not a material substance:

> The flesh is not matter, is not mind, is not substance. To designate it, we should need the old term 'element', in the sense that it was used to speak of water, air, earth, and fire, that is, in the sense of a general thing, midway between the spatio-temporal individual and the idea. (VI 139)

Merleau-Ponty discourages us from thinking of the flesh as mere metaphor, claiming that it is 'no analogy or vague comparison and must be taken literally' (VI 132). As the 'formative medium of the object and the subject', flesh discourages an opposition between perceiver and perceived, visible and invisible, but links them together as belonging to a common element that supports their reversibility (VI 147). This description of the invisible as a 'flesh' of things presents it as belonging to the same general being as the visible, which is merely a particular aspect or view of a larger whole.

Given that there is but one world or being, any innovation must develop from a renegotiation of the manner in which the invisible becomes visible. This passage of the invisible into visibility may involve the articulating work of a creative or 'operant' language. This, for Merleau-Ponty, makes the work of expressive language ontological – bound up with attempts to explore and organise being. A vivid passage of *The Visible and the Invisible* imagines a language that would permit the things themselves to 'speak' instead of severing (as ordinary language does) the connection between a speaking subject and the world. This 'living' language is one that Merleau-Ponty claims for philosophy; it is a language that creates meaning (*sens*) by making articulations within a common element.[6]

In the final section of *The Visible and the Invisible*, 'The Intertwining – The Chiasm', Merleau-Ponty describes relations of reversibility between subject-object, visible-invisible, active-passive and seer-seen. The chiasm (literally 'crossing' from the Greek) signals the continual possibility of reversal which, for Merleau-Ponty, makes possible bodily sentience as well as the work of expressive language. This continual possibility of reversal signalled by the chiasm suggests that opposed terms, such as subject and object, seer and seen, are not only (chiastically) intertwined but mutually constituting. The invisible, for instance, is not opposed to the visible, but doubles it and coexists with it as its inner lining – a latency that can, at any moment, be converted into visibility (VI 132). In order to be a subject, one must have the capacity to be an object (and, more uncomfortably, vice versa). One of the most important features of Merleau-Ponty's philosophy is his insistence that our ability to exist as subjects of perception – to see and to touch – is founded on our capacity to *be seen* and *be touched*. Merleau-Ponty writes:

> We say therefore that our body is a being of two leaves, from one side a thing among things and otherwise what sees them and touches them; we say, because it is evident, that it unites these two properties within itself, and its double belongingness to the order of the 'object' and to the order of the 'subject' reveals to us quite unexpected relations between the two orders. (VI 137)

When we see and touch, we are subjects. When we are seen and touched, we are objects. Between the seeing body and the visible body there is 'reciprocal insertion and intertwining of one in the other' (VI 138), but while we can shift our awareness from touching to being touched, reversing between the two, we cannot be both subject and object at the same time.[7]

Merleau-Ponty's discovery of a 'strange adherence' between the seer and the visible leads him to describe the structure of the flesh as a reflexive 'coiling' of the visible upon itself. He illustrates this 'coiling' through the image of a wave, the crest of which is able to peer over itself and look at its underside. 'There is vision, there is touch', Merleau-Ponty writes, 'when a certain visible, a certain tangible, turns back upon the whole of the visible, the whole of the tangible, of which it is a part' (VI 139). Merleau-Ponty goes on to describe the 'commerce' or exchange between this part of the visible or tangible (the body) and the whole (the world); the vision or touch that develops in their exchange belongs strictly to neither, 'as upon two mirrors facing one another where two indefinite series of images set in one another arise'. In the reflections produced by the two mirrors, Merleau-Ponty writes,

> since the seer is caught up in what he sees, it is still himself he sees: there is a fundamental narcissism of all vision. And thus, for the same reason, the vision he exercises, he also undergoes from the things,

such that, as many painters have said, I feel myself looked at by the things, my activity is equally passivity. (VI 139)

Perception (visibility, touch) occurs when a seer folds back upon the whole of which it is part. It is in this sense that 'the seer is caught up in what he sees'. The fact that it 'is still himself he sees' leads Merleau-Ponty to ascribe a 'fundamental narcissism' to vision, aptly reinforced by his metaphor of two mirrors facing one another. He adds that the intertwining of activity and passivity is the 'more profound meaning of narcissism' (VI 139). Insofar as visibility occurs as a continual exchange between seer and seen, the seer feels herself looked at by things. This aspect of Merleau-Ponty's thinking has been influential for philosophers who attribute agentic capacities to matter (for instance, Bennett 2010). Visibility also extends beyond the purview of any one subject.[8]

The flesh of the body and the flesh of the world, for Merleau-Ponty, share a structure – one characterised by a dual belonging to the order of objects and to the order of subjects.[9] Merleau-Ponty writes that our gaze 'clothes' the things we perceive with its flesh (*le regard les habille de sa chair*) (VI 131; Vi 171), and he describes fleshy being (*l'être charnel*) as 'a prototype of Being, of which our body, the sensible sentient, is a very remarkable variant, but whose constitutive paradox already lies in every visible' (VI 136). The body perceives things because, 'being of their family, itself visible and tangible, it uses its own being as a means to participate in theirs [. . .] the body belongs to the order of the things as the world is universal flesh' (VI 137). To say that there is a 'flesh' of the world is not anthropomorphism. Merleau-Ponty insists on this point. Rather than projecting some human attribute onto the world, the flesh conveys the sense that the human body's imbrication within the world is what makes it capable of perceiving it: '[the subject or seer] is one of the visibles, capable, by a singular reversal, of seeing them – he who is one of them' (VI 135). The flesh, then, is not something one 'has' but rather, as Judith Butler puts it, 'the web in which one lives' (2005: 181). Butler describes the flesh conditioning the possibility of touch (and vision) in a way that 'cannot be reducible to a unilateral action performed by a subject' (181). Our ability to see and touch is founded on our capacity to *be seen* and *be touched*. Butler accents the flesh as both active and passive.[10]

This Merleau-Pontian idea, that subjectivity is constituted on the basis of a fundamental, ontological passivity, is the subject of

Butler's article 'Merleau-Ponty and the Touch of Malebranche'. Butler transfers to the domain of language the idea that one must be capable of being touched in order to touch. One must be capable of being addressed in order to speak. Butler describes 'a passivity prior to the emergence of the "I", a relation that is, strictly speaking, nonnarratable by the "I", who can begin to tell its story only after this inauguration has taken place' (2005: 190). Merleau-Ponty imagines the sensed body (*corps senti*) and the sentient body (*corps sentant*) as 'two segments of one sole circular course' (VI 138). If we were to flatten the circle and look only at its top half, we would see a movement from left to right. The bottom half would appear as a movement from right to left: two lines moving in opposite directions. And yet, as part of a circle, they are two phases of the same movement. It is in this way that flesh is structured such that subjectivity and objectivity, passivity and activity, are continually reversible.

The flesh founds a reversibility between visible and invisible, active and passive, subject and object, sensing and sensed. But thinking these opposites together does not involve a collapsing of difference, a relation of identity or a synthesis, and this makes flesh and the chiasm successful alternatives to the dialectic. In Chapter 4 I discussed a critique of Merleau-Ponty – that his thinking does not leave adequate room for difference – and yet his ontology entails an *écart* (a gap). Merleau-Ponty underscores the point that while reversal is always possible, a difference is maintained between subject and object such that the two never coincide:

> It is time to emphasize the fact that it is a reversibility always imminent and never realized in fact. My left hand is always on the verge of touching my right hand touching the things, but I never reach coincidence; the coincidence eclipses at the moment of realization (*je ne parviens jamais à la coïncidence; elle s'éclipse au moment de se produire*). (VI 147; Vi 191)

The thickness of the flesh supports reversibility without dissolving difference into identity (through the *écart*).[11]

Merleau-Ponty's emphasis on the self-reflexive structure of the flesh is especially relevant to a reading of *Worstward Ho*. As a surface phenomenon, the flesh can coil up over itself, and we've seen how Merleau-Ponty figures subjectivity as a fold or a wave, the crest of which peers over its mass – a certain visible turning back on the whole of which it is a part (VI 139). Merleau-Ponty's description of the flesh as a 'mirror phenomenon' (which he expands in a working note) further accents its self-reflexivity (VI 255). For Merleau-Ponty, it is the self-reflexive structure of the flesh – the 'coiling up' of the visible or tangible – that founds the possibility for sentience. A body that is merely visible remains an object, incomplete (*inachevé*). Though a circuit is in place, no live current runs through it. It is only with the self-reflexive folding of the flesh – 'when the body sees itself, touches itself seeing and touching the things' – that the 'current' of the visible wakens to course through circuits that have been prepared for it, making 'of a visible a seer and from a body a mind (*esprit*) or, at least, a flesh' (VI 146–7). In order to become a sensing body (and not a mere object), the body must *see its own visibility*. Self-reflexivity – an ability to see oneself seeing – structures the flesh and founds bodily sentience.

The flesh subtends reversibility not only between subject and object but also between language and being. Like the body and like being, language belongs to a generalised flesh and shares its self-reflexive structure: 'no locutor speaks without making himself in advance allocutary, *be it only for himself*' (VI 154; emphasis in the original). For Merleau-Ponty, culture and 'ideality' (*idéalité*) are incarnate:

> It is as though the visibility that animates the sensible world were to emigrate, not outside of every body, but into another less heavy, more transparent body, as though it were to change flesh, abandoning the flesh of the body for that of language. (VI 153)

This image of a 'language body' suggests that language, like being, may be reconfigured by the movement of a particular way of saying (*la parole*). Merleau-Ponty links the work of philosophical ontology to the signifying work of creative or operant language. For Merleau-Ponty, philosophy is an operant language involved in 'an effort of articulation' (VI 127). *Articulation*, like *sens*, spans bodily and linguistic registers. In the body, it is a joint, cut or separation that permits movement. It is also the 'utterance of distinct elements of speech'. The idea that articulation divides language (as it does the body) evokes Saussure's sense that meaning derives not from the relation between sign and signifier, which is arbitrary, but from the manner in which a sign distinguishes itself by differing from other signs. But articulation can also mean 'the manifestation or expression of something immaterial' (*OED*), which implies that meaning can be made also by creating 'joints' within the fabric of being. The idea of a 'flesh' of language suggests a new approach to reading the dense reworkings of the English language we find in *Worstward Ho*.

In 'Literature and Life', Deleuze writes that 'through the creation of syntax, [literature] not only brings about a decomposition or destruction of the maternal language but also the invention of a new language within language' (1997: 229). Deleuze's theory of style aptly describes the strange idiom that develops in *Worstward Ho*, which indeed becomes a language within a language as Beckett renders his native English foreign. *Worstward Ho*'s language resembles English while differing from it in significant ways: the conspicuous absence of clarifying articles, the clipped, cryptic rhythm of the prose and the absence of the first person pronoun, as in the first line: 'On. Say on. Be said on. Somehow on. Till nohow on. Said nohow on' (NH 89). Enoch Brater remarks that the prose resembles an archaic form of English, citing the appearance of expressions such as 'pox', 'ooze' and 'vasts atween' as a 'high modernist attempt to reinvent a forgotten but still muscular Jacobean theater vocabulary' (1994: 137). Echoes from Edgar's speech in *King Lear* resound as well – 'The worst is not so long as one can say, This is the worst' – lines Beckett copied into his commonplace notebook (Knowlson 1996: 593). But the overriding feature of the strange (yet not wholly foreign) language is the manner in which its self-reflexivity initiates readers to its style. It is not true to say that *Worstward Ho* gets easier as we get used to the strangeness of its dialect (as happens with most dialects), for something curious happens: the dialect becomes more complex, more turned in on itself. We must rely on what the text has told us about its substitutions. And, so, we rely on our past experiences of the text to understand what is in front of us. In this way, the self-reflexive logic of its language recreates the conditions whereby the perceiving body orients itself in space. Just as the body relies on its past experiences, recognising a street because of a landmark seen before, so the reader of *Worstward Ho* relies on signals in the text that recur more minimally later on, as the prose becomes increasingly cryptic.

Worstward Ho signals a relation between language and physical space through the directional term in its title. Worst*ward* puns on 'worst *word*', conflating spatial direction (*ward*) with language, just as the French language blends signification and spatial direction in the term '*sens*'. The title also adapts 'Westward Ho!', with its evocations of pioneering and the westward course of empire. It refers also to Viola's enthusiastic utterance in *Twelfth Night*, to the title of a Renaissance play by Webster and Dekker (1607), and to Charles Kingsley's *Westward Ho!* (1855), an adventure novel about an expedition to the New World set in Elizabethan times (Brater 1994: 137). Beckett's parody of the rallying cry evokes the idea of movement towards a frontier, and emphasis on movement is underscored by the repetition of the propulsive word 'on'. There is a tendency, too, among readers, to refer to Beckett's work in spatial terms: Drew Milne calls the void of *Worstward Ho* a 'prose-scape' (1999: 94) while Gontarski refers to Beckett's work more generally as creating 'a land without soil' (2004: xv), referring to the aberrant qualities of Beckettian spaces and the critic's difficulty in 'mapping' them. Perhaps the most explicit treatment of space in Beckett's oeuvre is the short piece *Le dépeupleur* (1970) (translated as *The Lost Ones* in 1971) in which a cylinder with exact measurements is described as an '[a]bode where lost bodies roam each searching for its lost one' (CP 202). Gontarski reads *The Lost Ones* as an outline for the late 'closed space' tales (2004: xv), which suggests that *Worstward Ho*, too, is deeply preoccupied with questions of spatial orientation, especially as they relate to the remaking of linguistic meaning. Gontarski's recent work, a Bergsonian reading of Beckett, observes an alternation of disintegration and reinvention traversing *Worstward Ho* (a 'stuttering of failure and renewal') (2015: 67). In *Worstward Ho*, language becomes the scene or setting where, as in ritual, forms are brought into being through the work of articulation.

In the prose-scape of *Worstward Ho* we find orienting cues or signposts that enable us to make sense of the idiom. In order to make our way within the text, we must remember prior instances in the work in which a rule, code or associative phrase is given. Pascale Casanova rightly observes the text's rigorous systematicity, its 'strict rules of composition and organization' (2006: 16). The shades that populate the dim void are given epithets, for example: 'the as one plodding twain' for the old man and child. This practice, reminiscent of Homeric techniques for sustaining epic meter, depends on associations reinforced through repetition. In this way, the language of *Worstward Ho* initiates readers: we rely on what the text tells us about its substitutions. The text, like a landscape, makes sense to us as we map our way within it. We rely on its 'rules' to orient us.

The most cogent example of this occurs in the numeric catalogue of the shades.[12] Each shade is designated by a number (one, two or three), which enables a self-referential language that will refer 'from now' to the code it lays out. The following lines show the text's struggle to mean and to re-mean:

> Something not wrong with one. Meaning – meaning! – meaning the kneeling one. As from now two for the twain. The as one plodding twain. As from now three for the head. The head as first said missaid. So from now. For to gain time. Time to lose. Gain time to lose. (98)

The text begins to refer to the first shade, but, as if it cannot find the referent – 'Meaning – meaning!' – it resolves to lay out a system by which it will refer, in the future, to the shades: from now 'one' will refer to the kneeling figure. This saves time, for it will not be necessary to conjure anew the image of the figure of a woman, to describe her pain and her oscillations between standing and kneeling. This 'rule making' creates a system of reference that weaves its way into the text's language. On the next page, when we read, 'First back on to three', we know that three is the head sunk on crippled hands. We familiarise ourselves with a manner of meaning and reference that has been invented within the pages of the text itself (even as the idea of gaining time to lose lodges a critique of such efficient, indexical forms of reference). We have the chance to experience the cryptic economy such designations allow when, a few pages later, a dense interlude devoted to the 'dim' reinforces the way in which *Worstward Ho*'s syntax rearticulates language. A sentence such as 'First on back to unsay dim can go' (102) doesn't make sense unless we remember earlier moments in the prose poem that teach us how to read it. We must know to treat 'dim' as a substantive, and we must know that it has been wondered whether the dim is capable of disappearing, and, if so, whether for good (forever). A few lines later: 'One can go not for good. Two too. Three no if not for good' (103). In order to make sense of these lines, we must refer back to the numeric catalogue of the shades. 'Three no if not for good', for example, means something like: The third shade (skull) cannot disappear (unless it disappears forever). This new 'grammar' of substitution both reveals the workings of language – its 'logic' of substitution and reference – and modulates usual ways of meaning such that we realise the self-referential quality of sense-making. Meaning emerges as a variation on its preceding or surrounding text.

We are initiated into modes of meaning as we 'make sense' by reference to our acquired context. Multiple readings, as well as listening to the text, facilitate the learning of this strange tongue, opaque at first to our eyes and ears, like Watt's invented language in the garden. Its making 'sense' (*sens*), more precisely, reconfigures existing language by means of a self-reference exaggerated by hermetic closure (restricted vocabulary, words mostly monosyllabic and with similar sounds). As in a piece of music, refrains return (leitmotifs) that we associate with each of the shades. Appropriately, these 'epithets' undergo variations as the shades worsen. But, though they change, the refrains are always variations of their earlier versions, which allows the reader to track the decline of each of the three shades. For instance, we know that 'Three pins. One pinhole. In the dimmest dim' at the close of the text was once a woman, a man and child (three pins) and the skull (the pinhole) (115–16). Associated refrains for each of the shades enable us to negotiate the strange, quick-changing terrain of the text.

The first shade is associated early on with bones: 'Say yes that the bones may pain till no choice but stand' (90). This association permits the text to return to the first shade later by announcing: 'First the bones. On back to them' (96). The image of bones is replaced by kneeling: 'Forever kneeling. Better forever kneeling. Better worse forever kneeling. Say from now forever kneeling' (96). By the time we reach the cataloguing of the shades, we have: 'From now one for the kneeling one' (98). The first shade is then worsened: 'Bow it down. Be bowed down. Deep down. Head in hat gone. More back gone. Greatcoat cut off higher. Nothing from pelvis down. Nothing but bowed back. Topless baseless hindtrunk. Dim black. On unseen knees' (99). The 'bowed back' of the first shade is what is taken up in the next variation: 'Somehow again on back to the bowed back alone. Nothing to show a woman's and yet a woman's. Oozed from softening soft the word woman's. The words old woman's' (108). Before shade one worsens to a pin in the dim void (116), it reappears as a woman on 'unseen knees' whose stooping is likened to that of a gravestone with its name and dates worn away: 'Nothing and yet a woman. Old and yet old. On unseen knees. Stooped as in loving memory some old gravestones stoop. In that old graveyard. Names gone and when to when' (115). Thus, in the case of the first shade, the text abides by a rigorous logic of association. Variations on leitmotifs recur so that the reader recognises the shade in all its variations (bones, kneeling, old woman, stooped gravestone, pin).

It is important that this structuring and innovation take place within a closed space. *Worstward Ho* insists on immanence, both temporally and spatially: 'No once. No once in pastless now' (110). 'No place but the one. None but the one where none.' Finally: 'Beyondless. Thenceless there. Thitherless there. Thenceless thitherless there' (92). Though the text's title announces a journey (a direction, onwardness), the work remains stubbornly within the confines of a fixed, imagined space, a 'dim void' that is both inescapable – 'No place but the one' (92) – and ubiquitous: 'At bounds of boundless void' (116), as any possibility of going beyond is denied: 'A place. Where none. For the body. To be in. Move in. Out of. Back into. No. No out. No back. Only in. Stay in. On in. Still' (89). The paradoxical link between a closed space in which the body must stay (on in) and the possibility for reconfiguration relates to Merleau-Ponty's notion of the flesh, which, as a common element, provides a closure that permits reversals. (The closed space could also be the body itself, suggested by the widespread idea that certain scenes in Beckett take place inside a skull.) *Worstward Ho*'s insistence on immanence also discourages the fantasy of a perpetually inaccessible beyond, a fantasy that can only slow our ability to alter our world by inhabiting it. This insistence on immanence suggests that innovation is not achieved by rupture or by going beyond but develops instead from differentiating movements within a closed, limited space.

Just as the diametrically opposed bodies in *Quad* circle around each other and exchange places, so do opposed terms in *Worstward Ho*, such as progress-regress, affirmation-negation, visibility-invisibility, better-worse, change into their opposites. The 'worsening' of language in *Worstward Ho* has been usefully compared to Blanchot's notion of *désoeuvrement*, or 'unworking' (Krance 1990: 140). There are a number of ways in which ordinary, indexical language is unsettled in *Worstward Ho*, but perhaps most striking is its undoing of oppositions. Words usually thought to be incompatible (such as *on* and *no*) are revealed as, quite literally, reversible. 'On' is the propulsive call to movement with which the text begins and ends, and 'no' is its negation. The text begins 'On.

Say on' (89) and ends 'Nohow on. Said nohow on' (116). Yet we are made to see, by the proximity in which the words appear, that they differ only in the order of their letters. We feel the precariousness of meaning, its vulnerability to the slightest alteration (we might read, for example, from right to left). The text then mingles progress with regress: 'on' is identified with 'back', and the imperative 'on back' is repeated: 'Back is on. Somehow on. From now back alone. No more from now now back and now back on. Back for back on. Back for somehow on' (109). Ordinary language is further defamiliarised as received idioms (such as 'at all costs', 'gone for good', and 'at most/at least') are unravelled. The sense of these sayings, under scrutiny, reveals itself as pure convention. Why do we say gone for good? What is good about permanence?

Reversibility of meaning is also enacted in the text by the way in which it breaks down the opposition between better and worse. The refrain, often repeated, 'Better worse so', unsettles the difference between amelioration and deterioration: 'Better than nothing so bettered for the worse' (103). The allusion to *King Lear* is instructive here – in particular the idea that the worst is not the worst because, in the case of the worst, the only change possible would be for the better: 'The lamentable change is from the best. The worst returns to laughter' (Shakespeare 1972: IV:1). We can see this, too, in the work's approach to failure. Within the first three pages, 'Fail better' (89) becomes 'Worse failed' (91) then 'Fail better worse now' (91). According to the text's inverted system (better is worse), is 'failing better' worse because closer to the 'goal'? While critics have pointed out how the ambition to proceed from 'somehow' to 'nohow' stands progress on its head – Casanova describes 'somehow' and 'nohow' as 'two points on a line, given as a beginning and an end between which the book will be written' (2006: 17; see also Bersani and Dutoit 1993: 89–90) – the play of interchanging meanings also undermines the oppositions that sustain the idea of progress. In *Worstward Ho*, meanings are subject to chiastic reversals (one thing can also mean its opposite), but what does this radical destabilisation of conventional meaning in language enable us to see?

Part of what comes to light in the dim of *Worstward Ho* is that not just idioms but *all* language is convention, a missaying and thus a worsening of 'what is'. The text insists that words speak only of themselves: 'Nothing save they' (104). If words can only say themselves (rather than refer to things in the world), then there must be a slippage between what words can say and what is. Words can bring into being a world that is *not* what is: 'Say bones. No bones but say bones. Say ground. No ground but say ground' (90). Because language can falsify 'what is', a worsening of language may paradoxically be for the better, since it may enable something other than language (things, the world) to peek through. But it also suggests that the space constructed by language may be an alternative to the status quo – a space in which we can envision concretely how things might be otherwise.

This is one implication of a pair of readings of *Worstward Ho* that I find among the most compelling. These readings find in the text's work of negation – and in its focus on failure and 'worstness' – if not innovative potential then at least a way of resisting the status quo in such a way as to hold open a space in which something different might emerge. Drew Milne's reading of *Worstward Ho* as a 'sustained articulation of the dissident imagination' suggests that it is a 'determinate negation' (in Adorno's sense, borrowed from Hegel) of both capitalist ideology and the protestant work ethic. Milne's suggestion that Beckett's work could be read as 'an investigation into the ethics of imagination within capitalism' explains the compulsion to 'go on' in Beckett as a compulsion to work even without belief in the values sustaining the work in progress.[13] 'Beckett's dissidence', Milne argues further, 'challenges readers who are used to writing which is on better speaking terms with the resources of fiction' (1999: 97). *Worstward Ho*'s challenge to conventional ideas about what fiction should be, for Milne, operates a social critique in the spirit of determinate negation. By self-cancelling or negating its own (self-differentiating) negation, the text might open space for something other than the status quo.

In a similar vein, Shane Weller finds in *Worstward Ho* a resistance to nihilism. Weller's idea, echoing Nietzsche, is that nihilism taken to its extreme would reveal the impossibility of nihilism: nihilism would negate itself so as to leave an 'other-than-nothing' (2005: 189). This, Weller argues, is the 'unlessenable least of longing' and the 'gnawing to be naught' of *Worstward Ho*. This space between 'gnawing' and 'naught', Weller argues, 'the space which, in Adorno's reading of Beckett, is the "slightest difference" between "nothingness" and "coming to rest"', the sole '"haven of hope" in the face of nihilism' appears in *Worstward Ho* as irreducible. 'Worse in vain. Never to be naught,' for Weller, shows the impossibility of nihilism, gesturing towards 'an affirmation beyond the dialectic of affirmation and negation' (2005: 193).

Milne and Weller find in *Worstward Ho* radical creative potential, which may open possibilities for meaning and for relating to others and to our surroundings differently. But this mode of reading risks limiting the power of *Worstward Ho* to determinate negation – that is, to a critique that is fundamentally reactive. My argument is that the self-reflexivity of the text's language – its saying itself saying – enables it to achieve something equivalent in the domain of language to bodily sentience as Merleau-Ponty describes it: an awareness of its double belonging to the realm of subject (sayer) and object (said). We see this, for example, in the image of the held-holding hands (the second shade) and in the description of the skull (the third shade) as the scene/seen and seer of all.

This reversibility of subject and object, active and passive, is evident in a sonorous description of the second shade, the old man and child: 'Hand and hand with equal plod they go' (93). This line echoes the closing lines of Milton's *Paradise Lost*: 'They hand and hand with wand'ring steps and slow./Through Eden took their solitary way' (641–9). Beckett admitted to James Knowlson a more personal association also; this image evoking father and son was among the most 'obsessional' of his childhood memories, carrying a great deal of emotional resonance (though we are, as Knowlson puts it, 'light-years' away from simple autobiography) (1996: 594–5):

> Backs turned both bowed with equal plod they go. The child hand raised to reach the holding hand. Hold the old holding hand. Hold and be held. Plod on and never recede. Slowly with never a pause plod on and never recede. Backs turned. Both bowed. Joined by held holding hands. Plod on as one. One shade. Another shade. (93)

The play of sounds here aptly mimics the intertwining of the hands, which are, as the text repeats, both holding and being held. The 'held holding' hands give us an image of the intertwining of passivity and activity in an arrestingly tender image of father and son, refined away from autobiography to comment on the passivity necessary to relationality more generally: one must be held in order to hold. The physical image of intertwining in *Worstward Ho*, holding and being held, suggests the interdependence of activity and passivity as well as the idea that our being objects – able to be held – conditions our subjective activity.

The intertwining of subject and object, active and passive comes up also in the description of the third shade: the skull – seat and germ of all. The (unfleshly) skull is posited as the creator that has brought the other shades into being. As such, it has the same role as language in the text we're reading. It is the 'so-said seat and germ of all' (100). The third shade is worsened, deprived of its 'crippled hands': 'No hands. No face. Skull and stare alone. Scene and seer of all' (101). The homophony of scene and seen evokes seer-seen (*voyant-visible*), Merleau-Ponty's idea that in order to see we must *be seen*; a fundamental passivity permits subjective perception. But the literal meaning of 'scene' returns us to spatiality. We 'see' but we are also the arena in which what is seen takes place. When the skull stares, it sees its own stare: 'Clenched eyes clamped to clenched staring eyes' (100); 'Stare clamped to stare' (114). As it sees itself seeing, the third shade emerges as seer-seen, creator-created. S. E. Gontarski describes how this self-reflexivity threatens to block the narrative, for if the skull is the 'germ of all', then it must have produced itself: 'If of all of it too?' (NH 97; Gontarski 1996: xxv). If the skull has produced itself, if it is inside itself, from what perspective might it look at itself? Self-reflexivity tends towards infinite regress (as we saw in Chapter 3). 'Such paradoxes', Gontarski writes, 'shift the narrative focus from image to language and the latter's complicity in the act of representation' (1996: xxv). Language says and is said – 'Say on. Be said on' (89) – and language, it would seem, only ever speaks (of) itself:

> Worsening words whose unknown. Whence unknown. At all costs unknown. Now for to say as worst them may only they only they. Dim void shades all they. Nothing save what they say. Somehow say. Nothing save they. What they say. Whosoever whencesoever say. (104)

Just as everything is within the skull, so is everything within language. The dim void and the shades are merely 'they' – that is, words. There is nothing besides words: 'Nothing save they. What they say.' And yet, in the process of saying themselves saying, *something* may be caught in their mesh. Language coiling up over itself brings into being an experience of a world to which we didn't have access before.

Worstward Ho's interrogation of the conditions of its own (literary) creation motivates Mark Byron to observe in the text a 'mode of reflexive self-conception'. He reads *Worstward Ho* as asking what it means for a text to imagine itself in the process of its own creation (2017: 127). Byron explains: '[*Worstward Ho*] faces off with itself as a subjectivity bringing itself into existence and as an object of its contemplation'. What seems to be a 'mirroring effect', Byron argues, 'is more complicated and more fundamental: it is textual map and cartographer in one, its agency enfolded into its material structure' (128). The fact that the text is both map and cartographer, creat*ed* and creat*or*, makes an author figure seem incidental. Instead, language says itself saying. The text's agency is in its 'material structure'. In other words, *Worstward Ho* stages (literary) creation as a self-creation, as the work of words themselves, as material agency. The text's saying itself saying enacts the self-reflexivity Merleau-Ponty posits as fundamental to sentience (we must see ourselves seeing in order to see, touch ourselves touching in order to touch); the 'flesh' is structured so that by folding up over the whole of which it is a part, sentience is possible. In *Worstward Ho*, self-reflexivity occurs in language; in addition to conjuring the shades, the dim and the void (formerly known as characters), language conjures itself too. *Worstward Ho* makes use of the material agency of the 'flesh', enfolded also in the self-reflexive structure of language.

The reversibility of subject and object supported by the flesh – seer-seen, toucher-touched – similarly enacts itself in *Worstward Ho* at the level of language: 'Say for be said. Missaid. From now say for be missaid' (89). We are instructed that whenever 'say' occurs in the text, we should replace it with 'be said' then (preferably) with 'be missaid'. A line later, we have the opportunity to apply this. 'Say a body. Where none' (89) should become, according to the text's rule: 'Be missaid a body. Where none.' Added to the algebra of 'say' for 'be missaid' is: 'See for be seen. Misseen. From now see for be misseen' (93). We read 'say' or 'see' and replace them with 'be said' or 'be seen', holding both subject and object, active and passive, in the mind at once. If 'see' and 'be seen', for instance, can be exchanged, it implies that 'seeing' and 'being seen' are intertwined. Instructions to replace 'say' with 'be said', similarly, suggest a constitutive passivity in language (we must be addressed in order to speak). But seeing and saying are predicated not only on being seen and being said but also on being *mis*seen, *mis*said. This emphasis on error further complicates the self-transparency of a subject who would be able to see and say with any certainty, returning us, perhaps, to Beckett's fondness for Saint Augustine: *'Fallor, ergo sum!'* [I err, therefore I am] (CPEF 4).

This 'self-consciousness' of language reminds us that language is a texture of substitutions and exchanges. It operates by *missaying*, by substituting *words* for what may or may not be there. *Worstward Ho* is transparent about the way it calls into being what isn't there: 'Say bones. No bones but say bones. Say ground. No ground but say ground' (90). Words have fashioned the space of the text we're reading; they have created bodies where none. Language is creative in that it brings worlds into being. We hear this in the incantatory quality of the prose, which, resounding as if it were a spell, conjures the shades, the dim and the void. Enoch Brater calls attention to the acoustic effects of *Worstward Ho*, cataloguing its repetition of vowel sounds, arguing that the work's ability to surround its audience in auditory fashion creates an experience more than it conveys a meaning: 'the sounds in these stanzas is the sense' (1987b: 169).[14] But sound play and repetition are also ways in which language calls attention to the opacity of its surface, to its own operation. A line like 'Nothing save what they say. Nothing save they. What they say' (104) dies away like an echo against the walls of an empty room, *say they say* repeating the 'a', creating a play of sound that leads us to suspect that there is nothing beyond the words that spin around each other playfully, refusing to point to anything beyond themselves.

In addition to self-reflexivity at the level of sound, *Worstward Ho* is a dense reworking of scraps of language culled from the English literary canon as well as from Beckett's own work – so much so that critics have claimed that the text cannot be thoroughly understood without an intimate knowledge of Beckett's whole canon. This is the thesis of Adriaan van der Weel and Ruud Hisgen, whose *The Silencing of the Sphinx* offers a comprehensive interpretation of the *Worstward Ho* manuscripts.[15] Andrew Renton also shows how *Worstward Ho* draws from Beckett's earlier works, calling it the 'rhetorical sublime' of Beckett's oeuvre, integrating all that has come before. Renton finds traces of *Imagine Dead Imagine*, *Ohio Impromptu*, *Endgame*, *A Piece of Monologue* and *Ill Seen Ill Said*. The manner in which *Worstward Ho* refers to earlier works underscores the self-reflexivity of the Beckett canon as a whole.[16]

In Beckett's late prose, drama and television work S. E. Gontarski identifies spectral fragements of a 'persistent and ineluctable past' that commingle with the present. These ghostly images, Gontarski suggests, are 'not so much a debilitating haunting as a regenerative desire, but desire as a creative force, as reinvention or creation' (2015: 66). Gontarski finds in the propulsive 'onwardness' of Beckett's oeuvre a driving force on the order of Bergson's *élan vital*, an energetic current that is neither linear nor teleological but 'part of a continual, self-regenerative creative process, even as the flow is towards "Lessness"' (2015: 5).[17] This onwardness – manifest also in Beckett as an 'obligation to express' – encompasses lessness and disintegration as part of a more capacious, cyclical process. Such a perspective 'puts the lie to the reading of Beckett as a poet of despair, preoccupied with misery, death, suicide and the like, and refocuses the work on the impulse to go on' (2015: 28). This impulse to 'go on' is, as we know, both impossible and necessary. Gontarski's reading points to the unsettling vitality of creation as a regenerative process that is continual but not teleological, since disintegration is part of its movement too.[18]

Merleau-Ponty claims that philosophical problems are not solved in language but reiterated there. Insofar as it creates meaning self-reflexively (by an 'operation of language upon language' (VI 96)), language is itself a world or a stage upon which philosophical problems are exposed: 'language is itself a world, itself a being – a world and a being to the second power' such that language 'redoubles' the enigma of being and the world (VI 96). This idea of language as a stage on which philosophical problems are recreated aptly describes the particular labour of *Worstward Ho*: 'Ooze on back not to unsay but say again the vasts apart' (NH 108). By *saying again*, we gain insight into the problems of being as they repeat themselves in language.[19]

Merleau-Ponty describes how the physical body's active-passive movement restructures its surroundings, forging directions (*sens*). Similarly, operant language (*la parole parlante*) recreates its medium (*la parole parlée*) as it navigates among existing significations. As a 'language body', it remakes language, and Merleau-Ponty describes operant language in bodily terms, as a 'language-thing which counts as an arm, as action' (VI 126). Even without naming the Word *dramatis persona*, as one critic does, we might read the manner in which language operates upon itself in *Worstward Ho* as exhibiting a mode of agency germane to the active-passive, self-articulating element Merleau-Ponty names the 'flesh'.[20] In *Worstward Ho*, there is a folding of the 'flesh' of language. Its work of rearticulation mirrors the manner in which a body orients its space, instantiating a paradigm for creative innovation that is both active and passive.

Worstward Ho also meditates on aesthetic creation; the text could be read as a parable of the authorial process in the absence of an external creator. Innovation happens instead as a self-reflexive operation, the text's saying itself saying, which gives it – if not 'sentience' – then at least a version of agency enfolded in its material structure. The voluntarist agency of an author is displaced, as meaning in *Worstward Ho* emerges not as the unilateral work of a God or author or transcendental subject but as an operation of bodies and language. Because 'flesh' spans bodies, language and being, its passive agency affects not only language (rearticulating it) but also being, as language intertwines with the physical world.

Notes

1. Beckett's remarks echo his 1956 interview with Israel Shenker: '[Joyce is] tending towards omniscience and omnipotence as an artist. I'm working with impotence, ignorance' (qtd in Knowlson: 686). In his dialogues with Georges Duthuit, Beckett describes an art 'weary of pretending to be able, of being able, of doing a little better the same old thing, of going a little further along a dreary road' (PTD 103).
2. Fragments of a French translation by Beckett of *Worstward Ho* were recently discovered in the archives of Les Éditions de Minuit. Anthony Cordingley compared these fragments with Edith Fournier's published translation, finding 'remarkable similarities' between them (2017).
3. Casanova dispenses with 'the prejudice of non-meaning and confusion associated with Beckett's writing', a prejudice she associates with Blanchot's critical legacy. She emphasises instead the 'strict rules of composition and organization' that characterise Beckett's work, particularly the combinatorial method: '*Worstward Ho* is a summit of Beckett's *ars combinatoria*, prodigiously controlled and devised' (2006: 16). Like Bersani, she identifies the text's organisation, its movement from 'somehow on' to 'nohow on' as it worsens language by lessening it. She argues that this procedure is laid out in a series of 'rules' in Beckett's text, finding 'proof of a formidable

formal ambition, without precedent in the history of literature, of a logical, combinatory option in the service of a new literary form' (26).
4. I cannot hope to do full justice in these pages to the complexity of the chiasm or the flesh, the explication of which has filled entire volumes. What I hope to do instead is highlight the manner in which these notions present the interdependence of activity/passivity and subjectivity/objectivity, so as to explore how Beckett's prose might harness the foundational 'agency' of passivity in its 'living' language.
5. Robert Vallier, for instance, makes the case that Merleau-Ponty's *Institution and Passivity: Course Notes from the Collège de France (1954–1955)* sets the tone 'for an ontological radicalization of his work', constituting a 'turn' in his thinking that distinguishes the *Phenomenology* from *The Visible and the Invisible* (281).
6. Merleau-Ponty writes: 'philosophy is an operative language, that language that can be known only from within, through its exercise, is open upon the things, called forth by the voices of silence, and continues an effort of articulation which is the Being of every being' (un essai d'articulation qui est l'Être de tout être) (VI 126–7; Vi 166).
7. Hiroshi Kojima convincingly argues that Merleau-Ponty moves from a dialectical position in which subject and object would be fused, to a position of reversibility that characterises his late ontology. Kojima points out that Merleau-Ponty's 'hyperdialectic' is an early version of his chiasmus, which I discuss at greater length in Chapter 4 (Kojima 2002: 95–115).
8. The self-reflexive structure of the flesh – its ability to fold so as to look back at itself – also founds the subjectivities of others: 'if there is a relation of the visible with itself that traverses me and constitutes me as a seer, this circle which I do not form, which forms me, this coiling over of the visible upon the visible, can traverse, animate other bodies as well as my own. And if I was able to understand how this wave arises within me [. . .] I can understand a fortiori that elsewhere it also closes over upon itself and that there are other landscapes beside my own' (VI 140–1).
9. Renaud Barbaras suggests that Merleau-Ponty does not go far enough: 'The ontological transfer from my flesh (a body) to the world (as Flesh) would require an ontological shift much more radical than that which Merleau-Ponty makes in *The Visible and the Invisible*' (2002: 19–27).
10. This interdependence of activity and passivity has been used to discuss Merleau-Ponty's thought in conjunction with creativity in the arts (Menasé 2003).

11. Of the *écart*, Merleau-Ponty writes (in a working note): '*reversibility* is not actual *identity* of the touching and the touched [. . .] the fabric of possibilities that closes the exterior visible in upon the seeing body maintains between them a certain *divergence (écart)*. But this divergence is not a *void*, it is filled precisely by the flesh as the place of emergence of a vision, a passivity that bears an activity – and so also the divergence between the exterior visible and the body which forms the upholstering *(capitonnage)* of the word' (VI 272).
12. Andrew Renton schematises the shades as follows: 'S(hade) 1 The pained body of bones that rises and kneels. S(hade) 2 The combined image of man and child. S(hade) 3 The perceiving head or skull, "germ of all"' (1992: 102).
13. Milne describes how *Worstward Ho* dramatises the necessity of going on in the absence of 'know how': '"nohow on" plays on the denial of "know-how" as the "no" which nevertheless goes "on". "On", the flip side of "no", is a command to "go on" simultaneously imagined as a description of a journey which knows no "how" to get on with. The exploration of this narrative terrain forms a continuous and reflexively self-canceling oeuvre' (1999: 94). Milne's implication is that this self-cancelling might open space for something different (in the spirit of determinate negation). But I argue that *Worstward Ho* already shows us – in its aberrant articulations, play of sounds and texture of reversals (no–on) – alternative modes of meaning.
14. Brater claims that Beckett's late prose brings the drama of live performance into the text: 'meaning is impossible to divorce from verbal gesture. [. . .] The drama here is always in the play of language' (1994: 69).
15. They call *Worstward Ho* 'hermetic in the very literal sense that it can only properly be understood from a thorough knowledge of Beckett's entire *oeuvre*' (1998: 361).
16. Erik Wessler's *La Littérature face à elle-même* argues that the 'auto-reflexivity' of Beckett's body of work is what constitutes its radical literary innovation.
17. Gontarski writes, 'There is something of a Bergsonian driving force in Beckett's "obligation", delivered as advice to the painter Tal Coat, some inexplicable yet powerful force of rejuvenation, which Bergson deemed an *élan vital*' (2015: 28).
18. Gontarski's reading further suggests that Bergson's challenge to Western philosophical tradition incites a new way of thinking and of reading – 'one that "neither depends on a point of view nor relies on any symbol". Instead it requires of the reader a "kind of *intellectual sympathy* by which one places onself within an object in order to coincide with what is unique in it and consequently inexpressible"'

(Bergson as qtd in Gontarski 2015: 67). Gontarski then argues that Beckett's texts 'are best read from the inside, the reader part of the process rather than apart from it' (67). He contends, in a way most relevant to the argument of the present volume, that Beckett's work intersects with Bergson's 'new narrative of the human with its emphasis on consciousness and perpetual process' (67). In *Worstward Ho*, certainly, the reader feels herself caught up in the process of the text's creation.

19. Carla Locatelli notes that this constitutes a change in Beckett's attitude to language. Rather than trying to get rid of language or move beyond it (a desire expressed in his German Letter of 1937), Beckett's work seems to treat language more like an arena in which certain problems may be worked through (1990: 227).

20. Brater identifies the *dramatis persona* of *Worstward Ho* as the Word, which conforms to the lineage of Beckett protagonists with names beginning with M or W (1994: 137).

Conclusion
Embedded in the World: Beckett, Late Modernism, Earth-Body Art

> Now that I'm entering night I have kinds of gleams in my skull. Stony ground but not entirely. Given three or four lives I might have accomplished something.
>
> Beckett, 'Enough'

The short prose piece *Assez* (1966), translated as 'Enough', joins writerly difficulty – 'When the pen stops I go on. Sometimes it refuses' – with descriptions of sexual and intellectual subjection: 'I did all he desired. I desired it too. For him [. . .] All I know comes from him' (CP 186, 187). A version of agency based on will and intention is troubled here as the pen 'refuses' and the narrator's desires are not her own. The story ends with the narrator and her companion eating flowers; munching the petals has a 'calming' effect. If the Romantic ideal of fusion with the natural world is fulfilled comically, by way of ingestion, and if the idea of nature as 'calming' or as a palliative is mocked, then this parody is made more complex by the fact that the world of the story is not wholly our world, though forests, hills and storms are refracted in it. Flowers are off-kilter, 'stemless and flush with the ground like water-lilies' (191), and the story's physical environment is also the windless space of the page. In the end, the narrator says she will 'wipe out' everything but the flowers: 'No more rain. No more mounds. Nothing but the two of us dragging through the flowers' (192). Embedded within her textual-physical world (and her textual-physical world embedded in her), the narrator shapes it: stony ground (*terre ingrate*) but not entirely.

Beckett is most often described as a writer who embraces impotence, powerlessness, materiality and mortality. His aesthetic opposes a high modernist, godlike ambition to heal the breach between the word and the world, and he disdains the discourse of postwar French humanism, which (re)assures us that we will persevere and triumph in the face of adversity. Here, instead, is a writer who compares the Bible to morphine (in early drafts of *Fin de Partie)*, who refuses palliatives of any kind and who drills relentlessly into the bedrock of what is real. Here is a writer who reveals words as flimsy things, changeable, fickle and threadbare but also occluding and viscous, refusing to take form. Here is a writer who refuses to idealise the body and instead emphasises its materiality, its odours and secretions, which links it to the muddy viscosity of words and to the earth around us, to which, one day – as Beckett's writing makes us all too aware – we shall return.

Where does this portrayal of the human body as netted up with the earth and with language leave us in terms of thinking about human action or agency? Are we dealt into a deterministic universe where we drive on towards death, holding fast to a misguided sense of freedom? Although Merleau-Ponty and Beckett diverge sharply in their sensibilities – one can imagine Beckett's parodic genius running riot with some of the more rhapsodic passages in *The Visible and the Invisible* – Merleau-Ponty's understanding of bodily passivity nevertheless makes his phenomenology a valuable resource for rethinking embodiment in Beckett, a preoccupation that runs like a live wire through his long and varied career. My reading of Beckett with Merleau-Ponty shows how bodily passivity paradoxically illuminates a limited, material agency, different from the voluntarism of a humanist subject.

Merleau-Ponty's radical rethinking of passivity and embodiment has been developed and extended by contemporary phenomenologists, for instance by Don Beith, who proposes a theory of 'generative passivity'. Passivity, for Beith, is not inertness, rather it refers to a 'generative temporal openness, where meaningful structures or institutions of activity take time to developmentally unfold' (2). Beith theorises a 'passive genesis of sense' that is prior to any constituting activity and that subtends the vital body as well as our ideas about personhood. This has political and ethical implications that move us 'beyond' social constructivism, thinning the divide between nature and culture by demonstrating their interdependence (3). In the introduction to this volume, we saw how Merleau-Ponty's phenomenology has often explicitly influenced posthumanist and new materialist challenges to both voluntarism and constructivism. In their work on phenomenology and philosophy of mind, Shaun Gallagher and Dan Zahavi point out the resonance between Merleau-Ponty's ideas about embodied subjectivity, neuroscientific theories of embodied cognition (Varela, Clark) and enactivist models of mind, such as that of Alva Noë, who argues that perception is not limited to neuronal networks but involves the whole organism coping with and exploring its environment (Noë as qtd in Gallagher and Zahavi 2012: 110).

But how might such ideas about the extended mind, material agency and the importance of natural-material processes illuminate Beckett's austere, iconic images of bodily constraint, which might, at first (and even second) glance, seem to thwart any harmonious vision of integration between mind, body and world? Embodiment seems more a sentence to immobility than the condition of human agency. But it is worth remembering that even Beckett's 'skullscapes' (hints that his scenes are set 'inside a skull') do not limit the world to the mind so much as bring the world into the mind, challenging the opposition between inner and outer. It is also true that images of bodily restriction in Beckett – Murphy tied naked to his rocking chair with seven scarves – are comic. *Murphy* mirthfully depicts the impossibility of a mind 'free' of its body. Beckett gives us the body-as-object, joined to its material environment: ash, ooze, mud, cracked earth, grass, metal and clay. His embedded or machine-like bodies give us some indication of the conditions under which effective change might be possible – conditions that never involve abnegation of our material embodiment. They suggest that limitless dreaming is, ultimately, escapist, and that it is only by recognising and assuming our concrete limitations that we might work within them to expand the domain of what is possible.

In *Quad*, for instance, players move on predetermined tracks not by their own will but by the inertia of a manic tarantella that cannot stop. This 'performance' of passivity repeats an existing limitation in a different context – an aesthetic one. *Quad* dramatises a passivity which, insofar as it repeats the status quo – performing and reinscribing it – creates space for a subtle form of agency, a 'passive agency' I associate with embodiment in Beckett. More generally, *Quad*'s evocation of physiological processes (like the heartbeat) reminds us that, in the body, autonomic processes like breathing and the circulation of blood are necessary to activities that we think of as volitional, like running, dancing or speaking. The fact that the body is part of the world in which it moves and acts, far from inhibiting its freedom, is what secures its power to affect the environment of which it is a part.

I want to suggest briefly that this idea of embodiment as an enabling limitation, as the condition by which we have access not only to the world amenable to orientation but also to literary innovation, can be productively applied beyond the writings of Samuel Beckett, and with particular relevance to the mid-twentieth-century literary movement characterised (loosely) as 'late modernism'. Late modernism is defined against the high modernism of the early twentieth century, the tenets of which it inherits and modifies in the aftermath of the Second World War. On the other side, late modernism is bounded by (and perhaps anticipates) postmodernism, which Connor Carville calls a 'short-lived mannerist reaction to the pre-war period's classicism' (2018: 53). Yet while there are certainly parallels to be made between the self-reflexivity and infinite regress in Beckett's immediate postwar fiction and the stories of Jorge Luis Borges and Italo Calvino, a postmodern levity is lacking in the work of late modernists, who haven't entirely untethered their aims from those of the high modernists, even as these ambitions appear senselessly grandiose in the light of horrific historical circumstance.[1]

Tyrus Miller's influential book on late modernism identifies Beckett as a late modernist writer on the basis of the decline, decay, fragmentation, comic absurdity and formal innovation Miller finds in his work – all qualities Miller uses to define late modernism, which reacts to devastating historical circumstances that frustrate high modernist myths of mastery of form (1999: 14). Interestingly, Miller also finds in late modernism the tendency to intertwine oppositions, such as decline and renewal and despair and utopia. Miller compares Beckett to writers like Wyndham Lewis, Djuna Barnes and Mina Loy. Parting ways with Miller, Shane Weller articulates a novel conception of late modernism based on a reaction to language scepticism that is different from that of the high modernists. Instead of striving to overcome the schism between language and the world it represents, as Joyce did with his masterful wordplay in *Finnegans Wake*, Beckett embraced a literature of the 'unword' (detailed in his 1937 letter to Axel Kaun) and nominalism, making 'the *impossibility of expression* the very heart of the literary work' (Weller 2018: 45). Weller calls Beckett's practice of 'literary negativism' 'the epitome of European late modernism' – a movement which, 'in place of a faith in the power of the literary word to repair the breach between language and experience, takes as its matter the very experience of that breach' (45). For Weller, late modernist literature is 'the (highly paradoxical and indeed torturous) articulation of the inarticulability of experience' (45). In this, Beckett is joined not by Barnes and Lewis but by Paul Celan, Maurice Blanchot, W. G. Sebald and, proleptically, Kafka, a writer whose work Beckett read sparingly because, as he wrote to Morris Sinclair, he 'felt at home, too much so' in Kafka's work (LB2 464 as qtd in Weller 2018).

Kafka's inclusion in this list, despite his disruption of chronology, highlights the importance of impossibility and necessity to late modernism, a predicament to which Beckett refers, among other places, in his dialogues with Georges Duthuit: 'The expression that there is nothing to express, nothing with which to express, nothing from which to express, no power to express, no desire to express, together with the obligation to express' (PTD 103). Weller points out that Blanchot and Kafka describe a coupling of impossibility and necessity in similar terms – a coupling that arguably shapes their work.[2] Kafka is proleptic with respect to European late modernism insofar as his work depicts alienated, disempowered individuals subject to impersonal forces – an anticipation, perhaps, of the concentration camps, where the boundaries between life and death, human and animal, and human and nonhuman were eroded in a horrific way (Weller: 48). Adorno compares Kafka's personae to those of *Endgame*, likening them to a fly that has been struck by a fly swatter but is not quite dead (Adorno as qtd in Weller: 48). While the historical circumstances of the Second World War – its anticipation and aftermath – shape late modernism, what formally distinguishes this movement from its predecessor is that it *enacts* (rather than merely articulates) the impossibility of expression (Weller: 48). While high modernists such as T. S. Eliot or Joyce may discourse eloquently on the inadequacy of language, linguistic failure for late modernists such as Beckett infects the prose itself. Weller cites the syntactic 'violence of unremitting epanorthosis' in *The Unnamable*, but we could just as easily refer to the truncated syntax of *How It Is* or *Worstward Ho*, the stuttering close of *Malone Dies* or Beckett's final poem, 'What is the Word' (49). Late modernism responds to the horror of history. As Weller aptly puts it, 'experience had come to beggar language in a manner unimaginably more extreme than at the turn of the century' (45) – but rather than allowing the impossibility of expression to remain at the level of theme, late modernists enact it by allowing it to alter their syntax, sonority and literary form. Weller's theory of late modernism rightly emphasises en*act*ment, a more material and embodied response to the horror of history, a performance of impossibility or passivity that reinscribes it within a different context – an aesthetic one.

In what ways, then, might a phenomenology of embodiment be appropriate for understanding the gestures of late modernism, a movement driven by its experience of the necessity and impossibility of expression? Insofar as late modernism 'enacts' linguistic failure, or the inability of words to capture experience, it might be said to embody this failure, responding 'materially' as it were, reproducing the problem (rather than merely speaking about it, holding it at a distance). There is, then, an attempt to dramatise the problem within the work, to make it part of the material of the work itself. We see this in the fragmentation and tireless remaking of form, in syntactic 'violence' and in the stripping away of illusions of competence and mastery. A phenomenology of embodiment demonstrates the extent to which assuming and becoming part of one's surroundings leads to an awareness of the limits and possibilities of human agency. Such recognition and awareness contrasts not only with modernist myths of mastery but also with a French postwar humanist discourse that touted will, action and an empty solidarity that Beckett mocked with *éclat*.[3] In his dialogues with Duthuit, Beckett praises the painter Bram Van Velde for being

> the first to accept a certain situation and to consent to a certain act [. . .] The situation is that of him who is helpless, cannot act, in the event cannot paint, since he is obliged to paint. The act is of him who, helpless, unable to act, acts, in the event paints, since he is obliged to paint. (PTD 119)

This recognition and acceptance of what is necessary, this 'going on' in the face of impossibility, involves a refusal to look away or to receive succour in the form of illusions, especially an inflated sense of the human will and what it can control.

Looking at embodied agency in relation to late modernism reveals itself as a promising area for future research. Merleau-Ponty's thinking is especially apt in this respect because of the way in which it conceives of language in spatial terms. It addresses the imbrication of the human not only within the physical world but also within language. This embeddedness of the human within a linguistic 'space' or milieu is, as we've seen, a major preoccupation in Beckett's work. 'I'm in words, made of words, others' words' (TN 386) is its most literal expression, but we find strong affinities between the materiality of language and the muddy setting of *How It Is*, as discussed in Chapter 5.[4] Positing an analogy between space and language in the *Phenomenology of Perception* and developing it during his engagement with structuralism in the 1950s, Merleau-Ponty goes on to refer, in his ontological writings, to a 'flesh' of language. As we saw in Chapter 7, flesh, in Merleau-Ponty's thinking, is an element that encompasses the body, language and the world, distinguished by its self-reflexive structure (it can fold back to look at itself).

Merleau-Ponty's philosophy gives us a sense of our belonging to the earthy environment and to a linguistic terrain. Our orientation of our material surroundings according to our perceptions and projects, for Merleau-Ponty, offers more robust possibilities for 'agency' than does the will of a transcendental subject separate from its world. But Merleau-Ponty's sense of the body's power to shape existing space and language by speaking, writing and moving differently is ultimately more harmonious than the intimations of material agency we find in Beckett; there is pathos in Beckettian bodies imbricated within their linguistic and physical environments – a sense of disappointment, even of indignation at earthly limits. Nagg and Nell in their bins and Winnie in her mound of earth may evoke laughter as they dream beyond their bounds, paying too little attention to their embodied condition, which is, for the audience, all too palpable. Embeddedness in the world, in Beckett, is by no means empowering in a straightforward sense.

In the late twentieth and early twenty-first centuries, theoretical movements such as posthumanism, new materialisms and certain branches of eco-criticism (especially eco-phenomenology) have brought into the critical mainstream ideas that are fundamental to Merleau-Pontian phenomenology, most importantly the idea that the human body and its physical and linguistic world are materially intertwined in such a way as to be mutually dependent. What further unifies these movements (posthumanism, eco-criticism and phenomenology) and makes them especially pertinent to a reading of embodiment in Beckett is their interrogation of the 'limit' of the human. 'Limit' here applies both to human capabilities (power to affect change in the world, or agency) and to borders or boundaries: where does the human end and the world begin? This is a question germane to Beckett's work, which enacts it with affecting force. The Unnamable confesses: 'There's no end to me' (399) (*Je n'arrête pas*), and Malone's body expands expressionistically into space as he feels his feet beyond the reaches of the most powerful telescope, his turds coming out in Australia. Bodies flicker between presence and absence in Beckett's television and dramatic plays and in his later prose, a spectrality that S. E. Gontarski attributes not to haunting but to regenerative desire, the persistence of the past in the present that reveals a force of continuation moving through them (Gontarski 2015: 66). Bodies extend prosthetically in *Endgame* (in bins), in *Play* (in urns), in the trilogy (by means of crutches, pencils and jars) and in *Krapp's Last Tape* (in spools of audio recordings). Beckett's narrators have also a great love for ditches, in which they lie tangled in grass and mud or pummelled by the rain, able to hear the sighing of the earth or the turning of the planet. The boundaries of the human are abrogated as bodies intertwine with the material world around them, intuiting the sentience of the earth (in the immediate postwar writing) and the sentience of language as it says bodies into being (*Worstward Ho*).

Beckett's interrogation of the 'limit of the human' has been observed by Jean-Michel Rabaté in *Think Pig! Beckett at the Limit of the Human*, which kindled an interest in 'Beckett and the Nonhuman' (Atkinson et al. 2020). Earlier studies devoted to animals in Beckett have, similarly, observed an unsettling of the hierarchy that takes for granted human mastery over other 'creatures' (Bryden 2013; Anderton 2016). Beckett's interrogation of the limit of the human resonates also with contemporary theoretical attempts to decentre the human in favour of a more holistic view of the human in relation to objects, technology and ecology. The work of Jane Bennett, Katherine Hayles, Rosi Braidotti, Karen Barad, Donna Haraway and many others has challenged anthropocentric models of agency, urging attention to the nonhuman, a category that includes the environment, objects, technology, animals and language. In different ways, these theorists argue for the existence of diverse agentic forces at work in our material surroundings. In this sense, human agency requires acknowledgement of our complex imbrication within material systems (economic systems, traffic patterns, meteorological conditions, technological networks, language and cultural systems).

Although posthumanism, like Merleau-Pontian phenomenology, shares certain characteristics with poststructuralism – for instance, its challenge to the idea of a voluntarist subject – posthumanism differs by locating a limited, material agency in our embodied collaboration with objects and with the environment. Posthumanism demonstrates, eloquently, that dispensing with a voluntarist view of agency does not mean dispensing with agency altogether. We find similar intimations of a material agency also, I have argued, in Beckett's representations of human bodies embedded in their material surroundings.

The chapters in this volume have traced the way in which Merleau-Ponty's phenomenology relocates agency away from a transcendental subject and into a material body moving within its world. Merleau-Ponty's body-subject alters our conception of the relation between the human and the nonhuman by drawing attention to our imbrication within the nonhuman, implicating us in the fate of the environment. This facet of Merleau-Ponty's thinking has inspired eco-phenomenology as well as movements in contemporary theory aligned with posthumanism. Diana Coole, for instance, finds in Merleau-Pontian phenomenology a foundation for theories of material agency. The concrete, everyday implications of these phenomenological ideas (about material subjectivity and agency) have been the focus of Sara Ahmed's work. Ahmed draws on Merleau-Ponty to propose a spatial, material basis for sexual and romantic desire and for emotion more generally. *Queer Phenomenology* (2006) interrogates 'orientation' as that which draws us to certain things and bodies rather than others, enabling us to construct meaning. Ahmed derives human subjectivity and desire from the body's mode of interacting with its environment.

Eco-phenomenology is likewise concerned with the practical implications of more integrated mind-body ontologies. It works to unsettle the oppositions and hierarchies that undergird our instrumentalist, extractionist rapport with the environment. The human view of itself as separate and superior vis-à-vis the natural world has culminated in anthropogenic global warming, natural disasters, aridity, heat waves, wildfires, melting glaciers, floods and air pollution. Eco-phenomenology applies Merleau-Ponty's ideas (and those of other phenomenologists) to ecology, demonstrating that the fate of the human is aligned with that of the planet and urging ecological stewardship. In his reading of *Endgame*, Greg Garrard draws on a different tradition of eco-criticism: Timothy

Morton's argument for 'ecology without nature', which urges us to resist Romantic fetishisations of nature at the expense of ecology. Garrard notes that *Endgame*, in part by withholding explicit descriptions of nature, allows us to feel a climate crisis already in motion. Representations of the human as imbricated within its environment urge a thorough rethinking of human limits and responsibilities regarding our environment in peril.

Given that embodiment in Beckett so often involves an image of a human body literally inserted into language, packed earth, mud, jars, urns, bins and so forth, I'll close with a short description of installation art involving earthbound bodies. A brief overview of the work of Giuseppe Penone and Ana Mendieta – two different approaches to the imbrication of the human in the material world – gestures towards radical enactments of these themes beyond experimental literature, following their extension into the art world. The work of these artists resonates with the reading of embodiment in Beckett that Merleau-Ponty's phenomenology encourages: a view of the human as ineluctably embedded in the earth, from which we draw our power and possibility, even as we participate in a ceaseless though non-teleological process of disintegration and reinvention.

Giuseppe Penone (1947) is best known for his sculptural explorations of the interface between the human and the natural world, working with natural materials like wood, granite, marble, clay, bronze and glass. His earliest series, *Alpi Marittime* (*Maritime Alps*), is composed of works in the forest near Garessio, his childhood village in Piedmont. To create his 1968 sculpture *Continuerà a crescere tranne che in quel punto* (*It Will Continue to Grow Except at That Point*), Penone arranged for a steel cast of his hand and forearm to grasp a young tree trunk, forcing the tree to grow around the steel cast of his body. Penone further compares the growth and lifespan of trees with that of the human in his series *Alberi* (*Trees*), in which he sculpted large trunks of trees along their growth rings to reveal the tree as a sapling, its physical form at an earlier stage of its life. In 1999, Penone wrote: 'The desire for an equal relationship between my person and things is the origin of my work. Man is not a spectator or actor but simply nature' (Marks). We find these sentiments echoed in the series begun in 1981, *Essere fiume* (*Being the River*); Penone took one stone from a river bed that had been carved by the water flowing across it and one stone of the same material from the source of the river. He carved the latter stone to

Figure 8.1 Giuseppe Penone, *Continuerà a crescere tranne che in quel punto* (*It Will Continue to Grow Except at That Point*), 1968. © Artists Rights Society (ARS), New York/ADAGP, Paris.

match the former, imitating, in his sculptural work, the action of the river to shape the stone, becoming, in a sense, the river, imitating its work by means of his own art-making. Penone wrote that his work derived from his collaboration with his material: 'Not having a direct relationship with the material, but only a concept, or an idea of making a work to match an image conceived in the mind, isn't fertile over time – it doesn't produce many things' (Marks).

Penone's artist's book *Svolgere la propria pelle* (*Developing One's Own Skin*) (1970) is composed of hundreds of projected images of his skin on sheets of glass, giving the impression that human skin records and reacts like any other material in nature. The imprint (of the skin), Penone writes, 'has the intelligence of the material, a universal intelligence, an intelligence of the flesh of the material of man' (Penone, 222). Penone's sculpture has been described as accepting or 'acceding to man's place in the natural world; acknowledging human transience [. . .] and recognising that the body assumes a sculptural relationship to the spaces it inhabits'. In this context, Penone's *Soffi di creta* (*Breaths of Clay*) series (1978) has been described as 'making visible a projection of the body into space that is a fundamental condition of being alive. "Breath is automatic, involuntary sculpture", Penone wrote in 1977, "that brings us closer to osmosis with things"' (qtd in Marks). Finally, Penone's *L'albero delle vocali* (*The Tree of Vowels*) (1999–2000), a permanent installation piece in the Jardin des Tuileries in Paris, is a work I would pass almost daily on my way to teach. In all seasons, I would see it lying on a bed of earth; from a certain distance it was indistinguishable from a tree felled by a storm, its roots exposed. Seeing it there – or, more precisely, marking the moment at which it became discernible from nature, visible as dark bronze, as a human creation – never failed to give me pause. But if I happened to look back as I continued walking, it would look again like an ordinary tree. Like Merleau-Ponty and like Beckett, Penone explores the limit between the human and material world, showing us our imbrication within it.

We find a similar – though not identical – gesture in the 'earth-body art' of Ana Mendieta (1948–1985), a Cuban American artist known for capturing fleeting encounters between the body and earth in photographs and in short Super-8 films. On a trip to Mexico, Mendieta made *Imágen de Yágul* (1973), a photograph of her naked body in a ditch, a Zapotec tomb, covered with small white flowers that appear to be growing out of it. Her face and features are obscured, leaving only patches of skin, her toes and her arms visible beneath the bed of flowers and vines. Mendieta writes: 'In 1973 I did my first piece in an Aztec tomb that was covered in weeds and grasses – that growth reminded me of time. I bought flowers at the market, lay on the tomb, and was covered with white flowers. The analogy was that I was covered by time and history' (Mendieta 1988: 66). Silhouetted figures appear throughout Mendieta's work across a variety of landscapes (the US, Mexico and Cuba). In earlier work, Mendieta's body appears in the earth; later she would film or photograph the trace of its absence, or its mark or indentation on the environment. Mendieta would often fill the silhouettes created by her body with rocks, flowers, twigs, gunpowder or blood. A short film, *Burial Pyramid* (1974), shows Mendieta's body covered in stones, almost indistinguishable from the ruins of a Mesoamerican archeological site. At first it is difficult to see the body there, embedded in the ruin, but eventually we notice her breathing by the way it affects the landscape; the grasses flutter, a few stones roll away. The three-minute colour film gives us the impression that Mendieta's body, like the ruin, is involved in the earth's natural processes of growth and decay.

Figure 8.2 Ana Mendieta, *Imagen de Yagul*, from the series *Silueta Works in Mexico 1973–1977*, 1973. © The Estate of Ana Mendieta Collection, LLC. Courtesy Galerie Lelong & Co. Licensed by the Artists Rights Society (ARS), New York.

Given Mendieta's fondness for performing, photographing and filming the body's imbrication with the natural world, it isn't surprising that she should be cited among artists thought to be 'posthumanist' *avant la lettre*. Mendieta's environmental art, in which her body merges with the earth and other objects (grass, water, rocks), has been said to contrast with the more 'monumental alterations' (dependent on heavy machinery) of her male contemporaries in the Land Art movement, such as Robert Smithson (Ferrando 2016; Osterweil 2015). Mendieta's *Siluetas* series (1973–80), on the contrary, has been said to 'remind us that all flesh returns to the earth' and to mark 'an exchange [between body and world] characterized by a mutual, albeit transient recognition. The artist's body made a temporary indentation in the earth that the earth reclaimed and redistributed' (Osterweil 2015). In *Siluetas*, 'the human figure – sometimes reproduced in fire or blood – is not separate from the environment, in a holistic approach that resonates with posthuman environmental awareness and an overcoming of dualistic ontologies' (Ferrando 2016). Mendieta's earth-body art embeds the body within the natural environment, either by physically joining her body with the landscape or by recording its outline, making visible our embeddedness in the earth and our human involvement in its cycles of growth and decay. Mendieta and Penone's art draws our attention to our mortal condition as bodies intertwined within our material environment, and their images parallel those we find Beckett (though they lack Beckett's impulse for comedy).

Beckett's gesture, his way of embedding the human in a material world of earth, words or objects, is repeated often enough over the span of his career to carry the force of artistic obsession. His representation of embodiment reveals not only its affinity with phenomenological ideas about the intertwining of body and world, but also its contemporaneity, its pertinence to a conversation that spans posthumanism and eco-criticism, urging, for ethical and ecological reasons, greater attention to the imbrication of the human within its material world.

Notes

1. In France, the neatness of this periodisation is challenged by OULIPO, in particular the writings of Georges Perec, where whimsy joins a late modernist powerlessness. Pathos and high emotion emerge amid rigorous and playful structural constraint. A late modernist remaking

of form is discernible also in the works of certain writers of the *nouveau roman*, including contemporaries of Beckett whose work he admired: Maurice Blanchot, Robert Pinget, Marguerite Duras and Alain Robbe-Grillet.

2. Weller cites *Faux Pas* (1943): 'The writer finds himself in the increasingly ludicrous condition of having nothing to write, of having no means with which to write it, and of being constrained by the utter necessity of always writing it' (Blanchot: 3 as qtd in Weller 2018: 46). In a 1921 letter to Max Brod, Kafka lists three impossibilities for Jewish writers in Prague: 'The impossibility of not writing, the impossibility of writing German, the impossibility of writing differently. One might also add a fourth impossibility, the impossibility of writing' (Kafka: 289 as qtd in Weller 2018: 47).

3. At the close of his 1948 essay 'Peintres de l'Empêchement', Beckett writes: 'Pour finir parlons d'autre chose, parlons de l'humain . . .' In a mocking tone, he quips that the word 'human' is reserved for times of great massacres, and goes on to describe the importance of what he calls 'true humanity' (*humanité vraie*) in art. This is the 'humanity' of solitude that reaches out its hand (*la solitude qui tend le bras*). If we are interested in time, we should kill it, in space, we should crack it apart, in goodness, we should suffocate it; Beckett excoriates a polite 'arts and craft' that would not truly explore what is at hand (1983: 131–2).

4. The relation between the body and language is a guiding preoccupation of *The Edinburgh Companion to Samuel Beckett and the Arts*; it features in several of the essays collected in the volume. For further discussion of this subject, see my review (Dennis 2017).

Bibliography

Ackerley, C. J. (2004), *Demented Particulars: The Annotated Murphy*, Edinburgh: Edinburgh University Press.
Ackerley, C. J. (2009), '"Ever Know What Happened?": Shades and Echoes in Samuel Beckett's Plays for Television', *Journal of Beckett Studies* 18, pp. 136–64.
Ackerley, C. J. (2010), *Obscure Locks, Simple Keys: The Annotated Watt*, Edinburgh: Edinburgh University Press.
Ackerley, C. J. and S. E. Gontarski, eds (2004), *The Grove Companion to Samuel Beckett: A Reader's Guide to His Works, Life, and Thought*, New York: Grove Press.
Adorno, Theodor (1982), 'Trying to Understand *Endgame*', trans. M. T. Jones, *New German Critique* 26, pp. 119–50.
Adorno, Theodor (1997), 'Cultural Criticism and Society', *Prisms*, trans. Samuel and Sherry Weber, Cambridge, MA: The MIT Press.
Ahearn, Laura (2001), 'Language and Agency', *Annual Review of Anthropology* 30, pp. 109–37.
Ahmed, Sara (2006), *Queer Phenomenology: Orientations, Objects, Others*, Durham, NC and London: Duke University Press.
Anderton, Joseph (2016), *Beckett's Creatures: Art of Failure After the Holocaust*, London: Bloomsbury.
Anzieu, Didier (1999), *Beckett*, Paris: Gallimard.
'articulation, n.' (June 2020), *OED Online*, Oxford University Press, <www.oed.com/view/Entry/11196> (last accessed 25 August 2020).
Atkins, Anselm (1967), 'Lucky's Speech in Beckett's "Waiting for Godot"': A Punctuated Sense-Line Arrangement', *Educational Theatre Journal* 19:4, pp. 426–32.
Atkinson, Douglas, Amanda Dennis and Thomas Thoelen, eds (2020), *SBTA 32: Beckett and the Nonhuman*.
Badiou, Alain (1995), *Beckett: L'Increvable désir*, Paris: Hachette Littératures.

Badiou, Alain (2003), *On Beckett*, ed. Alberto Toscano and Nina Power, trans. Bruno Bosteels, Nina Power and Alberto Toscano, London: Clinamen.

Bair, Deirdre (1990), *Samuel Beckett: A Biography*, 2nd ed., London: Vintage.

Barad, Karen (2007), *Meeting the Universe Halfway: Quantum Physics and the Entanglement of Matter and Meaning*, Durham, NC and London: Duke University Press.

Barbaras, Renaud (1991), *De l'être du phénomène: sur l'ontologie de Merleau-Ponty*, Grenoble: Jérôme Million.

Barbaras, Renaud (2002), 'The Ambiguity of the Flesh', *Chiasmi International 4: Figures et fonds de la chair*, pp. 19–27.

Barbaras, Renaud [1991] (2004), *The Being of the Phenomenon: On Merleau-Ponty's Ontology*, trans. Leonard Lawlor and Ted Toadvine, Bloomington: Indiana University Press.

Barry, Elizabeth (2006), *Beckett and Authority: The Uses of Cliché*, Houndmills, Basingstoke and New York: Palgrave Macmillan.

Barry, Elizabeth (2008), 'One's Own Company: Agency, Identity and the Middle Voice in the Work of Samuel Beckett', *Journal of Modern Literature* 31:2, pp. 115–32.

Barthes, Roland (1974), *S/Z*, trans. Richard Miller, New York: Hill and Wang.

Bates, David (2001), 'Idols and Insight: An Enlightenment Topography of Knowledge', *Representations* 73, pp. 1–23.

Beckett, Samuel (1953), *L'Innommable*, Paris: Minuit.

Beckett, Samuel (1961), *Comment c'est*, Paris: Minuit.

Beckett, Samuel [1961] (2013), *Happy Days: A Play in Two Acts*, New York: Grove Press.

Beckett, Samuel (1983), *Disjecta: Miscellaneous Writings and a Dramatic Fragment*, ed. Ruby Cohn, New York: Grove Press.

Beckett, Samuel (1988), *L'Image*, Paris: Minuit.

Beckett, Samuel (2006), *Samuel Beckett: The Complete Dramatic Works*, London: Faber and Faber.

Beckett, Samuel (2010), *The Collected Shorter Plays*, New York: Grove Press.

Beckett, Samuel (2014), *Echo's Bones*, ed. Mark Nixon, New York: Grove Press.

Begam, Richard (1996), *Samuel Beckett and the End of Modernity*, Palo Alto: Stanford University Press.

Beith, Don (2018), *The Birth of Sense: Generative Passivity in Merleau-Ponty's Philosophy*, Athens: Ohio University Press.

Beloborodova, Olga (2020), *Postcognitivist Beckett*, Cambridge: Cambridge University Press.
Bennett, Jane (2010), *Vibrant Matter: A Political Ecology of Things*, Durham, NC and London: Duke University Press.
Ben-Zvi, Linda (1980), 'Samuel Beckett, Fritz Mauthner, and the Limits of Language', *PMLA* 95:2, pp. 183–200.
Bergson, Henri [1911] (1998), *Creative Evolution*, trans. Arthur Mitchell, Mineola and New York: Dover Publications.
Bergson, Henri (2001), *Time and Free Will: An Essay on the Immediate Data of Consciousness*, trans. F. L. Pogson, Mineola, NY: Dover.
Bergson, Henri [1899] (2008), *Laughter: An Essay on the Meaning of the Comic*, trans. Cloudesley Brereton and Fred Rothwell, Rockville, MD: Arc Manor.
Bersani, Leo and Ulysse Dutoit (1993), *Arts of Impoverishment: Beckett, Rothko, Resnais*, Cambridge, MA: Harvard University Press.
Bixby, Patrick (2012), 'The ethico-politics of homo-ness: Beckett's *How It Is* and Casement's Black Diaries', *Irish Studies Review* 20:3, pp. 243–61.
Blanchot, Maurice (1982), 'Where Now? Who Now?', in *The Siren's Song*, ed. G. Josipovici, London: The Harvester Press Ltd, pp. 192–9.
Blanchot, Maurice (1993), *The Infinite Conversation*, trans. Susan Hanson, Minneapolis: University of Minnesota Press.
Blanchot, Maurice (1995), *The Madness of the Day*, trans. Lydia Davis, Barrytown, NY: Station Hill Press.
Blanchot, Maurice (2001), *Faux Pas*, trans. Charlotte Mandel, Palo Alto: Stanford University Press.
Blau, Herbert (1986), 'Notes From the Underground: "Waiting for Godot" and "Endgame"', in S. E. Gontarski (ed.), *On Beckett: Essays and Criticism*, New York: Grove Press, pp. 255–79.
Boulter, Jonathan (2008), *Beckett: A Guide for the Perplexed*, London: Continuum.
Boulter, Jonathan (2012), '"We have our being in justice": Samuel Beckett's *How It Is*', in Mariko Tanaka, Yoshiki Tajiri and Michiko Tsushima (eds), *Samuel Beckett and Pain*, Amsterdam and New York: Rodopi, pp. 173–200.
Boulter, Jonathan (2019), *Posthuman Space in Samuel Beckett's Short Prose*, Edinburgh: Edinburgh University Press.
Bourne-Taylor, Carole and Ariane Mildenberg, eds (2010), *Phenomenology, Modernism and Beyond*, Oxford: Peter Lang.
Braidotti, Rosi (2013), *The Posthuman*, Cambridge: Polity Press.

Brater, Enoch (1987a), *Beyond Minimalism: Beckett's Late Style in the Theater*, Oxford and New York: Oxford University Press.

Brater, Enoch (1987b), 'Voyelles, Cromlechs and the Special (W)rites of *Worstward Ho*', in James Acheson and Kateryna Arthur (eds), *Beckett's Later Fiction and Drama: Texts for Company*, London: Macmillan, pp. 160–94.

Brater, Enoch (1994), *The Drama in the Text: Beckett's Late Fiction*, Oxford: Oxford University Press.

Brazil, Kevin (2013), 'Beckett, Painting and the Question of "the human"', *Journal of Modern Literature* 36:3, pp. 81–99.

Brienza, Susan (1987), *Samuel Beckett's New Worlds: Style in Metafiction*, Norman and London: University of Oklahoma Press.

Brown, Charles S. and Ted Toadvine, eds (2003), *Eco-Phenomenology: Back to the Earth Itself*, Albany: State University of New York Press.

Bryden, Mary (1995), '*QUAD*: Dancing Genders', in Catharina Wulf (ed.), *The Savage Eye/L'œil fauve: New Essays on Samuel Beckett's Television Plays*, SBT/A 4, pp. 109–23.

Bryden, Mary (1996), 'The Schizoid Space: Beckett, Deleuze, and L'Épuisé', *SBT/A* 5, pp. 85–94.

Bryden, Mary (2002), 'Deleuze Reading Beckett', in Richard Lane (ed.), *Beckett and Philosophy*, New York: Palgrave, pp. 80–93.

Bryden, Mary, ed. (2013), *Beckett and Animals*, Cambridge: Cambridge University Press.

Butler, Judith (1993), *Bodies That Matter: On the Discursive Limits of 'Sex'*, London and New York: Routledge.

Butler, Judith (2005a), *Giving an Account of Oneself*, New York: Fordham University Press.

Butler, Judith (2005b), 'Merleau-Ponty and the Touch of Malebranche', in Taylor Carman and Mark B. N. Hansen (eds), *The Cambridge Companion to Merleau-Ponty*, Cambridge: Cambridge University Press, pp. 181–205.

Butler, Judith (2015), *Senses of the Subject*, New York: Fordham University Press.

Butler, Lance St John (1984), *Samuel Beckett and the Meaning of Being: A Study in Ontological Parable*, London: Macmillan.

Byron, Mark (2017), 'Mind, Brain, and Text Immanent Thinking in *Worstward Ho*', *SBT/A* 29, pp. 126–37.

Cadava, Eduardo, Peter Connor and Jean-Luc Nancy, eds (1991), *Who Comes After the Subject?*, London and New York: Routledge.

Cahn, Stephen M. (2007), *Classics of Western Philosophy*, 7th ed., Indianapolis: Hackett.

Calder, John (2002), *The Philosophy of Samuel Beckett*, London: Calder.
Campbell, Julie (1993), 'Pilgrim's Progress/Regress/Stasis: Some Thoughts on the Treatment of the Quest in Bunyan's *Pilgrim's Progress* and Beckett's *Mercier and Camier*', *Comparative Literature Studies* 30, pp. 137–52.
Carman, Taylor and Mark B. N. Hansen (2005), 'Introduction', in Taylor Carman and Mark B. N. Hansen (eds), *The Cambridge Companion to Merleau-Ponty*, Cambridge: Cambridge University Press, pp. 1–25.
Carman, Taylor (2012), 'Foreword', in Maurice Merleau-Ponty, *Phenomenology of Perception*, London and New York: Routledge, pp. vii–xvi.
Casanova, Pascale (2006), *Samuel Beckett: Anatomy of a Literary Revolution*, trans. Gregory Elliott, London and New York: Verso.
Caselli, Daniela (2005), *Beckett's Dantes: Intertextuality in the Fiction and Criticism*, Manchester and New York: Manchester University Press.
Cataldi, Suzanne L. and William S. Hamrick, eds (2007), *Merleau-Ponty and Environmental Philosophy*, Albany: State University of New York Press.
Coetzee, J. M. (1972), 'The Manuscript Revisions of Beckett's *Watt*', *Journal of Modern Literature* 2:4, pp. 473–80.
Cohn, Ruby (1962a), 'Plays and Player in the Plays of Samuel Beckett', *Yale French Studies* 29, pp. 43–8.
Cohn, Ruby (1962b), *Samuel Beckett: The Comic Gamut*, New Brunswick: Rutgers University Press.
Cohn, Ruby (1965), 'Philosophical Fragments in the Works of Samuel Beckett', in Martin Esslin (ed.), *Samuel Beckett: A Collection of Critical Essays*, Englewood Cliffs, NJ: Prentice-Hall, pp. 169–77.
Connor, Steven (1988), *Samuel Beckett: Repetition, Theory and Text*, Oxford: Basil Blackwell.
Connor, Stephen (2010), 'Preface', in Samuel Beckett, *The Unnamable*, London: Faber and Faber, pp. [vii–xxv].
Connor, Steven (2014a), *Beckett, Modernism and the Material Imagination*, Cambridge: Cambridge University Press.
Connor, Steven (2014b), '"Was That a Point?": Beckett's Punctuation', in S. E. Gontarski (ed.), *The Edinburgh Companion to Samuel Beckett and the Arts*, Edinburgh: Edinburgh University Press, pp. 269–81.
Connor, Steven (2019), *Giving Way: Thoughts on Unappreciated Dispositions*, Palo Alto: Stanford University Press.
Coole, Diana (2005), 'Rethinking Agency: A Phenomenological Approach to Embodiment and Agentic Capacities', *Political Studies* 53:1, pp. 124–42.

Coole, Diana (2007), *Merleau-Ponty and Modern Politics after Anti-Humanism*, Lanham, MD: Rowman and Littlefield.
Coole, Diana (2010), 'The Inertia of Matter and the Generativity of the Flesh', in Diana Coole and Samantha Frost (eds), *New Materialisms: Ontology, Agency, and Politics*, Durham, NC: Duke University Press, pp. 92–116.
Coole, Diana and Samantha Frost, eds (2010), *New Materialisms: Ontology, Agency, and Politics*, Durham, NC: Duke University Press.
Cordingley, Anthony (2007), 'Psychoanalytic Refuse in *Comment c'est/ How It Is*', in Caroline Hamilton, Michelle Kelly, Elaine Minor and Will Noonan (eds), *The Politics and Aesthetics of Refusal*, Newcastle-upon-Tyne: Cambridge Scholars Publishing, pp. 111–29.
Cordingley, Anthony (2017), 'Samuel Beckett and Édith Fournier Translating the "Untranslatable" *Worstward Ho*', *Journal of Beckett Studies* 26:2, pp. 239–56.
Cordingley, Anthony (2018), *Samuel Beckett's How It Is: Philosophy in Translation*, Edinburgh: Edinburgh University Press.
Cousineau, Thomas (1999), *After the Final No: Samuel Beckett's Trilogy*, Cranbury, NJ: Associated University Presses.
Dastur, Françoise (2001), *Chair et langage: essais sur Merleau-Ponty*, La Versanne: Encre marine.
Davies, Paul (2006), 'Strange Weather: Beckett from the Perspective of Ecocriticism', in S. E. Gontarski and Anthony Uhlmann (eds), *Beckett After Beckett*, Gainesville: University of Florida Press, pp. 66–78.
De la Durantaye, Leland (2016), *Beckett's Art of Mismaking*, Cambridge, MA: Harvard University Press.
De Saint Aubert, Emmanuel (2003), 'La co-naissance: Merleau-Ponty et Claudel', in Marie Cariou, Renaud Barbaras and Etienne Bimbenet (eds), *Merleau-Ponty aux frontières de l'invisible*, Milan: Associazione Culturale Mimesis, pp. 249–81.
Deleuze, Gilles (1985), *Cinéma II: L'Image-Temps*, Paris: Minuit.
Deleuze, Gilles (1992), 'L'Épuisé', in Edith Fournier (ed.), *Quad et autres pièces pour la télévision*, Paris: Les Editions de Minuit, pp. 80–106.
Deleuze, Gilles (1995), 'The Exhausted', trans. Anthony Uhlmann, *SubStance* 24:3, issue 78, pp. 3–28.
Deleuze, Gilles (1997), 'Literature and life', trans. Daniel W. Smith and Michael A. Greco, *Critical Inquiry* 23:2, pp. 225–30.
Deleuze, Gilles and Félix Guattari (1983), *Anti-Oedipus: Capitalism and Schizophrenia*, trans. Robert Hurley, Mark Seem and Helen R. Lane, Minneapolis: University of Minnesota Press.

Dennis, Amanda M. (2015), 'Poets of Their Own Acts: Tactics, Style and Occupation in Beckett's "Nouvelles"', *SBT/A* 27, pp. 43–55.

Dennis, Amanda (2017), 'A Theater of the Nerves: Samuel Beckett's Non-Representational Art', *Journal of Modern Literature* 40:4, pp. 134–43.

Dennis, Amanda M. (2019), 'Samuel Beckett et la langue maternelle- Ambivalence et expatriation linguistique', in Yann Mével (ed.), *Samuel Beckett et la culture française*, Paris: Éditions Minard, pp. 95–114.

Derrida, Jacques (1979), *Spurs: Nietzsche's Styles/Eperons: Les Styles de Nietzsche*, Chicago: University of Chicago Press.

Derrida, Jacques (1992), 'This Strange Institution Called Literature', in Derek Attridge (ed.), *Acts of Literature*, New York and London: Routledge, pp. 33–75.

Derrida, Jacques (1993), *Aporias*, trans. Thomas Dutoit, Palo Alto: Stanford University Press.

Derrida, Jacques [2000] (2005), *On Touching – Jean-Luc Nancy*, trans. Christine Irizarry, Palo Alto: Stanford University Press.

Descartes, Réné (1988), *Descartes: Selected Philosophical Writings*, ed. and trans. John Cottingham, Robert Stoothoff and Dugald Murdoch, Cambridge: Cambridge University Press.

Descombes, Vincent [1979] (1980), *Modern French Philosophy*, Cambridge: Cambridge University Press.

Dillon, M. C. (1991), 'Preface: Merleau-Ponty and Postmodernity', in M. C. Dillon (ed.), *Merleau-Ponty Vivant*, Albany: State University Press of New York, pp. ix–xxxv.

Doherty, Francis (1992), 'Mahaffy's Whoroscope', *Journal of Beckett Studies* 2:1, pp. 27–46.

Dreyfus, Hubert L. (1996), 'The Current Relevance of Merleau-Ponty's Phenomenology of Embodiment', *The Electronic Journal of Analytic Philosophy* 4, <https://ejap.louisiana.edu/ejap/1996.spring/dreyfus.1996.spring.html> (last accessed 9 January 2021).

Esslin, Martin (1969), *The Theatre of the Absurd*, Garden City, NY: Doubleday.

Esslin, Martin (1982), 'Patterns of Rejection: Sex and Love in Beckett's Universe', in Linda Ben-Zvi, *Women in Beckett: Performance and Critical Perspectives*, Urbana and Chicago: University of Illinois Press, pp. 61–7.

Federman, Raymond (1970), 'Beckettian Paradox: Who is Telling the Truth?', in Melvin J. Friedman (ed.), *Samuel Beckett Now*, Chicago: The University of Chicago Press, pp. 103–17.

Fehsenfeld, Martha (1982), 'Beckett's Late Works: An Appraisal', *Modern Drama* 25:3, pp. 355-62.
Feldman, Matthew (2006), *Beckett's Books: A Cultural History of Samuel Beckett's 'Interwar' Notes*, New York and London: Continuum.
Feldman, Matthew (2009), '"But what was this pursuit of meaning, in this indifference to meaning?": Beckett, Husserl, Sartre and "Meaning Creation"', in Ulrika Maude and Matthew Feldman (eds), *Beckett and Phenomenology*, London: Continuum, pp. 13-38.
Ferrando, Francesca (2016), 'A Feminist Genealogy of Posthuman Aesthetics in the Visual Arts', *Palgrave Communications* 2, <https://doi.org/10.1057/palcomms.2016.11> (last accessed 9 January 2021).
Finney, Brian (1987), '*Still* to *Worstward Ho*: Beckett's Prose Fiction since the Lost Ones', in James Acheson and Kateryna Arthur (eds), *Beckett's Later Fiction and Drama: Texts for Company*, London: Macmillan, pp. 65-79.
Fletcher, John (2000), *Samuel Beckett: Waiting for Godot, Endgame, Krapp's Last Tape*, London: Faber.
Foucault, Michel [1969] (1977), 'What is an Author', in Michel Foucault, *Language, Counter-Memory, Practice: Selected Essays and Interviews*, ed. Donald Bouchard, trans. Sherry Simon, Ithaca: Cornell University Press, pp. 113-38.
Foucault, Michel [1970] (1980), 'Theatrum Philosophicum', in Michel Foucault, *Language, Counter-Memory, Practice: Selected Essays and Interviews*, ed. Donald Bouchard, trans. Sherry Simon, Ithaca: Cornell University Press, pp. 165-92.
Franklin, Seb (2013), 'Humans and/as Machines: Beckett and Cultural Cybernetics', *Textual Practice* 27:2, pp. 249-68.
Friedman, Alan Warren (2017), *Surreal Beckett: Samuel Beckett, James Joyce, and Surrealism*, New York and London: Routledge.
Gallagher, Shaun (1986), 'Body Image and Body Schema: A Conceptual Clarification', *The Journal of Mind and Behavior* 7:4, pp. 541-54.
Gallagher, Shaun (2005), 'Dynamic Models of Bodily Schematic Processes', in Helena de Preester and Veronik Knockaert (eds), *Body Image and Body Schema: Interdisciplinary Perspectives on the Body*, Amsterdam: J. Benjamins, pp. 233-50.
Gallagher, Shaun and Dan Zahavi (2012), *The Phenomenological Mind*, 2nd ed., London and New York: Routledge.
Garner, Stanton B. (1993), '"Still living flesh": Beckett, Merleau-Ponty, and the Phenomenological Body', *Theater Journal* 45:4, 'Disciplinary Disruptions', pp. 443-60.

Garrard, Greg (2011), '*Endgame*: Beckett's "ecological thought"', *SBT/A* 23, pp. 383–97.
Gasché, Rodolphe (2007), 'Aporetic Experience', in Rodolphe Gasché, *The Honor of Thinking: Critique, Theory, Philosophy*, Palo Alto: Stanford University Press, pp. 327–48.
Gibson, Andrew (2006), *Beckett and Badiou: The Pathos of Intermittency*, Oxford: Oxford University Press.
Gibson, Andrew (2014), 'French Beckett and French Literary Politics 1945–52', in S. E. Gontarski (ed.), *The Edinburgh Companion to Samuel Beckett and the Arts*, Edinburgh: Edinburgh University Press, pp. 103–16.
Gontarski, S. E. (1985), *The Intent of Undoing in Samuel Beckett's Dramatic Texts*, Bloomington: Indiana University Press.
Gontarski, S. E. (1996), 'Introduction: The Conjuring of Something out of Nothing: Samuel Beckett's "Closed Space" Novels', in Samuel Beckett, *Nohow On: Company, Ill Seen Ill Said, Worstward Ho*, New York: Grove Press, pp. vii–xxviii.
Gontarski, S. E. (2001), 'The Body in the Body of Beckett's Theater', *SBT/A* 11, pp. 169–77.
Gontarski, S. E. (2002), 'Style and the Man: Samuel Beckett and the Art of Pastiche', *SBT/A* 12, pp. 11–20.
Gontarski, S. E. (2004), 'Introduction: Anywhere and Nowhere: Mapping the Beckett Country', in C. J. Ackerley and S. E. Gontarski (eds), *The Grove Companion to Samuel Beckett: A Reader's Guide to his Works, Life and Thought*, New York: Grove Press, pp. ix–xvi.
Gontarski, S. E. (2015), *Creative Involution: Bergson, Beckett, Deleuze*, Edinburgh: Edinburgh University Press.
Gontarski, S. E. (2018), 'An End to Endings: Samuel Beckett's End Game(s)', in S. E. Gontarski, *Revisioning Beckett: Samuel Beckett's Decadent Turn*, London: Bloomsbury, pp. 145–56.
Goodall, Jane (2006), 'Lucky's Energy', in S. E. Gontarski and Anthony Uhlmann, *Beckett After Beckett*, Gainesville: University Press of Florida, pp. 187–96.
Grossman, Evelyne (2012), 'Structuralism and Metaphysics', *Journal of Beckett Studies* 21:1, pp. 88–101.
Gutting, Gary (2001), *French Philosophy in the Twentieth Century*, Cambridge: Cambridge University Press.
Haraway, Donna (2016), *Staying with the Trouble: Making Kin in the Chthulucene*, Durham, NC and London: Duke University Press.

Hayles, Katherine (1999), *How We Became Posthuman: Virtual Bodies in Cybernetics, Literature, and Informatics*, Chicago: University of Chicago Press.
Head, Henry (1896), 'On Disturbances of Sensation with Especial Reference to the Pain of Visceral Disease', *Brain* 19, pp. 153–276.
Helsa, David (1971), *The Shape of Chaos*, Minneapolis: University of Minnesota Press.
Hill, Leslie (1990), *Beckett's Fiction: In Different Words*, Cambridge: Cambridge University Press.
Hisgen, Rudd and Adriaan van der Weel (1998), *The Silencing of the Sphinx*, Leiden: privately printed.
Hoefer, Jacqueline [1959] (1965), '*Watt*', in Martin Esslin (ed.), *Samuel Beckett: A Collection of Critical Essays*, Englewood Cliffs, NJ: Prentice Hall, pp. 62–76.
Husserl, Edmund [1913] (1983), *Ideas Pertaining to a Pure Phenomenology and to a Phenomenological Philosophy*, first book, trans. F. Kersten, The Hague: Martinus Nijhoff publishers.
Idhe, Don (1990), *Technology and the Lifeworld: From Garden to Earth*, Bloomington: Indiana University Press.
Ingold, Tim (2004), 'Culture on the Ground: The World Perceived Through the Feet', *Journal of Material Culture* 9:3, pp. 315–40, <http://doi.org/10.1177/1359183504046896> (last accessed 9 January 2021).
Inkpin, Andrew (2017), 'Was Merleau-Ponty a "transcendental" Phenomenologist?' *Continental Philosophy Review* 50, pp. 27–47, <http://doi.org/10.1007/s11007-016-9394-0> (last accessed 9 January 2021).
Israel, Nico (2011), 'At the End of the Jetty: Beckett, Smithson, Spirals and Global Modernity', *Journal of Beckett Studies* 20:1, pp. 1–31.
Kafka, Franz (1978), *Letters to Friends, Family and Editors*, trans. Richard and Clara Winston, London: Calder.
Kanelli, Katerina (2010), '"Fall and Recovery" de Lucky; ou, Les premiers pas de danse dans le théâtre de Samuel Beckett', *Limit(e)*, Beckett 0, pp. 27–38.
Katz, Daniel (1999), *Saying 'I' No More: Subjectivity and Consciousness in the Prose of Samuel Beckett*, Evanston, IL: Northwestern University Press.
Kennedy, Sean (2014), '"Bid us sigh on from day to day": Beckett and the Irish Big House', in S. E. Gontarski (ed.), *The Edinburgh Companion to Samuel Beckett and the Arts*, Edinburgh: Edinburgh University Press, pp. 222–36.

Kenner, Hugh (1959), 'The Cartesian Centaur', *Perspective* 11:3, pp. 132–41.
Kenner, Hugh (1973), *A Reader's Guide to Samuel Beckett*, London: Thames and Hudson.
Kenner, Hugh (1987), *The Mechanic Muse*, New York: Oxford University Press.
Knowlson, James (1996), *Damned to Fame: The Life of Samuel Beckett*, New York: Grove Press.
Knowlson, James (2003), *Images of Beckett*, Cambridge: Cambridge University Press.
Kofman, Sara (1988), 'Beyond Aporia', trans. David Macey, in Andrew Benjamin (ed.), *Post-structuralist Classics*, London and New York: Routledge, pp. 7–44.
Kojima, Hiroshi (2002), 'From Dialectic to Reversibility: A Critical Change of Subject-Object Relation in Merleau-Ponty's Thought', in Ted Toadvine and Lester Embree (eds), *Merleau-Ponty's Reading of Husserl*, Dordrecht: Kluwer Academic Publishers, pp. 95–115.
Krance, Charles (1990), '*Worstward Ho* and *On*-words: Writing to(wards) the Point', in Lance St. John Butler and Robin J. Davis (eds), *Rethinking Beckett: A Collection of Critical Essays*, New York: St Martin's Press, pp. 124–40.
Kristeva, Julia (1982), *Powers of Horror: An Essay on Abjection*, trans. Leon S. Roudiez, New York: Columbia University Press.
Lamont, Rosette (2002), 'Fast-Forward: Lucky's *Pnigos*', *SBT/A* 11, ed. Angela Moorjani and Carola Veit, pp. 132–9.
Landes, Donald A. (2012), 'Translator's Introduction', in Maurice Merleau-Ponty, *Phenomenology of Perception*, London and New York, Routledge, pp. xxx–li.
Latour, Bruno [1991] (1993), *We Have Never Been Modern*, trans. Catherine Porter, Boston, Harvard University Press.
Lavery, Carl (2018), 'Ecology in Beckett's Theatre Garden: Or How to Cultivate the Oikos', *Contemporary Theatre Review* 28:1, pp. 10–26, <http://doi.org/10.1080/10486801.2017.1403912> (last accessed 9 January 2021).
Léoni-Figini, Margherita (2007), 'Dossiers pédagogiques: Parcours Exposition Samuel Beckett', <http://mediation.centrepompidou.fr/education/ressources/ENS-beckett/ENS-beckett.html> (last accessed 9 January 2021).
Levinas, Emmanuel [1983] (1990), 'Intersubjectivity: Notes on Merleau-Ponty', trans. Michael B. Smith, in Galen Johnson and Michael B.

Smith (eds), *Ontology and Alterity in Merleau-Ponty*, Evanston, IL: Northwestern University Press, pp. 55–60.

Lewis, Jim (1990), 'Beckett et la caméra', in Mikel Dufrenne and Olivier d'Allonnes (eds), *Revue d'Esthétique, numéro hors série*, Paris: Éditions Jean-Michel Place, pp. 371–9.

Lhermitte, Jean (1939), *L'Image de notre corps*, Paris: Éditions de la Nouvelle Revue Critique.

Lieber, Jean-Claude (1998), 'Pensée de la mort, mort de la pensée', in Didier Alexandre and Jean-Yves Debreuille (eds), *Lire Beckett: En attendant Godot, Fin de partie*, Lyon: Presses Universitaires de Lyon, pp. 75–85.

Liedman, Sven Eric and Douglas Moggach (1997), 'Hegel and the Enlightenment Project', *The European Legacy* 2:3, pp. 538–43, <http://doi.org/10.1080/10848779708579771> (last accessed 9 January 2021).

Locatelli, Carla (1990), *Unwording the World: Samuel Beckett's Prose Works after the Nobel Prize*, Philadelphia: University of Pennsylvania Press.

Magessa O'Reilly, Edouard (2001), *Samuel Beckett: Comment C'est/ How It Is and/et L'image – A Critical-Genetic Edition/Une Edition Critico-Genetique*, New York and London: Routledge.

Magessa O'Reilly, Edouard (2009), 'Preface', *How It Is*, London: Faber and Faber.

Marks, Tom (2015), 'Force of Nature: Interview with Giuseppe Penone', *Apollo: The International Art Magazine*, 19 September, <https://www.apollo-magazine.com/force-of-nature-interview-with-giuseppe-penone/> (last accessed 9 January 2021).

Maude, Ulrika (2009), *Beckett, Technology and the Body*, Cambridge: Cambridge University Press.

Maude, Ulrika and Matthew Feldman, eds (2009), *Beckett and Phenomenology*, London: Continuum.

Maude, Ulrika (2014), 'Convulsive Aesthetics: Beckett, Chaplin and Charcot', in S. E. Gontarski (ed.), *The Edinburgh Companion to Samuel Beckett and the Arts*, Edinburgh: Edinburgh University Press, pp. 44–53.

Maude, Ulrika (2020), '"All that inner space one never sees": Beckett's Inhuman Domain', *SBT/A* 32, pp. 255–71.

Mauthner, Fritz [1901] (1923), *Beiträge zu einer Kritik der Sprache*, Leipzig: Felix Meiner.

McMullan, Anna (2010), *Performing Embodiment in Samuel Beckett's Drama*, London: Routledge.

McTighe, Trish (2013), *The Haptic Aesthetic in Samuel Beckett's Drama*, Houndmills, Basingstoke and New York: Palgrave Macmillan.
Ménasé, Stéphanie (2003), *Passivité et creation: Merleau-Ponty et l'art moderne*, Paris: Presses Universitaires de France.
Mendieta, Ana (1988), 'An Interview with Ana Mendieta by Linda Montano', *Sulfur* 22.
Merleau-Ponty, Maurice (1960), *Signes*, Paris: Gallimard.
Merleau-Ponty, Maurice (1963), *The Structure of Behavior*, trans. Alden L. Fisher, Pittsburgh: Duquesne University Press.
Merleau-Ponty, Maurice (1964a), *L'oeil et l'esprit*, Paris: Gallimard.
Merleau-Ponty, Maurice (1964b), *Signs*, trans. Richard C. McCleary, Evanston, IL: Northwestern University Press.
Merleau-Ponty, Maurice (1969), *La prose du monde*, Paris: Gallimard.
Merleau-Ponty, Maurice [1947] (1989), *Le primat de la perception et ses consequences philosophiques*, Grenoble: Cynara.
Merleau-Ponty, Maurice (1993), 'Eye and Mind', trans. Michael B. Smith, in Galen A. Johnson and Michael B. Smith (eds), *The Merleau-Ponty Aesthetics Reader: Philosophy and Painting*, Evanston, IL: Northwestern University Press, pp. 121–49.
Merleau-Ponty, Maurice (2000), 'Titres et travaux – Projet d'enseignement', *Parcours Deux 1951–1961*, Paris: Verdier, pp. 9–35.
Merleau-Ponty, Maurice (2003a), *L'institution. La passivité: Notes de cours au Collège de France 1954–1955*, ed. Dominique Darmaillacq, Stéphanie Ménasé, Claude Lefort, Paris: Belin.
Merleau-Ponty, Maurice (2003b), *Nature: Course Notes from the Collège de France*, trans. Robert Vallier, Evanston, IL: Northwestern University Press.
Merleau-Ponty, Maurice (2010), *Institution and Passivity: Course Notes from the Collège de France (1954–1955)*, trans. Leonard Lawlor and Heath Massey, Evanston, IL: Northwestern University Press.
Mildenberg, Ariane, ed. (2018), *Understanding Merleau-Ponty, Understanding Modernism*, New York and London: Bloomsbury.
Miller, Tyrus (1999), *Late Modernism: Politics, Fiction, and the Arts Between the World Wars*, Berkeley and Los Angeles: University of California Press.
Milne, Drew (1999), 'The Dissident Imagination: Beckett's Late Prose Fiction', in Rod Mengham (ed.), *An Introduction to Contemporary Fiction: International Writing in English since 1970*, Cambridge: Polity Press, pp. 93–109.

Milton, John (2005), *Paradise Lost*, ed. Gordon Teskey, New York: W. W. Norton & Company.
Mintz, Samuel (1959), 'Beckett's *Murphy*: A Cartesian Novel', *Perspective* 11:3, pp. 156–65.
Mood, John (1971), '"The Personal System" – Samuel Beckett's *Watt*', *PMLA* 86:2, pp. 259–62.
Moorjani, Angela (1991), 'A Cryptanalysis of Beckett's *Molloy*', in Joseph H. Smith (ed.), *The World of Samuel Beckett*, Psychiatry and the Humanities XXII, Baltimore and London: Johns Hopkins University Press, pp. 53–75.
Morin, Emilie (2017), *Beckett's Political Imagination*, Cambridge: Cambridge University Press.
Morton, Timothy (2007), *Ecology without Nature: Rethinking Environmental Aesthetics*, Cambridge, MA: Harvard University Press.
Morton, Timothy (2010), *The Ecological Thought*, Cambridge, MA: Harvard University Press.
Mounin, Georges (1968), 'La "Mise en question du langage" dans la literature actuelle', *La Linguistique* 4:1, pp. 21–9.
Murphy, P. J. (1994), 'Beckett and the Philosophers', in John Pilling (ed.), *The Cambridge Companion to Beckett*, Cambridge: Cambridge University Press, pp. 222–40.
Nancy, Jean-Luc (2003), *A Finite Thinking*, ed. Simon Sparks, Palo Alto: Stanford University Press.
Neimans, Astrida (2017), *Bodies of Water: Posthuman Feminist Phenomenology*, London: Bloomsbury.
Nixon, Mark (2006), 'Beckett and Romanticism in the 1930s', *SBT/A* 18, pp. 61–76.
Nixon, Mark (2011), *Samuel Beckett's German Diaries 1936–1937*, London: Continuum.
Noë, Alva (2004), *Action in Perception*, Cambridge, MA: MIT Press.
Noland, Carrie (2009), *Agency and Embodiment: Performing Gestures/Producing Culture*, Cambridge, MA: Harvard University Press.
Okamuro, Minako (2003), 'Alchemical Dances in Beckett and Yeats', *SBT/A* 14, pp. 87–105.
Oppenheim, Lois (2000), *The Painted Word: Samuel Beckett's Dialogue with Art*, Ann Arbor: University of Michigan Press.
Osterweil, Ara (2015), 'Bodily Rites: The Films of Ana Mendieta', *Artforum* 54:3.
Ovid (2014), *The Metamorphoses*, trans. A. S. Kline, 2nd ed., CreateSpace Independent Publishing Platform.

Penone, Giuseppe (2007), *Giuseppe Penone: Sculture di linfa*, exhibition catalogue, Biennale di Venezia.

Perloff, Marjorie (1996), *Wittgenstein's Ladder: Poetic Language and the Strangeness of the Ordinary*, Chicago: University of Chicago Press.

Pilling, John (2006), 'Beckett and Mauthner Revisited', in S. E. Gontarski and Anthony Uhlmann (eds), *Beckett after Beckett*, Gainesville: University Press of Florida, pp. 158–66.

Porter Abbott, H. (1996), *Beckett Writing Beckett: The Author in the Autograph*, Ithaca and London: Cornell University Press.

Pountney, Rosemary (1988), *Theatre of Shadows: Samuel Beckett's Drama 1956–1976*, Gerrards Cross: Colin Smythe.

Proust, Marcel (1920), 'À propos du «style» de Flaubert', *La Nouvelle Revue Française* XIV, pp. 72–90.

Rabaté, Jean-Michel (2005), 'Unbreakable B's: From Beckett and Badiou to the Bitter End of Affirmative Ethics', in G. Riera (ed.), *Alain Badiou: Philosophy and its Conditions*, Albany: State University of New York Press, pp. 87–108.

Rabaté, Jean-Michel (2014), 'Beckett's Masson: From Abstraction to Non-Relation', in S. E. Gontarski (ed.), *The Edinburgh Companion to Samuel Beckett and the Arts*, Edinburgh: Edinburgh University Press, pp. 131–45.

Rabaté, Jean-Michel (2016), *Think Pig! Beckett at the Limit of the Human*, New York: Fordham University Press.

Renton, Andrew (1992), '*Worstward Ho* and the End(s), of Representation', in John Pilling and Mary Bryden (eds), *The Ideal Core of the Onion: Reading Beckett Archives*, Bristol: The Longdunn Press Ltd, pp. 99–136.

Reynolds, Jack (2004), *Merleau-Ponty and Derrida: Intertwining Embodiment and Alterity*, Athens: Ohio University Press.

Reynolds, Jack and Jon Roffe (2018), 'Neither/Nor: Merleau-Ponty's Ontology in "The Intertwining/The Chiasm"', in Ariane Mildenberg (ed.), *Understanding Merleau-Ponty, Understanding Modernism*, New York: Bloomsbury, pp. 100–14.

Robinson, Michael (1974), *The Long Sonata of the Dead: A Study of Samuel Beckett*, New York: Grove Press.

Roche, Anthony, 'The "Irish" Translation of Samuel Beckett's *En Attendant Godot*', in S. E. Gontarski (ed.), *The Edinburgh Companion to Samuel Beckett and the Arts*, Edinburgh: Edinburgh University Press, pp. 199–208.

Salisbury, Laura (2012), *Samuel Beckett: Laughing Matters, Comic Timing*, Edinburgh: Edinburgh University Press.
Salisbury, Laura (2014), 'Gloria SMH and Beckett's Linguistic Encryptions', in S. E. Gontarski (ed.), *The Edinburgh Companion to Samuel Beckett and the Arts*, Edinburgh: Edinburgh University Press, pp. 153–69.
Saunders, Paul (2011), 'Samuel Beckett's *Trilogy* and the Ecology of Negation', *Journal of Beckett Studies* 20.1, pp. 54–77, <http://doi.org/10.3366/jobs.2011.0005> (last accessed 9 January 2021).
Schilder, Paul (1923), *Das Körperschema*, Berlin: Springer.
Schilder, Paul [1935] (1950), *The Image and Appearance of the Human Body: Studies in the Constructive Energies of the Psyche*, London: Routledge.
Schlosser, Markus (2015), 'Agency', in Edward N. Zalta (ed.), *The Stanford Encyclopedia of Philosophy*, <https://plato.stanford.edu/archives/fall2015/entries/agency/> (last accessed 9 January 2021).
Schmidt, James (1984), *Maurice Merleau-Ponty: Between Phenomenology and Structuralism*, London: Macmillan.
Schulz, H. J. (1973), *This Hell of Stories: A Hegelian Approach to the Novels of Samuel Beckett*, The Hague: Mouton.
Scruton, Roger (1983), 'Beckett and the Cartesian Soul', in Roger Scruton, *The Aesthetic Understanding: Essays in the Philosophy of Art and Culture*, London and New York: Methuen, pp. 222–41.
Shakespeare, William (1972), *King Lear*, ed. George Hunter and Kiernan Ryan, London: Penguin.
Silverman, Hugh (1980), 'Merleau-Ponty and the Interrogation of Language', *Research in Phenomenology* 10, pp. 122–41.
Silverman-Zinman, Toby (1995), 'Lucky's Dance in *Waiting for Godot*', *Modern drama* 3, pp. 311–12.
Simon, Anne and Nicolas Castin (1998), 'Avant-Propos', in Anne Simon and Nicolas Castin (eds), *Merleau-Ponty et le littéraire*, Paris: Presses de l'École Normale Supérieure, pp. 9–19.
Singer, Linda (1993), 'Merleau-Ponty on the Concept of Style', in Galen A. Johnson (ed.), *The Merleau-Ponty Aesthetics Reader*, Evanston, IL: Northwestern University Press, pp. 233–44.
Skerl, Jennie (1974), 'Fritz Mauthner's "Critique of Language" in Samuel Beckett's *Watt*', *Contemporary Literature* 15.4, pp. 474–87.
Smith, Justin E. H., ed. (2017), *Embodiment: A History*, Oxford: Oxford University Press.
Smith, Russell (2008), *Beckett and Ethics*, London: Continuum.

Stevens, Brett (2010), 'A Purgatorial Calculus: Beckett's Mathematics in "Quad"', in S. E. Gontarski (ed.), *A Companion to Samuel Beckett*, Oxford: Wiley-Blackwell, pp. 164–81.

Stewart, Paul (2006), *Zone of Evaporation: Samuel Beckett's Disjunctions*, Amsterdam and New York: Rodopi.

Stewart, Paul (2014a), 'Sexual Indifference in the Three Novels', in S. E. Gontarski (ed.), *The Edinburgh Companion to Samuel Beckett and the Arts*, Edinburgh: Edinburgh University Press, pp. 67–77.

Stewart, Paul (2014b), 'Suffering Fiction in *The Unnamable*', *SBT/A* 26, pp. 165–79.

Szafraniec, Asja (2007), *Beckett, Derrida, and the Event of Literature*, Palo Alto: Stanford University Press.

Tadashi Naito, Jonathan (2008), 'Writing Silence: Samuel Beckett's Early Mimes', *SBT/A* 19, pp. 393–402.

Tajiri, Yoshiki (2007), *Samuel Beckett and the Prosthetic Body: The Organs and Senses in Modernism*, Houndmills, Basingstoke, Hampshire: Palgrave Macmillan.

Thierry, Yves (1987), *Du corps parlant: Le langage chez Merleau-Ponty*, Brussels: Ousia.

Toadvine, Ted (2009), *Merleau-Ponty's Philosophy of Nature*, Evanston, IL: Northwestern University Press.

Toadvine, Ted (2017), 'Phenomenology and Environmental Ethics', in Stephen M. Gardiner and Allen Thompson (eds), *The Oxford Handbook of Environmental Ethics*, Oxford: Oxford University Press, pp. 174–86.

Toadvine, Ted (2019), 'Maurice Merleau-Ponty', in Edward N. Zalta (ed.), *The Stanford Encyclopedia of Philosophy*, <https://plato.stanford.edu/archives/spr2019/entries/merleau-ponty/> (last accessed 9 January 2021).

Tonning, Erik (2007), *Samuel Beckett's Abstract Drama: Works for Stage and Screen 1962–1985*, Oxford: Peter Lang.

Tresize, Thomas (1990), *Into the Breach: Samuel Beckett and the Ends of Literature*, Princeton: Princeton University Press.

Tubridy, Derval (2018), *Samuel Beckett and the Language of Subjectivity*, Cambridge: Cambridge University Press.

Tucker, David (2012), *Samuel Beckett and Arnold Geulincx: Tracing 'a literary fantasia'*, London: Continuum.

Uhlmann, Anthony (1999), *Beckett and Poststructuralism*, Cambridge: Cambridge University Press.

Uhlmann, Anthony (2006), *Samuel Beckett and the Philosophical Image*, Cambridge: Cambridge University Press.

Vallier, Robert (2005), 'Institution: The Significance of Merleau-Ponty's 1954 Course at the Collège de France', *Chiasmi International* 7, pp. 281–302.

Van Hulle, Dirk (2012), 'The Extended Mind and Multiple Drafts: Beckett's Models of the Mind and the Postcognitivist Paradigm', *SBT/A* 24:1, pp. 277–90.

Van Hulle, Dirk and Mark Nixon (2013), *Samuel Beckett's Library*, Cambridge: Cambridge University Press.

Van Hulle, Dirk and Pim Verhulst (2017), *The Making of Samuel Beckett's Malone Dies/Malone meurt*, Antwerp: University Press Antwerp.

Van Hulle, Dirk and Shane Weller (2014), *The Making of Samuel Beckett's The Unnamable/L'Innommable*, London: Bloomsbury Academic.

Van Hulle, Dirk, Eduoard Magessa O'Reilly, Pim Verhulst and Mark Nixon (2017), *The Making of Samuel Beckett's Molloy*, London: Bloomsbury.

Van Ruler, Han and Anthony Uhlmann, eds (2006), *Arnold Geulincx: Ethics – with Samuel Beckett's Notes*, trans. Martin Wilson, Leiden and Boston: Brill.

Wall, Brian (2009), '. . . *but the clouds*. . ., *Quad, Nacht und Träume*: Fantasy, Death, Repetition', *Journal of Beckett Studies* 18, pp. 88–104.

Wall, John (2002), 'A Study of the Imagination in Samuel Beckett's *Watt*', *New Literary History* 33.3, pp. 533–58.

Wasser, Audrey (2012), 'A Relentless Spinozism: Deleuze's Encounter with Beckett', *SubStance* 41:1 issue 127, pp. 124–36.

Watson, David (1991), *Paradox and Desire in Samuel Beckett's Fiction*, New York: Palgrave Macmillan.

Weller, Shane (2005), *A Taste for the Negative: Beckett and Nihilism*, London: Legenda.

Weller, Shane (2006), *Beckett, Literature, and the Ethics of Alterity*, New York: Palgrave.

Weller, Shane (2018), 'From Language Revolution to Literature of the Unword: Beckett as a Late Modernist', in Olga Beloborodova, Dirk Van Hulle and Pim Verhulst (eds), *Beckett and Modernism*, London: Palgrave, pp. 37–52.

Weller, Shane (2020), 'Negative Anthropology: Beckett and Humanism', *SBT/A* 32, pp. 161–75.

Wessler, Erik (2009), *La littérature face à elle-même: L'écriture spéculaire de Samuel Beckett*, Amsterdam: Rodopi.

Wiener, Norbert (1948), *Cybernetics, or Control and Communication in the Animal and the Machine*, Cambridge, MA: The MIT Press.

Wittgenstein, Ludwig (1967), *Zettel*, eds G. E. M. Anscombe and G. H. von Wright, trans. G. E. M. Anscombe, Blackwell: Oxford.

Wood, David (2003), 'What is Ecophenomenology?', in David Wood, *The Step Back: Ethics and Politics after Deconstruction*, Albany: State University of New York Press, pp. 149–68.

Zahavi, Daniel (2018), *Phenomenology: The Basics*, London and New York: Routledge.

Index

Page numbers in italics refer to illustrations and those followed by n are notes. Works by Beckett appear under their titles whereas works by other people appear under the author's name, with the exception of *The Phenomenology of Perception* by Merleau-Ponty which is discussed at length throughout this book and therefore has its own separate entry.

abject bodies, 1–2, 15, 138, 158n, 172
Ackerley, Chris, 32, 49n, 50n, 159n
Adorno, Theodor, 85, 104, 111n
   Dialectic of Enlightenment, 154
Ahmed, Sara, *Queer Phenomenology*, 209
All Strange Away, 161
Anouilh, Jean, 83n
anthropometry, 73–4, 83n
anthropomorphism, 62, 163, 173n
   representations of landscape, 44, 51–3
anti-anthropomorphism, 14–15, 22, 41
Anzieu, Didier, 157n
aporia, 114–33, 133n
Aristophanes, 70
Aristotle, 63, 123, 131, 133n, 159n
'Assumption', 36
Atkins, Anselm, 71, 83n
Augustine, 31

Badiou, Alain, 116, 125, 132–3n, 133n, 140
Baillet, Adrien, *La Vie de Descartes*, 30
Bair, Deirdre, 55, 81n

Barad, Karen, agential realism, 13
Barbaras, Renaud, 47n, 132n
Barry, Elizabeth, 4–5, 150
Barthes, Roland, *S/Z*, 95
Beaufret, Jean, 8, 29, 47n
Begam, Richard, 82n, 119, 133n
Beith, Don, 202
Beloborodova, Olga, 49n
Bennett, Jane, 13, 41
Ben-Zvi, Linda, 57, 81n
Bergson, Henri, 38, 47n, 66–7
   Time and Free Will, 66–7
Bernal, Olga, 94
Bersani, Leo, 135, 140, 158n
Big House novel, 81n
binary logic, 55–6, 60–1
Bixby, Patrick, 140
Blanchot, Maurice, 115–16, 132n, 139–40, 205
   Faux Pas, 215n
   La folie du jour, 131
body schema, 27–8, 48n, 97–8, 112n
body-objects, 2
body-subject
   and the abject, 138
   agency, 48n, 162
   endings, 97–8

body-subject (cont.)
  human and nonhuman environment, 209
  interaction with its world, 25–7, 29, 45–6
  transcendence, 22
borders
  abject and, 158n
  between art and life, 128
  of body and words, 126–7
  closed, 123
  of the human body, 20
  'limit of the human', 207–8
  of sense and nonsense, 65
  subjectivity, 119–20
Borges, Jorge Luis, 204
  'The Circular Ruins', 94
Boulter, Jonathan, 14, 80n, 154
Bourdieu, Pierre, 145, 159n
Bowles, Patrick, 87
Braidotti, Rosi, 13, 14, 20n
  The Posthuman, 135
Bray, Barbara, 135
Brazil, Kevin, 53, 80n
Brod, Max, 215n
Brunschvicg, Leon, 23, 47n
Bryden, Mary, 17n, 164–5, 166–7, 169, 173n
Butler, Judith, 18–19n
  Bodies That Matter, 164
  Giving an Account of Oneself, 5
Butler, Lance St John, 111n

Cadava, Eduardo, *Who Comes After the Subject?* 5
Calder, John, 83n
'The Calmative' ('Le Calmant'), 40–1
Calvino, Italo, 204
capitalism, 166, 170–1, 191
Carman, Taylor, 159n
Carroll, Lewis, *Alice's Adventures in Wonderland*, 81n
Carville, Connor, 204
Caselli, Daniella, 152
Casement, Roger, 158n
  Black Diaries, 138
Castin, Nicolas, 121–2, 160n
Catastrophe, 10, 172, 175n
Celan, Paul, 205

Centre Pompidou, Paris, exhibition, 1, 164, 173n
Cézanne, Paul, 41, 51–4, 80n
chiasm
  flesh, 183, 198n
  'hyperdialectic', 198n
  language and, 178–9, 190
  Merleau-Ponty, Maurice, 12, 15, 117, 132n
  reversibility, 26, 101, 112n, 114, 180–1
'circuits', 2, 51–84, 82n, 166
Claudel, Paul, 29
  Ars Poetica, 25
climate in crisis, 108–10, 113n
'closed spaces', 2, 17, 127, 161, 173n, 186, 189
Coetzee, J. M., 63–4
Cohn, Ruby, 49n
Collège de France, 171, 174–5n
Come and Go, 82n
Company, 176
compulsive bodies, 161–75
Connor, Peter, *Who Comes After the Subject?* 5
Connor, Steven
  'circuits', 166
  'finite thinking', 108
  Giving Way: Thoughts on Unappreciated Dispositions, 18n
  non-agential materialism, 138–9
  partitioning, 148–9, 158n
  phenomenology, 8
  punctuation, 160n
  repetition, 4, 56
  terminus, 116
constructivism, 6, 20n, 135, 202–3
Coole, Diana, 6, 13, 18–19n, 132n, 162, 173n, 209
Cordingley, Anthony
  intertextuality, 139–40, 147
  late modernist bricolage, 135, 152
  mud, 137
  Stoicism, 154, 156
  'worn down' subject, 149
Cousineau, Thomas, 93, 112n
creation, body and, 176–200
creative bodies, 161–75

Index 237

'cut out' system, 57
cybernetic theory, 61–2, 82n

dance and language, 77–8
Dante, *Inferno*, 92, 134–5, 152, 153–4, 166
Dastur, Françoise, 47n
Davies, Paul, 111n
de Beauvoir, Simone, 23, 40, 46n
de Saint Aubert, Emmanuel, 47n
decline
  of body and environment, 104–5, 109
  of humanity, 71–2, 79, 83n
defecation, 143–4
Deleuze, Gilles
  Anti-Oedipus, 169, 174n
  creativity, 38
  demotion of subjectivity, 173n
  'The Exhausted', 167–70
  language of image, 167–70
  'position statements', 164–5
  poststructuralism, 4
  potentiality, 174n
Democritus, 49–50n
Derrida, Jacques
  aporia, 114–15, 116, 119, 131
  Aporias, 123–4
  différance, 119
  and Husserl, 18n
  poststructuralism, 4
  reversibility, 118
  Speech and Phenomena, 132n
  'style', 142
  On Touching, 118
  'Tympan', 125, 133n
Descartes, René
  cogito, 24–5, 119
  Dioptrics, 145, 159n
  influence on Beckett's writing, 30–2, 132–3n
  Meditations, 49n
  navigation, 89–90
  parodies of, 15, 71
determinism, 34, 39, 50n, 163, 202
dialectic, 85–113, 117
  'hyperdialectic', 117, 132n
Dillon, M. C., 24
discomfort, bodily, 106–8
Discourse on Method, 32

Dream of Fair to Middling Women, 29, 51, 80n, 142
Dreyfus, Hubert, 173n
Dublin Bay, 102
Duthuit, Georges, 8, 52, 80n, 119–20, 143, 205, 206

earth-body art, 201–15
'Echo's Bones', 134
eco-criticism, 4, 14, 111n, 209–10
École Normale Supérieure, 7–8, 23, 29
ecology, 1–20, 39–40
eco-phenomenology, 11–12, 14, 20n, 42, 209–10
The Edinburgh Companion to Samuel Beckett and the Arts, 158n
'The End' ('La Fin')
  anti-anthropomorphism, 22
  Dublin Bay, 102
  ecological reading of, 14, 39–46
  flesh, 1
  landscape, 36, 101
  mud, 137
Eh Joe, 161
Eleutheria, 86, 111n
En Attendant Godot see *Waiting for Godot*
enactivism, 11, 49n, 203
Endgame (Fin de partie), 14, 85–113, 151, 162, 205, 208, 209–10
endings, 96–110
Enlightenment
  Hegel, Georg Wilhelm Friedrich, 85, 111n
  progress, 116, 120
  subjectivity, 12, 15, 162
  values, 157
'Enough', 201
Esslin, Martin, 174n
expatriatism, 159n
'The Expelled' ('L'expulsé'), 40

'*Fallor, ergo sum!*', 31
Federman, Raymond, 94
Feldman, Matthew, *Beckett and Phenomenology*, 8
Film, 15, 161

'La Fin' *see* 'The End'
Fin de partie (Endgame), 14, 85–113, 151, 162, 205, 208, 209–10
'First Love' ('Premier Amour'), 40, 134
Flaubert, Gustave, 160n
Fletcher, John, 71, 83n
Footfalls, 2
Foucault, Michel, 4, 6, 46n
    'What is an Author', 4, 163
French language, 40–1, 68–79, 82n, 83n, 84n, 142
French phenomenology, 6, 7–8, 23; *see also* phenomenology
Frost, Samantha, 173n

Gadamer, Hans-Georg, 80n
Gaelic language, 65
Gallagher, Shaun, 20n, 48n, 203
Garner, Stanton B., 18n, 19n
Garrard, Greg, 14, 108–9, 209–10
Gasché, Rodolphe, 123
Geulincx, Arnold, 22, 33
    Ethics, 42–3, 92
    ethos of humility, 35
Giacometti, Alberto, 8
Gibson, Andrew, 50n
glitches, 55–6, 67, 71
godillot, 22–3, 46n
Godillot, Alexis, 46n
Goethe, Johann Wolfgang von, *Prometheus*, 133n
Gontarski, S. E.
    Beckett and Cézanne, 80n
    Beckett and Descartes, 32
    'closed spaces', 173n
    creativity, 38
    expatriatism, 159n
    'grafting', 49n
    The Intent of Undoing, 113n
    spectrality, 208
    'style', 141–2
Goodall, Jane, 83n
'grafting', 49–50n, 147
Grossman, Evelyne, 82n
Grünbaum, A. A., 'Aphasie und Motorik', 29
Guattari, Felix, *Anti-Oedipus*, 169, 174n
Gunn, Dan, 143
Gutting, Gary, *French Philosophy in the Twentieth Century*, 47n

habitus, 145, 159n
Hansen, Mark B. N., 159n
Happy Days, 125, 137
Haraway, Donna, 12, 20n
Havel, Vaclav, 172, 175n
Hay, Louis, 127
Hayles, Katherine, 3, 13
    How We Became Posthuman, 94–5
Head, Henry, 27
Hegel, Georg Wilhelm Friedrich, 48n, 85–6, 111n, 117–18
    'hole in being', 26
    Phenomenology of Spirit, 111n
Heidegger, Martin, 8, 14
Hill, Leslie, 118–19
Hoefer, Jacqueline, 56, 57–8
Holocaust, 85, 104
Horkheimer, Max, 111n
How It Is, 15, 132n, 133n, 134–60, 173n, 205, 207
humour, 63–7
Husserl, Edmund
    Beckett and, 132–3n
    body and senses, 21
    Derrida, Jacques, 18n
    Ideas, 23
    lived experience of the body, 3, 23
    Les méditations cartésiennes, 46–7n
    Merleau-Ponty, Maurice, 8, 160n
    Paris Lectures 1929, 23, 46–7n
    reversibility, 118
    transcendental idealism, 10, 19n, 47n
'hyperdialectic', 117, 132n

Ihde, Don, *Technology and the Lifeworld*, 20n
Ill Seen Ill Said, 176
Imagine Dead Imagine, 161
Ingold, Tim, 46n
L'innommable see *The Unnamable*
intertextuality, 138–40
Irishness, 65, 82n
Israel, Nico, 130, 133n

Index   239

jaillir, 72–3
James, William, 139
Joyce, James, 14, 81n, 82n, 142
  Finnegans Wake, 157n, 204
  Ulysses, 149
justice, 153–5

Kafka, Franz, 205, 215n
  'In the Penal Colony', 156–7
Kanelli, Katerina, 84n
Kant, Immanuel, 154
Katz, Daniel, 119, 132n
Kaun, Axel, 59, 204
Kennedy, Seán, 81n
Kenner, Hugh, 56
  'Cartesian Centaur', 17n, 49n
Knowlson, James, 30, 39, 81n,
    111n, 116, 166, 174n
Koestler, Arthur, *Darkness at
    Noon*, 80n
Kofman, Sarah, 122
Kojève, Alexandre, 48n
Kojima, Hiroshi, 'From Dialectic
    to Reversibility: A Critical
    Change of Subject-Object
    Relation in Merleau-Ponty's
    Thought', 132n
Krapp's Last Tape, 50n, 173n,
    208
Kristeva, Julia, 112n, 158n

Laertius, Diogenes, 156
Lamont, Rosette, 70–1
Landes, Donald, 111n, 159n
language
  automation of, 61–2, 66–7
  and the body, 28, 76–8, 79
  and dance, 77–8
  deterioration of, 71–4, 79
  disarticulation of, 135–6
  dismantling of, 51–84
    as environment, 7
    mutations of, 68–79
    as a rational system, 51–84
    repetitive, 56–7
    of resistance, 56–7
late modernism, 201–15, 214–15n
Latour, Bruno, *We Have Never
    Been Modern*, 12
laughter, 62–4, 67
Lavery, Carl, 113n

Lefort, Claude, 158n
Leibniz, Gottfried Wilhelm,
  appetition, 169–70
The Letters of Samuel Beckett
  vol. I, 39, 51, 52, 81n, 143
  vol. II, 55, 119, 142, 143, 205
  vol. III, 135
Levinas, Emmanuel, 118, 140,
    158n
Lewis, Jim, 165–6
LeWitt, Sol, 164
Lhermitte, Jean, 27
Lieber, Jean-Claude, 71–2, 76, 83n,
    84n
Liedman, Sven-Eric, 111n
life cycles, 85–113
'Lightning Calculation', 40
L'Image, 135
'limit of the human', 207–9, 215n
lived body, 8–9
The Lost Ones, 186

machines, 61–2, 66–7
Magessa O'Reilly, Edouard, 148
Mahaffy, J. P., 30–1
Mallarmé, Stephane, 142, 145–6
Malone Dies (Malone Meurt),
    85–113, 112n, 205
Malraux, André, 144
  'The Voices of Silence', 141
Maude, Ulrika
  abject bodies, 138–9, 158n
  agency, 150
  *Beckett, Technology and the
    Body*, 8–10
  Beckett and Phenomenology, 8
  and Bergson, 66–7
  deteriorating bodies, 88
  'habit body', 48n
  and Kenner, 17n
  langauge and agency, 158n
  phenomenology, 15
  radio plays, 173n
Mauss, Marcel, 'Techniques du
    Corps', 159n
Mauthner, Fritz, 62
  *Beiträge zu einer Kritik der
    Sprache*, 57–9, 81n
McGreevy, Thomas, 39
McMullan, Anna, 17n, 18n, 19n,
    104–5, 109, 166

McMullan, Anna (*cont.*)
  Performing Embodiment in Samuel Beckett's Drama, 10–11
McTighe, Trish, 174n
meaning
  breakdown of, 51–84
  physical body and, 64–7
Meditations, 32
Mendieta, Ana, 210, 212–14
  Burial Pyramid, 212
  Imágen de Yágul, 212, 213
  Siluetas series, 214
Mercier and Camier, 32, 86, 111n
Merleau-Ponty, Maurice
  agency-oriented philosophy, 10–11, 17n
  aporia, 116–18
  and Beckett, 7–8, 19n
  'beneath' (*en deçà de*), 85–6
  Bergson, 47n
  bodily movement, 173n
  body and interaction with the world, 104
  body and language, 48–9n
  body and senses, 21
  body image, 97–8
  body-organism, 46n
  Cézanne, 41, 51–4
  'Cézanne's Doubt', 51–2, 80n
  chiasm, 12, 101, 112n
  childish painters (*peintre-enfants*), 143–4
  cogito, 24–7, 31, 47n, 48n
  cognition, 20n
  creative novelty, 171
  dialectical exchanges, 116–18
  'The End', 42
  Eye and Mind, 121, 145, 159n
  'flesh of the world', 153, 207
  'habit body', 48n
  Humanism and Terror, 80n
  'hyperdialectic', 132n
  idealism, 47n
  incarnate subjectivity, 9
  'incompossibles', 52
  'Indirect Language and the Voices of Silence', 141, 142–5
  intellectualism, 47n
  internal focalisation, 160n
  language, 80–1n
  language as environment, 15
  lectures, 146, 174–5n
  lived body, 8–9
  motricity, 29
  nature, 48–9n
  organic intentionality, 88
  'paradox of expression', 159n
  perception, 23–4, 36
  phenomenology, 3, 18n, 202–3, 207–10
  The Phenomenology of Perception see separate entry under title
  'On the Phenomenology of Language', 146
  'The Philosopher and His Shadow', 118
  posthumanism, 13
  The Prose of the World, 141, 144–5, 158n
  prosthetic body, 68
  reflective attitude in philosophy, 111n
  reflexivity, 6
  relaxation, 91–2
  reversibility, 79, 114–15, 118
  sense, 26–8
  Signs (Signes), 158n
  space, 145–6
  space and language, 206–7
  'speaking body', 49n
  speech, 145–6
  The Structure of Behaviour, 111n, 141
  'style', 136, 139, 140–50, 152, 157, 158n, 159n, 171
  subjectivity, 6–7
  'suspension', 121–2
  transcendental ego, 48n
  and transcendental idealism, 10–11
  The Visible and the Invisible, 47n, 101, 116–18, 202
  see also body schema; body-subject
Miller, Tyrus, 204
minimalism, 164
Mintz, Samuel, 'Beckett's Murphy: A Cartesian Novel', 49n
Molloy, 65, 85–113, 111n, 112n, 163, 167

Index   241

Mood, John, 56
Moorjani, Angela, 87, 111n, 112n
Morin, Emilie, *Beckett's Political Imagination*, 175n
Morton, Timothy, 14, 109, 209–10
    'ecocritical cliche', 89
Mounin, Georges, 82n
moving body, 6
mud, 134–41, 152–3, 155, 157n, 202
Murphy
    bodily restriction, 203
    disembodied rationalism, 15, 21–2, 30, 31–9, 45–6
    exhaustion, 167
    'grafting', 49–50n
    speech, 163

Nancy, Jean-Luc, 118, 162
    'finite thinking', 108
    Who Comes After the Subject? 5
'narratracide', 115
Naumann, Hans, 142
'neutrality', 132n
'new materialisms', 12–13, 162, 202–3, 207
Niemans, Astrida, posthuman phenomenology, 13
Nietzsche, Friedrich, 1, 83n, 142
Nixon, Mark, 29, 40
Noë, Alva, 203
Noland, Carrie, 6, 17n, 19n
non-agential materialism, 138–41
Norris, Christopher, 18n
Not I, 2, 158n, 161
'nouvelles', 40–1

objective space, 51, 145
Occasionalism, 31–3, 43, 49n
Oppenheim, Lois, 7, 19n
OULIPO, 214–15n

parabasis, 70–1
paradox, 68, 93–4, 114–33, 143–4, 159n, 182, 193
Parmenides, 122
'partitioning', 148–9, 157, 158n
Pascal, Blaise, *Pensées*, 83n
passive receptivity, 86, 100
passivity, 201–4
    active, 3–4, 18–19n, 113n

and agency, 171–2
'beneath' (*en deçà de*), 85
bodily, 2–3, 202
dialectic, 106
generative, 202
institution, 171
intertwining, 192–3
language, 194–5, 198n
late modernism, 206
narcissism, 182
object-like, 25–6
prosthetic body, 104
receptive, 86
repetition, 164–6, 170, 177
reversibility, 199n
subjectivity, 182–3
suffering, 99–103, 160n
thing-like, 37
violence of, 134–60
'Peintres de l'Empêchement', 215n
Penone, Giuseppe, 210–12
    Alberi (Trees), 210
    Continuerà a crescere tranne che in quel punto (It Will Continue to Grow Except at That Point), 210, 211
    Essere fiume (Being the River), 210–11
    L'albero delle vocali (The Tree of Vowels), 212
    Alpi Marittime (Maritime Alps), 210
    Soffi di creta (Breaths of Clay), 211–12
    Svolgere la propria pelle (Developing One's Own Skin), 211
Perec, Georges, 214–15n
Perloff, Marjorie, 81n
    'language of resistance', 56–7
Perspective, 49n
phenomenology, 21–50
    auto-critique, 132n
    cognition, 20n
    definition, 6–7
    Derrida, Jacques, 115
    eco-phenomenology, 11–12, 14, 20n, 42, 207–10
    embodiment, 3–4, 10–15, 19n, 206
    flesh, 154

phenomenology (cont.)
  French, 6, 7–8, 23
  late modernism, 206–8
  'middle voice', 150
  passivity, 202–3
  poststructuralism, 18n
  see also Merleau-Ponty, Maurice
The Phenomenology of Perception
  body and language, 48–9n
  body image, 97–8
  body-organism, 46n
  body's interaction with the world, 22, 104
  body-subject, 29
  chiasm, 101
  cogito, 24–7, 31
  intellectualism, 47n
  prosthetic body, 68
  reflective attitude in philosophy, 111n
  relaxation, 91–2
  space, 145
  space and language, 207–8
  speech, 145–6
  'style', 141
  see also Merleau-Ponty, Maurice
'Philosophy Notes on Aristotle', 63
physical body and meaning, 64–6
Pike Theatre, 82n
Pilling, John, 81n
Plato, 123, 131, 133n
Play, 161, 163, 208
pnigos, 70–1
poros, 122
Porter Abbott, H., 86, 112n, 115, 120, 129, 132n
positivist science, 111n
postcognitivism, 11, 33, 49n
posthumanism, 4, 11–14, 20n, 202–3, 209, 214
postmodernism, 204
poststructuralism, 4–7, 18n, 95, 163, 209
postwar humanism, 42, 50n, 53, 80n, 206
Poulet, Georges, 47n
Pountney, Rosemary, 174n
'Premier Amour' ('First Love'), 40, 134
Prometheus, 133n

prosthetic body, 97–8, 102–3, 104, 125–6, 208
Proust, 89
Proust, Marcel, 50n, 89, 160n

Quad, 1–2, 17n, 161–75, 203–4
Quad II, 164, 165–6
A Quarterly Review, 114–33

Rabaté, Jean-Michel, 14, 61, 80n, 137–8, 153–4, 157n, 173n
  Think Pig! Beckett at the Limit of the Human, 208
radical indecision, 114–33
radio plays, 15, 173n
rational subjectivity, 91–2
repetition
  academic discourse, 82
  humour, 66–7
  intertextuality, 84n
  justice, 154
  language, 186–7
  paradox, 159n
  patterns, 147–9
  poststructuralism, 4–5
  Quad, 161–75
  sensory dimensions of language, 59
  sound, 195
  speech, 68, 71–2, 160n
  'style', 157
Robinson, Michael, 55
Roche, Anthony, 82n
Romanticism, 40–1
Routledge, 55
Royal Court Theatre, London, 103
Ryman, Robert, 164

Sade, Marquis de, 154
Salisbury, Laura, 57, 81n, 105
Sartre, Jean-Paul
  humanism, 80n
  'hyperdialectic', 132n
  and Merleau-Ponty, 158n, 160n
  'nothingness', 48n
  phenomenology, 8, 23, 46n
  'What is Literature?', 141
Saunders, Paul, 89–90, 111n
Saussure, Ferdinand de, 142
Schilder, Paul, 27, 97–8
  body schema, 112n

The Image and Appearance of the Human Body, 48n
Schiller Theatre, 103
Schmidt, James, 48n
Schopenhauer, Arthur, 89
Schulz, Hans Joachim, 111n
Sebald, W. G., 205
self-reference, 125, 179, 188
self-reflexivity
  ecology, 90
  embodiment, 6
  flesh, 183–5, 198n, 207
  Hayles, Katherine, 94–5
  late modernism, 204
  Merleau-Ponty, Maurice, 183–5
  Molloy, 94, 110
  The Unnamable, 45
  Worstward Ho, 179, 183–5, 192–7
'sensory poetics', 54, 57
Serra, Richard, 164
Shaw, George Bernard, *Man and Superman*, 83n
short-circuited rationalism, 51–84
Silverman, Hugh, 159n
Silverman-Zinman, Toby, 70
similes, 121–2
Simon, Anne, 121–2, 160n
Simpson, Alan, 82n
Sinclair, Morris, 205
Singer, Linda, 158n, 159n
Skerl, Jenny, 57, 59
'skullscapes', 203
Smithson, Robert, 133n
  'Earthwork,' *Spiral Jetty*, 130
sociality, 156–7
Socrates, 122, 131
solipsism, 133n
sound, 55–67
speech
  articulation, 184–5
  How It Is, 148–53
  Merleau-Ponty, Maurice, 145–6
  physiology of, 138–9
  rediscovered, 160n
  refiguring language, 177
  space, 179
  Waiting for Godot, 68–80, 83n
Spinoza, Baruch, 33, 35, 71
spirals, 129–30
Stewart, Paul, 81n, 126, 158n

Stoicism, 156
strophes, 148–9
structuralism, 141
'style', 134–60
subjectivity, 162–3
  abject bodies, 158n
  agency, 24
  aporia, 119
  and community, 135
  Deleuze, Gilles, 169, 173n
  embodiment, 6, 8, 40, 203
  flesh, 153
  human, 209
  humanism, 141
  incarnate, 9–10
  intertwining, 102–3
  material, 13, 19n, 209
  Merleau-Ponty, Maurice, 47, 182–4
  Nancy, Jean-Luc, 162–3
  'neutrality', 132n
  passivity, 25–6
  posthumanism, 14
  poststructuralism, 95
  radical, 23
  rational, 91–2
  self-styling, 20n
  sound, 173n
  'style', 136
  see also body-subject
Süddeutscher Rundfunk, 165–6
Szafraniec, Asja, 119

Tajiri, Yoshiki, 97–8, 112n, 125–6, 132n
  Samuel Beckett and the Prosthetic Body, 20n
television plays, 15, 161
Les Temps Modernes, 40, 141, 158n
Texts for Nothing, 4, 131, 132n, 134, 152, 163
Thierry, Yves, 49n
'thingness', 98–9
thinking as performance art, 68–71
'Three Dialogues', 52, 80n
Toadvine, Ted, 11–12, 20n
transcendental idealism, 19n, 23–4
Transition, 36, 52
travaux, 72–3

Tresize, Thomas, *Into the Breach*, 18n
Tubridy, Derval, 14, 19n, 119
Tucker, David, 92

The Unnamable (L'innommable), 114–33
  abject bodies, 158n
  dialectic, 111n
  language and agency, 112n
  late modernism, 205
  nature, 45
  paradox, 93
  space, 110

Vachon, André, 47n
Valéry, Paul, 26
  'Le cimetière marin', 48n
Van Hulle, Dirk, 29, 33, 110, 112n, 127–9, 133n
Van Velde, Bram, 52, 80n, 206
Van Velde brothers, 52
Verhulst, Pim, 110, 112n
Verlaine, Paul, *Sagesse*, 83n
voluntarism, 6–7, 18n, 86, 202–3, 209

Waiting for Godot (En Attendant Godot), 68–79
  Cezanne, 51–2
  godillot, 22
  Irishness, 82n
  language, 54, 62
  and Pascal, 83n
  subhuman, 84n
Wall, Brian, 170–1

Wall, John, 56
Watson, David, 112n, 125
Watt, 51–2, 54–67, 79, 81n, 82n, 167
Watt, James, 61
Weller, Shane, 50n, 127–9, 133n, 204–6, 215n
'What is the Word', 205
'Whoroscope', 30–1
'Whoroscope Notebook', 81n
Wiener, Norbert, *Cybernetics, or Control and Communication in the Animal and the Machine*, 82n
Windelband, Wilhelm, *A History of Philosophy*, 29, 170
Wittgenstein, Ludwig, 56, 57
Wood, David, 11
World War II, 51, 55–7, 81n, 205
'worsening', 176–200
Worstward Ho, 176–200
  abject bodies, 15
  late modernism, 205
  'limit of the human', 208
  mud, 136–7
  progress, 131
  repetition, 163
  speech, 173n
  'worsening', 2

Yeats, Jack, 14
Yeats, W. B., 166

Zahavi, Dan, 20n, 203
Zeno, 122

EU representative:
Easy Access System Europe
Mustamäe tee 50, 10621 Tallinn, Estonia
Gpsr.requests@easproject.com

www.ingramcontent.com/pod-product-compliance
Lightning Source LLC
Chambersburg PA
CBHW070325240426
43671CB00013BA/2366